THINKING ON PURPOSE

FOR PROJECT MANAGERS: OUTSMARTING EVOLUTION

by Bill Richardson

Second Edition

Oshawa, Ontario

Thinking on Purpose for Project Managers: Outsmarting Evolution
By Bill Richardson

Acquisitions Editor: Kevin Aguanno
Cover Design: Scott Russo
Cover Photo: James Steidl/istockphoto
Interior Layout: Peggy LeTrent and Tak Keung Sin
eBook Conversion: Agustina Baid

Published by:
Multi-Media Publications Inc.
Box 58043, Rosslynn RPO, Oshawa, Ontario, Canada, L1J 8L6

http://www.mmpubs.com/

Paperback ISBN-13: 9781554890255
Adobe PDF ebook ISBN-13: 9781554890262

Second Edition

First Edition originally published as ISBN 9780980958607 in 2008 by The Perdix Group Inc.

Published in Canada. Printed simultaneously in the United States and in England.

CIP Data available from the publisher.

Dedication

To my wife—best friend, soulmate, lover—and her unshakable belief in my ability to write this book.

Acknowledgements

Judy Richardson, for creating and shaking down the practical situations in this book drawn from her twenty-plus years in project management. She painstakingly applied the tools to ensure both their appropriateness and end point value. Judy made sure these tools really work.

Donna Steinhorn, for being, in my opinion, one of the top business coaches on the planet. She has worked tirelessly with me for over three years to not only help guide me through the unfamiliar territory of my first book, but to help me build my keynote speaking business, as well.

Soni Pitts, for being an expert editor with a very keen marketing mind. Soni is masterful with words, and her natural understanding of what makes people buy has been extremely valuable, both in terms of how we have marketed this book and built its companion website.

Jennifer Feeley, for being a personal assistant who works incredibly hard at taking care of our business as if it were her own. This book would not have met our publication deadlines if it weren't for her persistent organizing and close attention to detail. Jennifer is the front line for our company, and our clients constantly tell us how lucky we are.

Sylvie Edwards, project manager and speaker, for taking the time out from her own busy schedule to review our early drafts of the book. She was instrumental in influencing the direction of our skill assessment approach and how project managers like to see information displayed. Sylvie is the kind of peer reviewer every author needs.

Ben McColm and Eugene Stellato, two of my coaching clients, for volunteering to be guinea pigs for testing ideas, approaches, and theories as the book was being written. Both gentlemen know project management from both theoretical and practical perspectives, and were extremely generous with both their insights and feedback.

My kids, Brett Richardson and Geneva Stewart, for their patience in picking up extra family duties while I focused on this book over the past few months. Throughout this adventure they never wavered in their support and encouragement, which in retrospect I now realize is one of those things that makes dads so proud of their kids.

The late Mrs. Squires, my ninth grade English teacher, who saw promise in my ability to communicate and never let me forget it all through high school. Often, during our lengthy philosophical debates, she ended the conversation with, "Well, Bill, why don't you write a book?"

Foreword

This book is about both project managers, and project management. It's about helping PMs use their innate thinking skills more effectively to get things done, regardless of which project management methodology is in play—e.g. The Project Management Institute, the International Project Management Association, the Association for Project Management, etc. The principles and concepts in this book can integrate with any project management life cycle or project management methodology.

The premise of the book is simple: Evolution endowed us with a powerful, but manifestly automatic thinking process, in which our mindsets are created based on reactions to and interpretations of past experiences. Mindsets drive behavior; behavior drives performance; performance drives results. Therefore, poor mindsets lead to poor results.

Thinking On Purpose is about outsmarting evolution and choosing the right mindset so that you can enhance your thinking process and maximize your result—no matter what you're doing.

TABLE OF CONTENTS

SECTION 2—THE SOLUTION

SECTION 3—THE APPLICATION

Introduction

I entered the workforce right out of college, on February 2, 1969. My first position in corporate North America was in a Canadian bank. As I look back now, it does seem like a very long time ago. But the experiences and credentials I've called upon to write this book came in large part both from the various and challenging jobs and assignments I was fortunate to have experienced during my early career in banking and my four years working as a consultant and corporate coach.

Project management has always come easily to me. These days, I write about it, teach it, consult about it and coach it. Hang around me long enough and you'd be forgiven for thinking that I was born with a spreadsheet clutched in my tiny red fist. However, it wasn't until almost twenty-five years into my career that I really began to question the way the work I did got done and, most importantly, how I attacked problems and issues. During this same time, I came across Daniel Goleman's first book, "Emotional Intelligence." This was the book that ignited my quest for concrete answers about how we think, what role emotions play and how both of these dimensions affected the way we perform in our jobs.

After that, I read every book on the subject that I could get my hands on, and began continuously observing and paying attention to how my colleagues, team members, bosses, and clients behaved, made decisions and solved problems. By this time, I had been blessed with a number of senior project management opportunities and was beginning to manage programs consisting of multiple projects. Looking back, I cringe to see how my "make it up as I go" mindset delivered my success at the expense of my team. Sure, I got the accolades from the top. But I literally wore out my teams because of my steadfast belief in my ability to respond when necessary to any threat or problem (instead of using critical thinking and planning to avoid such problems in the first place).

From the mid-1990s until 2004—when I left banking to pursue my passion of writing, teaching and speaking on subjects I care about—I was fortunate to be able to refine my thinking and skills in such diverse roles as sales management and commercial account management. These roles really opened my eyes to a critical trait for successful project management: foresight. This period is responsible for the creation of my 30/60/10 rule for success in project management: Successful project management is 30% insight, 60% foresight, and 10% hindsight.

The 30/60/10 Rule of Successful Project Management

Thirty percent of your results should come from insight, which is the capacity to discern the true nature of a situation; in other words, your ability to sift through the information at hand and find the nuggets of genuine value in the mountain of raw data. Sixty percent of your results should come from *foresight*, which is the ability to focus on and predict what is likely to happen and doing what can be done now to prepare for it. Ten percent of your results should come from *hindsight*, which is the understanding of the significance and nature of things that have happened in the past.

Unfortunately, while foresight is a logical and desirable key trait for a project manager, my experience, interviews, and research over the past three years indicate that it is vastly underdeveloped in comparison to hindsight. Project managers rely far more heavily on hindsight than foresight in their day-to-day handling of projects. In fact, the granddaddy of all hindsight orientations, the post implementation review, is actually built into most project management methodologies. As a result, to use a military metaphor, project managers often end up fighting the previous war, instead of the one they're in.

From my point of view, a project manager who doesn't actively strive to develop a strong sense of insight and foresight is essentially driving around in a car with a rearview mirror, but no windshield. Without the ability to see plainly what lies ahead of them, and predict and plan for what lies beyond that, project managers are forced to rely on trial and error (acquired over many years of experience running directly into obstacles at full speed) in order to become successful. And even then, any further success relies heavily on the unlikely reality of the playing field remaining virtually unchanged from previous experiences. Unfortunately, while the PM may be able to wrest some degree of success from this process, the teams that are passengers on these hair-raising rides often pay a hefty price in terms of stress, exhaustion, and discouragement.

Planning Makes Foresight as Clear as Hindsight

Imagine for a moment how much more fun your job as a project manager would be if you were confident in your ability to clearly see the root cause of every problem. Imagine how much more enjoyable your work would be if you had an effective method for identifying problems *before* they were problems. And imagine how much easier you and your team would have it if you knew precisely where to start looking for solutions, options, and alternatives, no matter what situation you faced.

I believe that insight and foresight are skills we all possess to some degree, and all it takes is a little prodding, some information about how our brains are wired and a little structure to bring these innate skills to life. The key here is *structure*. Our brains, if left to their own devices without any sort of imposed, structured thinking, will automatically nudge us into taking intuitive, gut-reaction, seat-of-the-pants approaches. On the other hand, we don't always have the luxury of a completely structured approach, which is where the development of experience-based insight comes into play. The secret is to continually operate between these two polar opposites—intuitive versus structured thinking—based on the situation at hand and the time, people and resources, we have available to deal with it.

Thinking On Purpose

To become more purposeful in your actions, and to expand your insight and foresight, you need to do less of your thinking on autopilot and more of your thinking on purpose.

Thinking On Purpose involves a series of specific and deliberate steps:

- Frame Your Purpose, so that you know exactly what you are trying to accomplish and why.
- Qualify Your Information, so that you can distinguish between fact, fiction, and everything in between.
- Identify Your Mindsets, so that you know what types of automatic thinking may be in play and how to deal with them.
- Structure Your Thinking, so that you can escape the gravitational pull of autopilot thinking.
- Validate Your Outcome, so that activity and effort are rewarded with achievement of a goal.
  To make understanding and using this information easier, this book is divided into three sections:

Section One—The Problem

Chapters 1, 2 and 3 explain how the human brain is wired, and how thinking on autopilot is both entirely human and potentially risky. In Chapter 1, *Human Evolution*, I cover the basics of how our brains have evolved to their current state. In Chapter 2, *Key Traits of the Human Brain*, I discuss the universal human traits that served us well as we climbed up the evolutionary ladder, but that sometimes get in our way today. Finally, Chapter 3, *The Problems*, digs deeper into the specifics of how these good traits go bad when we attempt to deal with situations that have evolved faster than our innate responses have.

Section Two—The Solution

Chapter 4, *The Solution—Thinking On Purpose*, delves into how the Five-Step Process for ***Thinking On Purpose*** works, and provides a solution to our natural tendencies to think on autopilot. This chapter introduces an alternative to Auto Pilot Thinking (APT), called On Purpose Thinking (OPT), and the identifiable differences between the two. This chapter also defines the processes, pitfalls, best practices, and available tools provided to help you master the art of ***Thinking On Purpose***. Chapter 5, *Personal Evolution*, brings you full circle back to the way change happens and how paying attention to your thinking can influence your own personal evolution. This chapter challenges you to begin choosing your mindset instead of having it chosen for you.

Section Three—The Application

Chapters 6 and 7 are all about application of the TOP framework. Chapter 6, *Thinking On Purpose (TOP) in Action*, explains how the TOP framework can be applied to real life, using three typical project management scenarios as examples. Chapter 7, *The Thinking On Purpose Toolkit*, catalogues over forty thinking tools that can be used by novice and expert alike to gain leverage on problems and opportunities.

The comprehensive index found at the back of this book is designed to enhance the modular nature of this book and assist you in being able to zero in on the concept, process, or tool you need when you need it.

Project Leadership

I wrote this book because I believe in the value of project management and the project managers who actually go out there day in and day out and get things done. Four years ago, I left the comforts of corporate North America to pursue my dream of running my own company and my passion for expressing myself on subjects that I care about deeply: project management and the value of critical thinking in both our personal and professional lives. My goal is to promote leadership in project management, and to do so by putting the arrow of ***Thinking On Purpose*** into the quiver of every project manager on the planet. If this book helps you to make better decisions, foresee and avoid obstacles, and make life for your project management team even a little bit easier, than I will have achieved my goal.

***Thinking On Purpose* in Action—Applying TOP to Three Common Project Management Scenarios**

I believe that the true test of the validity of the principles of ***Thinking On Purpose*** is to apply these concepts to real-life project management problems and situations, and to demonstrate the strong connection between thinking on autopilot and the sorts of problems repeatedly encountered by project managers.

As part of my research in writing this book, I contacted several project managers to obtain their candid thoughts regarding problem areas in the profession. I have merged these various real-world issues into three hypothetical scenarios, similar to case studies, for the purposes of demonstrating how the principles of ***Thinking On Purpose*** can be applied to each situation.

In these scenarios, I have taken three of the most common types of PM difficulties and profiled how autopilot thinking and unfiltered mindsets prevailed to create outcomes that were not only unexpected, but also undesirable. Within each scenario, I have outlined how the application of ***Thinking On Purpose*** concepts and approaches can positively impact the outcome.

Below are brief summaries of the three scenarios we'll be using: *Red Light; Green Light*; a situation in which blind optimism leads to unforeseen problems, *All Together Now*, in which a disenfranchise and uninformed team results in project stagnation, and *But Wait, There's More!*, which explores the problematic issues of scope creep.

We'll delve into these scenarios in detail and walk through how the principles of ***Thinking On Purpose*** can be effectively applied to each situation later in the book, after I've laid the groundwork for why these projects likely went awry in the first place, and introduced the principles, concepts, and proper usage of the ***Thinking On Purpose*** process.

Scenario Summaries

Scenario One—Red Light, Green Light: How Miscommunication Derails Success

The first scenario, *Red Light, Green Light*, is about how miscommunication and failure to anticipate roadblocks derails a project timeline. George Green was overseeing a simple and seemingly bulletproof IT project. The implementation of a new application required some server and desktop upgrades—there was barely any development even required. Every week, his team met for a status update and every week it was the same: Network: green, Development: green, Infrastructure: green, Business: green. He didn't anticipate this week's meeting being any different; in fact, he almost cancelled it. It's a good thing he didn't.

Out of nowhere, Network dropped a bombshell: Not only were they unable to meet their deliverables on time, but they would need an additional six weeks to finish. But there were only four weeks to go until implementation, and Network's deliverables had to be in place in two! When George questioned the timeline slippage, Network said that the timeline was unrealistic and that Development was in trouble as well.

Flabbergasted, George turned to Development, who had already reported that they were green. They confirmed that they might be unable to meet their timeline, because their dates assumed they would be working with a senior developer who turned out to be unavailable. They were training a junior developer, but the training and his lack of experience were going to slow down their progress significantly. When George asked them why they had reported that they were green, they noted that they weren't actually late, yet, and that they were trying to keep George happy.

Stunned, George couldn't figure out what had gone wrong where. He had thought he had the project under control. Will he be able to get the project back in the green? Or will the whole thing get stuck at a red light, unable to proceed?

Scenario Two—All Together Now: When Teams Fall Apart

The second situation, *All Together Now...* shows how a project can fall apart when the team is neither properly informed nor engaged.

When Caroline, a seasoned project manager, was first transferred from the PMO at Acme's regional office to the head office to become the PMO's Program Director, she became directly responsible for mentoring and consulting the project managers in the PMO. Her first assignment was to work with the project management team that was implementing Acme's Regional Notification Program to extend the functionality of its Emergency Notification Group.

However, what Caroline found when she first started looking into the project wasn't encouraging. The project sponsor, Vice President of Operations Mike Kelly, was seriously concerned that the timeline was in jeopardy, but he made it quite clear to Caroline that timeline failure wasn't an option—too many other projects—including some that were critical to revenue production—were depending on the successful and timely completion of the RNP project.

Not only that, but the project charter was woefully short on details. Only the barest outlines of a plan were even in existence, the breakdown of the project tasks was barely sketched out at the highest level, and the timeline seemed to be arbitrary at best and completely unrelated to the nature and number of the component tasks.

The project sponsor's ultimatums and the plan's sketchy nature were the least of Caroline's concerns. After a round of meetings with the project team, it quickly became clear that not only were they almost completely unaware of the reasons for the project they were assigned to, several of them felt that the whole thing was unnecessary, that they were spread far too thin in their existing responsibilities to even consider working on and implementing the project and that the timeline was almost certainly untenable.

What a mess. Not only is Caroline faced with a nearly completely stalled project whose completion (or lack thereof) impacts several others, but her team is also unengaged, uninformed and desperately overstretched. Will she be able to turn this dismal state of affairs around? Or will the project become completely mired down in the mud of overworked and under-committed team members?

Scenario Three—But Wait, There's More: The Dangers of Scope Creep

The third scenario, called, *But Wait, There's More!* depicts the age-old problem of scope creep and how this bane of every project manager's existence can undermine a project if not properly addressed.

When Tom first initiated the project to implement the Corporate Audit Information Management Process, he had some trouble getting agreement on—or even input into—the project's scope. Finally, however, he managed to get the green light for what he thought was a workable project.

When it was time for his first update to the Executive Steering Committee, Tom was excited but pleased. He was going to be able to report that not only was his project moving along on time, but it would almost certainly come in under budget.

That's when it all started falling apart. The committee was thrilled to hear his good news, but almost immediately they started requesting more functionality and features be added to the final project. Tom was stunned. There was simply no way to add these features to the scope of the project without completely derailing it. Unwilling to make a scene at the committee meeting, however, Tom held his tongue until he could get a meeting with his boss, Dave Moody.

Dave shared Tom's concerns and his assessment of the situation. However, Dave pointed out that this was a delicate issue and needed to be handled with the utmost concern for proprieties and that any objections to increasing the scope needed to be researched and presented with the maximum objectivity and clarity in order not to create a rift in the company. Dave instructed Tom to use a new process, called the TOP Process, to look into the situation.

Will Tom be able to salvage his project? Or will scope creep turn a fast-moving project into a train wreck of blown budgets and mangled timelines? And just what is the TOP Process, anyway, and how can it help?

Stay Tuned...

We will return to these "case studies" later in the book to see how the application of the TOP Process is used to turn these disasters around. In the meantime, keep these scenarios (and any similar such issues you have faced yourself) in mind while you read the book. As you read, try to envision how each chapter applies to these issues, how the principles of ***Thinking On Purpose*** could have prevented the problems from occurring in the first place and how they can be used to correct the situations as they now stand.

SECTION 1

THE PROBLEM

Chapter 1

Human Evolution

"In the long history of humankind (and animal kind, too) those who learned to collaborate and improvise most effectively have prevailed." —Charles Darwin

"There is nothing sadder in this world than the waste of human potential. The purpose of evolution is to raise us out of the mud, not have us groveling in it."
—Diane Frolov and Andrew Schneider, writers
of the television series *Northern Exposure*

1.1 In the Beginning

Life strives to succeed.

That's why you're here. That's why we're all here, in fact. Because once life takes root somewhere, it throws everything it can into the process of staying alive and creating more life.

Life, or at least the building blocks for life, seems to have taken hold pretty much as soon as our planet had cooled down enough to permit it. And once life got a foothold, it was off to the races churning out new combinations, new mutations and new processes until it found something (or several somethings) that worked.

By the time Earth was only a few billion years old—hardly an eyeblink on the cosmic scale of time—basic life forms like bacteria were already taking off. And once that happened, there was no stopping it. Diversity exploded. The tree of life began branching and splitting off and branching again until it began to look less like something arboreal and more like a tangled and overgrown bramble thicket.

Out of this roiling stew of diversity came higher life forms, each more dizzyingly complex than the last. But at the same time, if you look closely enough you'll see that everything is built from the same basic building blocks that are simply rearranged into new patterns.

Life is efficient. It recycles. It reuses. It builds off of what works and evolves by adding new and interesting options to an already proven core, rather than reinventing everything from scratch every time. If the new options fail to offer any advantage, or put life at risk, they die out. On the other hand, if the changes further life's goals—persistence and procreation—those changes may live long enough to pass the new pattern on.

This is where we get into trouble.

1.2 The Power of Three: The Lizard, the Leopard and the Learning Brains

You see, back when our ancestors roamed the savannah, it was in our best interest to make snap judgments and base decisions on biases, stereotypes and other mental shortcuts. When something hidden in the tall grass started coming toward your group, evolution didn't favor the guy who stood around waiting for all the evidence to come in before making a decision on how to act! And woe to the fellow who refused to learn that the folks from downriver have a nasty habit of spearing first and asking questions later when they meet someone on the trail.

Most of the time, these "decisions" happened without any conscious awareness on our part that a decision was being made at all. Something happened and you reacted: that was it. Sure, those who learned to react quickly to their environment, rather than carefully and thoughtfully responding to it, may have made a few wrong judgments along the way, ("Whew, it was only a baby antelope lost in the grass. Hey…dinner!"). But, in the long run, they were right often enough to live longer than those who didn't. As a result, they were able to pass those reactions on to their offspring, and they onto theirs and so on. Darwin called this evolutionary process "natural selection."

During this phase in our evolution, these shortcuts served us very well—so well, in fact, that they became hardwired into our system. These days, unless you run a Vegas sideshow, you're unlikely to come face to face with giant predators or war-like neighbors, and while those mental shortcuts were very useful when hesitation could mean a quick and ugly death, today we almost always have the luxury of waiting around to review all of the evidence before coming to a considered decision. If only we could shut our automatic reactions off, that is.

Unfortunately, our environment has evolved far more quickly than our brains have. Your body may be sitting in a climate-controlled office calmly sipping a cup of coffee while you wrestle with the latest product distribution bottleneck, but your mind is still convinced that you're squatting in the jungle somewhere trying to find some lunch without becoming someone else's and it prods you to act accordingly, often without your consent or awareness. Needless to say, this state of affairs is hardly conducive to orderly, structured problem solving.

While it's impossible to circumvent your hardwiring altogether (and, quite frankly, it would be a bad idea to do so—there are still enough dangers in the world to warrant keeping these reflexes handy), there are ways to work around this mental programming when it's to your advantage to do so. But, in order to do so, you have to understand how it got this way in the first place.

The Lizard Brain

The first prototypical brains appeared in primitive fish around a million years ago, although they weren't much to look at—barely more than a few nerve cells huddled together for warmth around a tiny spark of thought, but it was enough to give those fish a clear advantage in the battle for life and procreation, and so they remained...and evolved.

Before long, evolutionarily speaking, our early reptile ancestors had enough brainpower that they could partition it off into distinct sections, each with its own purpose and function—a frontal area that handled smell, a middle region for vision, and a rear division that managed balance and coordination.

These sections fed into a central region called the diencephalon, which put all of the incoming sensory data the lizard was experiencing together into a coherent whole and used the resulting output to generate reactions. Over time, those reactions that were successful became instincts, which are basically just automatic mental shortcuts that prevent you from thinking yourself into an early grave when presented with a need for decisive action. It's at this point in evolution that the basic survival instincts (like the urge to procreate, to find food, and the fight-or-flight response) were hardwired into the brain.

Over time, bigger, better, and higher-powered brain structures have evolved as creatures branched off from the evolutionary tree and matured, but this early brain is still there underneath it all, sitting in the sun on a warm rock and scanning the horizon for predators. We still refer to this section of our brains as "the reptile brain" or "the lizard brain," and when we're faced with a life-or-death situation, it's often what keeps us alive.

Now, granted, at this point it still wasn't much of a brain from human perspectives, but it was a considerable advance over the basic lump of neurotissue that the fish were using, and light-years ahead of the simple receptors and reactions of primitive bacteria. In short, it worked, and thus it continued to survive, and evolve.

The Leopard Changes Its Spots

As mammals began to evolve, they built upon their reptilian brain and adapted those early instincts to help them navigate a completely different environment. But whenever an animal evolves to exploit a new environment or evolves into a new and more complex type of life, there are always tradeoffs. In mammals, evolution resulted in a far more complex body type (warm-bloodedness alone is a hugely complicated metabolic system whose delicately-balanced processes are still not entirely understood) that required a substantially longer period of time to develop and mature.

The tradeoff was that mammal offspring were usually born helpless, having spent all of their gestation period simply stringing the foundations of those complicated advancements into place. So mammals created entirely new instincts like parenthood and family groups, to cope with these changes. These changes allowed their young to survive to a point where they could fend for themselves.

Another environmental change required them to adopt a nocturnal lifestyle to avoid daytime predators. In this case, the tradeoff was a shift in the balance of their senses away from vision and into smell and hearing. This change altered the basic reptile brain that the mammals had inherited. As the sense of smell became more and more important, that region of the brain grew both in size and power, until it grew into what we recognize as the cerebrum.

Eventually, as mammals evolved into stronger, larger and more dangerous creatures that could walk in the light once more, those diminished areas devoted to vision rewired themselves to take advantage of the vast processing power of the cerebral cortex's enlarged neural networks. As a result, these mammals were able to hear and see with incredible depth, range, and clarity. These experiments were, by and large, a success, and mammals thrived. And so they lived and continued to evolve.

The Advent of the Human Mind: The Learning Brain

Over time, more layers, more input and more diversified data-handling pathways were added onto this basic structure, until finally it became what we recognize today as the human brain.

This snazzy new luxury model has all sorts of tweaks and perks. There's the huge frontal lobe, which gives us abstract thought, judgment, inhibitions, introspection and initiative, in addition to taking care of most concerns dealing with movement and physical reactions. There's the occipital lobe, which allows you to see and read this book: there's the parietal lobe, which helps us merge touch and perception so we don't fall over when we quit thinking about where our feet are: and there's the temporal lobe, which takes care of fancy stuff like music, speech, emotion, and visual memory.

Our brain is even further divided up into hemispheres, so that each of these lobes has two different versions, each doing things a little bit differently and relying on the corpus callosum to act as a sort of telecommunications bridge to coordinate action between them. This division and recombination gives the human brain incredible flexibility, wide adaptability and an almost unimaginable amount of thinking horsepower.

In fact, human brains have so much going on that our skulls have grown to massive proportions relative to our body size in order to contain them. But even with all that extra space, our brains still have to be folded up on themselves in a sort of biological origami in order to pack all that thinking power into the space available.

The end result of all this cranial evolution is a highly flexible, incredibly complex thinking machine that can take in an unbelievable amount of raw data and filter, sift, organize, file and react to it on the fly in such a way as to create a smooth-running, functioning interface with both the world outside of our brains and the world inside them.

It is, in fact, the most complicated brain on the planet, and, as you might imagine, all this intellectual horsepower doesn't come without a few tradeoffs of its own.

The Man with Three Brains

As complicated as all this high-level thinking machinery is, however, keep in mind that it's still all built on top of those very same primitive brain structures—the brain stem, the hypothalamus, and the cerebellum—that drove our reptilian and mammalian ancestors. In an emergency, the brain has no compunction about jettisoning all those fancy doo-dads and running straight from the core, using only those functions that are absolutely necessary to survive and disabling pretty much everything else.

As a result, we really are creatures with three brains. On the one hand, we have a complex, highly evolved cognitive brain capable of producing such things as the space program, the Magna Carta, irrigation, the Brahms concertos, the Internet, and the Sistine Chapel paintings. On the other hand, all of this is built on the foundation of two very powerful instinctive animal brains that run on quick-and-dirty subroutines, like emotion and instinct, and produce things like anger, aggression, fear, violence, and lust.

Usually, our advanced brain remains in charge, but the lizard and the leopard lie just underneath this civilizing outer layer, barely restrained and capable of exerting nearly irresistible influence over our bodies, our thoughts and our actions, on a moment's notice, should they see fit to raise their heads and roar.

1.3 Bits and Pieces

In addition to the three brains and the three minds, our thinking machinery is composed of various and sundry subparts, each of which contributes its own notes to the final melody of thought and behavior.

The Basic Building Blocks

First, we'll take a brief look at the component parts of the brain cells themselves, the neurons and the glial cells that help support them and coordinate connections.

Neurons are the basic cell structure of the brain, and they make up what we refer to as gray matter. As new information is processed, cable-like extensions of these neurons, called axons, reach out to each other to make connections. Guided by chemical signatures created by various genes, the axons link up in specific patterns to create the connections we need to process input, create memory and maintain basic life functions. These connections are called synapses.

You begin creating these connections in the womb in reaction to stimuli in your environment, and you continue creating them until you are about 10 years old. At this point, preliminary growth ends and the brain begins pruning and shaping the brain like a ruthless gardener,
snipping old connections that are no longer needed or used and strengthening those that remain. While this process strengthens and optimizes the functioning of the remaining connections, it also results in the loss of our early childhood ability to learn new things like language, academic subjects and other complex subjects easily and naturally.

As your brain grows, these neurons and their connections work together to form highly specialized networks that handle specific tasks. The network known as Broca's area, for instance, helps control speech, while a closely related network, called Wernicke's area, allows you to understand words. Working together, these and similar networks give us the power of speech and language.

String enough of these circuits and networks together, and you get some rather complicated and abstract results, such as memory and self-awareness. These are the hallmarks of the human brain, and they are founded in immense complexity and the tightly choreographed dance of chemicals, impulses, and feedback loops that form the body's central nervous system, which governs the functioning of the human brain.

Central Nervous System

Your brain is part of a bigger system called the central nervous system (CNS) The CNS is made up of your brain and your spinal cord. Signals that are generated in response to stimuli are carried to your brain by your spinal cord to be interpreted and acted upon. The spinal cord then transports these response signals back to the body so that it can take action. In some cases, such as touching a burning object, the signals to react can bypass the brain altogether, making a quick loop from the nerves to the spine and back again, taking you out of harm's way before you have time to think. Unfortunately, even in this case the pain signals still get sent straight to the brain for processing. Ouch.

Peripheral Nervous System

The peripheral nervous system is an extension of your CNS, and is made up of the nerve connections and other sensors in your body that take in signals for processing. Some parts of this system are under your control, such as muscle movement. Other parts, referred to as the autonomic and parasympathetic nervous systems, are automatic. They handle stuff like breathing, body temperature, digestion, glandular processes and so on.

It's good that these things are automatic—you'd hate to stop breathing or processing hormones simply because you got distracted! On the other hand, this means that your body and your mind are often controlled or at least strongly affected by processes over which you have no say. Mood swings, fight-or-flight reactions, chemical balances and other functions of these automatic systems dramatically affect our thoughts, and can either enhance and destroy our ability to think clearly.

1.4 A Delicate Balance

Your brain and nervous systems work in concert to create a functioning body and mind. However, this is a very delicately balanced system. Anger, depression, and other strong emotional states can distract us from taking care of ourselves and even encourage us to do ourselves harm. Illness, fatigue, and dehydration can cloud our judgment, weaken our resolve and blind us to danger. Malnutrition, poor health, chemical imbalances and the like can affect thinking in ways we still don't even begin to understand. Some studies have even shown that something as simple as giving vitamin supplements to prisoners can reduce violence by double-digit percentages, so strong is the effect of poor nutrition on judgment, behavior, and critical thinking.

This is why maintaining good health is so vitally connected to critical thinking and our ability to function as rational, functional human beings (a subject I'll touch on later in this book). Just let me briefly say now that your brain and body function together as a seamless whole—there is no separation between the two. Neglect the body, and the brain and all its activities suffer. Take care of yourself, and your ability to think clearly and behave appropriately and effectively will increase along with your health.

Chapter Summary

The human brain is a complex and marvelously adaptable tool, and it has brought us through the ravages of time and the pressures of survival to emerge as the predominant species on this planet in terms of our ability to shape our environment to our will and impose that will upon the world around us.

As with anything in nature, nothing functional is ever lost or discarded; it is simply built upon and adapted for new uses. Beginning with the most primitive neural structures, nature has built a thinking machine of such complexity that even at the furthest reaches of our current technical expertise and medical understanding we can only generate grossly simplified and flawed simulations of its most mundane and basic tasks.

As a result of this recycling process, our brains, magnificent as they are, are layered platforms of function and thought, each with its own purpose and its own strengths and weaknesses, and each complementing the other to create a whole that is far greater than the sum of its parts:

- **The Lizard Brain** is the most primitive region of our brain. It handles all the automatic functions of life, including metabolism, endocrine function, breathing, and heartbeat. It also initiates basic reactions to stimuli, such as fight-or-flight, hunger, lust, anger and so on.
- **The Leopard Brain** is somewhat more developed than the Lizard Brain. It provides us with higher-functioning instincts, like hunting, caring for our young, operating in social groups, etc. It is also responsible for our visual, auditory, and verbal development.
- **The Learning Brain** is what we often call the thinking brain or the cognitive brain. It is designed for higher reasoning, using language, storing memories, thinking about and manipulating the environment, and bringing all of this together to create consciousness.

These three brains work in concert with our **Central Nervous System** and our **Peripheral Nervous System** to keep our bodies running at as close to peak health as possible, keep us safe from predators and other hazards of the environment, and help us survive long enough to pass our genetic structures on to the next generation.

CHAPTER 2

The Nature of Thought and the Human Brain

"Thinking is hard work." —Thomas Edison

"There is nothing either good or bad, but thinking makes it so."
—William Shakespeare

All human brains share certain key traits, and these traits are responsible for much of what we consider to be "human nature." These traits are neither good nor bad—each serves a function in the fight for survival, and each can cause problems if allowed to run roughshod over the mind and body at inappropriate times. In this chapter, we'll explore what these traits are and how they affect the way you perceive and think about the world around you. But first, let's take a moment to talk about the nature of thought itself—what it is, what it isn't and how these key traits affect the quality and nature of the thinking process at a basic level.

2.1 What Is Thought?

Simply put, thinking is the process of perceiving and modeling the world around us in a way that allows us to interact with it in a way that makes sense to us. We think by taking in and interpreting input; forming and manipulating concepts; comparing them against existing memories and experiences; extrapolating and predicting future events and consequences; reasoning out appropriate responses based on our own desires, goals, intentions and needs; and then carrying out the processes necessary to generate those actions.

Another part of thinking is imagination. In fact, imagination plays a very big role in thinking, because it allows us to visualize things that haven't happened yet, or that have happened outside of our sphere of awareness. Imagination is a combination of the rational, reasoning parts of your brain and the more "gut level" constituents, like emotion, intuition, and feelings. Without imagination, we would be little more than basic robots, reacting to stimuli in a cold, clinical fashion and then shutting down until further reactions were required.

Since thought is the end result of a process involving very complex combinations of physical functions, anything that upsets or alters these physical functions will alter the thinking they produce. This is easy to see on any Saturday night at your local nightclub or bar.

The alkaloid poison known as alcohol interferes with the normal functioning of several chemical processes. It has the affect of changing the way we think and behave by suppressing inhibitions, diminishing our capability for critical judgment, dampening higher reasoning, limiting input and so on. Indeed, for many people, that is the whole point of drinking. Once the alcohol wears off, assuming the drinker hasn't seriously overdone it and permanently injured himself, the brain returns to normal. But any thinking done during inebriation can and often is rightly considered to be deeply suspect.

The point is that thought and thinking aren't intellectual processes that happen alongside physiological ones. They are physiological processes that have an intellectual component. Your thinking, quite simply, is the sum of your intellectual activity *plus* your emotional state *plus* your physical condition plus any ongoing instinctive reactions to your external environment plus any number of other factors.

It's the basic GIGO paradigm—Garbage In, Garbage Out. No matter how smart, educated or determined you are, you can't circumvent this reality. The best you can do is to recognize it and work toward optimizing it.

2.2 Plasticity

Plasticity is a trait shared by all healthy human brains, and one that is vitally important to our survival. Plasticity means that our brains are designed to be flexible. We are hardwired to be able to think in new ways, engage with new experiences and adapt to new environments that we haven't had experiences with in the past. Without this plasticity, we would be unable to cope effectively with new experiences, we couldn't learn anything new and we couldn't imagine anything that hadn't happened yet.

You may have seen what happens in the absence of plasticity in someone with a severe developmental disability that provokes violent and sometimes even self-destructive reactions to changes in the environment or her daily routines. For someone with this type of disability, living on her own is almost impossible, and certainly not without a great deal of training and personal effort on her part to manually implement coping mechanisms that do not come naturally. Considering how changeable and impermanent the world around us really is, it's obvious how powerful and necessary this trait can be.

2.3 Emotions

Humans—even project managers—are emotional creatures and as such, emotions often rule our thoughts. Emotions are strong motivators that originate in the lower brain structures upon which our higher thinking is based. Because of this we often wind up making decisions based on strong emotional feelings for or against something rather than on logical, rational thinking—even when we like to think we'd do the opposite.

To illustrate this, consider a recent study that offered participants the following two situations. In the first scenario, the participant is the 100,000th customer at a theater and wins a prize of $100. In the second, the person *in front of the participant* is the 100,000,000th customer and wins $1000. As a consolation prize, the participant is offered $150.

When asked which they'd rather be, most people said they would rather be the person in the first scenario, even though that meant receiving less money. The emotional value of winning, rather than coming in second, is consistently perceived as being greater than the logical benefits of winning an additional $50.

In the same study, most people also said they would prefer to make $50,000 a year when everyone else around them was making $25,000, rather than to be making $100,000 a year when everyone around them was making $500,000 a year. The emotional need to be more successful than others was strong enough to negate the logical advantage of $50,000.

Clearly, emotion is a much stronger motivator than logic, despite the fact that people will often argue strongly that their actions are more driven by logic than by emotion. Without careful attention and conscious manipulation, the lizard and leopard win out over the learning brain in these situations almost every time.

2.4 Pattern Recognition

The human mind is designed to detect and react to patterns. It's how we recognize the faces of our friends, find our way around town and deal with new situations that are similar to past ones. Pattern recognition has long been a key to our survival. During our evolution, we relied on pattern recognition to alert us to danger, help us find food and shelter, and prevent us from repeating past mistakes. And all of this happens well beneath our conscious level of awareness; we never realize it's happening, even when we are consciously acting on the results of this process.

Unfortunately, this means we often see patterns where none exist. One example of this is what I call the "Elephant's Tether." When a captive elephant is young, its trainer tethers it by securing a sturdy rope or chain around its foot and anchoring that chain to a strong peg or wall. At first the young elephant will panic or rebel and try to escape. But it is so small that it has no hope of pulling free. Eventually, the struggle exhausts the young pachyderm, and it accepts captivity.

Over time, however, that tiny little elephant grows into an enormous and immensely strong adult who could tear that chain away from its anchor as easily as you or I can break a piece of thread. So you'd think there would be a constant flood of escaped elephants running around.

But, in fact, the elephant has become so accustomed to the idea of the chain as an unbreakable tether attached to an unmovable object *that it doesn't even try*. It has learned helplessness so well that sometimes its owners even do away with heavy ropes and chains and simply tether it by a thin cable, the presence of which is more than enough to convince the elephant that it is firmly tethered and cannot escape.

As a result, adult elephants continue to remain captive not by the holding power of their chains, but by the holding power of their beliefs.

* * *

Our minds work the same way. We easily become attached to beliefs that hold us back, prevent us from seeing or taking opportunities. That makes us captive to beliefs, ideas, thoughts, concepts, and assumptions that are no longer true (if they ever were) but because our belief in them is so strong, we can't break free. The only way to foil the Elephant Mind is to show it that it can, indeed, pull free of its imaginary limits and break the bonds of helplessness it learned so long ago, and the only way to do this is to simply drive it forward until those bonds snap.

Another aspect of pattern recognition is seeing shapes, images, and other patterns where none exist. This is called matrixing, and it's the result of the brain's pattern-matching system being fooled by coincidental similarities.

It's matrixing that results in things like seeing canals on Mars and holy images in tortillas, finding recognizable shapes in passing clouds and star constellations, and imagining we can predict future occurrences of truly random events like coin tosses based on past results.

A third of pattern recognition is stereotyping. We assume we can "recognize" a type of person or situation because it fits a pattern we have seen in the past. This plays a valuable part in the game of survival, allowing us to make quick judgments based on limited evidence when waiting for more would be dangerous.

Unfortunately, it also causes a great deal of the pain, misery, and injustice humans deal with around the world, because stereotyping is, by and large, a highly inaccurate process when it comes to complicated situations like human relationships, foreign policy, and community dynamics.

Since pattern recognition happens so fast, and so far below the level of our conscious awareness, we most likely don't even know it's happening. And so it affects our thoughts, behaviors and actions—and puts us in the line of fire from the consequences of those thoughts, behaviors, and actions—without us realizing what's going on.

2.5 Biases and Assumptions

Biases are the brain's unconscious shortcuts that allow us to process tons of complex input effectively, efficiently and quickly. Biases do this by comparing what we're experiencing with what we've experienced in the past. With that information, the brain considers what happened before and generates feelings, preferences, concepts, and emotions about what's happening now that enable us to decide what to do without having to examine and judge every piece of input independently. Without this ability, we would be overwhelmed by the burden of trying to analyze every new bit of information and input individually and without reference to past experience. In computer terms, biases might be compared to your word processor's auto-complete function. As you type, the auto-complete sees what you've written and tries to complete the word or phrase for you based on its library of likely possibilities. Biases improve survival rates by cutting down on reaction time. Something happens, we react to it, and the results of those interactions produce biases that will influence the way we think and act when we find ourselves in the same (or even wildly dissimilar) situations later. However, just as with the auto-complete function, biases are often wrongly applied because they jump in too soon, before we truly have enough data to warrant a conclusion.

Plausible reasoning (also referred to as natural reasoning) is a good example of a common bias. We engage in plausible reasoning when we jump to a conclusion that is probably correct based on how similar one situation is to another. We assume this situation is like the other because aspects of it are the same. Confirmation bias is another. When confirmation bias is in play, we are drawn toward evidence that supports our existing beliefs, no matter how outrageous or unlikely, while ignoring any evidence to the contrary, no matter how strong or compelling.

Like all biases, plausible reasoning and confirmation bias can be good and bad. They make sense in a world where standing around trying to logically create a unique response to every situation is a good way to wind up as dinner. However, we are rarely faced with those situations these days, and we have a hard time giving up on our biases because they seem so natural and obvious to us (a function of their unconscious nature), even when they continually prove inadequate to deal with the complicated and often unique situations in which we continually find ourselves.

Biases and assumptions often result in something called "satisficing." Satisficing is a portmanteau (or word combination) of "satisfy" and "suffice," and was coined by Herbert Simon in 1955. It refers to our tendency to intuitively favor one answer over another and ignore other alternative answers. Unfortunately, we tend to latch onto the first option that appears satisfactory, or that will suffice, and then avoid "wasting time" by pursuing other (quite possibly more effective) options.

Satisficing is not in and of itself a bad thing. Sometimes, "good enough" really is good enough, and pursuing more perfect ends would never justify the means. However, problems occur when we satisfice in situations where optimization is mandatory.

It's wise to keep a continual eye out for this tendency, even when it's not a problem, just so you can learn to identify it when it happens. Always keep asking yourself if you prefer a solution because it is the best or simply because you *like* it best.

2.6 Mindsets

Mindsets might be considered uberbiases. As we experience life, we create biases for dealing with individual situations or events. Over time, these biases accrete into a framework for dealing with reality as a whole based on our past experiences. We call such frameworks *mindsets.*

But a mindset isn't just about your biases. It's actually the sum total of all of your biases, emotional responses and other mental shortcuts combined. Once we enter what we feel to be a familiar situation, our mindset regarding that situation triggers a cascade of biases, thoughts, emotions and other subroutines to help us quickly and decisively handle the situation.

All of this happens nearly instantaneously and almost entirely unconsciously. As such, mindsets exert a powerful influence on our thinking because they determine how we think about the world around us, usually without any awareness on our part that it's happening.

Mindsets are very useful in that they allow us to quickly and easily interpret complicated situations in ways that make sense to us. We acquire mindsets for every aspect of the world around us, from how we deal with relationships to which religion we practice and how we feel about concepts such as work, happiness, and community. Without mindsets, we would have to figure out how to deal with each situation from scratch every time we encountered one. The result would be confusing, stressful and exhausting, and probably resoundingly unsuccessful.

Mindsets, however, can be harmful as well. An inaccurate or outdated mindset—such as "all black males are criminals" or "all dogs are friendly"—can result in misunderstandings, physical harm and even death. We often have difficulty even realizing we have a particular mindset about some concept, let alone being able to determine what that mindset might be and how to change it. And even if we know we have a mindset and know that it is inadequate or dysfunctional, it's still hard to break free of it because mindsets are part of our unconscious thinking and come into play without our awareness or permission.

Examples of harmful mindsets in the project management world include, "if it worked for me in the past, it will work for me now" and, "since they made me the project manager, I must be the smartest person on this team." In my experience, both of these mindsets are common and deadly, both in terms of personal effectiveness and the ability to foster collaboration in a team.

The only way to create new mindsets is by exposure to new ideas, situations, and concepts. Fortunately, our brains' plasticity comes in handy in this regard—we can use this built-in flexibility to reshape our thinking about a particular subject and create new responses to familiar stimuli. However, this is a lengthy and difficult process, more a matter of erosion due to constant exposure to new ideas than a single, one-time change.

2.7 The Meaning of Life and the Need for Explanations

Curiosity may have killed the cat, but it's like oxygen to humans. The human brain has a need to find explanations for events, and doing so gives us great pleasure... even when those explanations are dead wrong.

This drive to explain is tied to the trait of pattern recognition; in this case cause and effect. Once we recognize a pattern in the effect, we feel satisfied that we understand the cause of what has happened. If we cannot identify the cause or isolate a pattern in the effect, however, we feel real, physical discomfort and will go out of our way to concoct a "logical" explanation simply to dispel those ill feelings, with no regard for whether or not that explanation is correct or even plausible. We even use this process to explain our own actions to ourselves and to others, never realizing that these explanations are often just as unlikely to be based in the truth as any other.

You can see this trait clearly in today's culture, where an answer of "I don't know" is considered to be all but an admission of personal inferiority and weakness. Whether we realize it or not, we are far more strongly driven to end our discomfort (by creating a solution) than to be right. Right or wrong, it seems, is not the point. It's uncertainty itself that's unacceptable.

2.8 Focus, Attention, and Concentration

Human brains are capable of great feats of focus and concentration. While all of our shortcuts and mental tricks play important roles in our survival, our ability to focus on what's important while ignoring irrelevant or distracting stimuli is one of the keys traits for our survival.

Back in the day, this ability enabled us to pick the tiger out from the surrounding grass, or hear a twig snap over the hum of a million insects. These days, that same ability enables us to read a book on a noisy train or paint a picture of a fountain in the park while hundreds of people pass between the fountain and our eyes throughout the day. Without it, we would be constantly awash in a sea of distraction, unable to discern the signal through all the noise. However, this trait also has its downside.

It's all too easy for us to get caught up in what feels important at the moment without realizing that we have, instead, become sidetracked from our true goals and are being led down an endless rabbit hole of distraction. There's a hilarious story in which this process is named yak shaving, based on a hypothetical story created by online celebrity Joi Ito. In this scenario, Joi wants to wax his car but can't because his hose is broken. So he decides to buy a new one, but needs to borrow an EZPass from his neighbor to pay for the tolls, which he can't do because he borrowed his neighbor's mooshi pillow, and his son tore out the yak hair stuffing. So in order to wax his car, Joi finds himself at the zoo shaving a yak.

Another downside to focus is its ability to lead us into confirmation bias, which we discussed earlier. Because of our mindsets, humans want to believe what we feel to be real, and thus we focus on evidence and actions that support this belief and easily block out what doesn't. If we are not careful to act consciously to avoid it, confirmation bias can easily be used by those who are adept in manipulating our perceptions to blind us to the truth and lead us into harm. Rationalization—our ability to convince ourselves that we're doing the right thing even in the face of overwhelming evidence to the contrary—does the rest.

Whatever our reasoning, one thing is clear—this sort of thinking prevents us from seeing when we are heading down a dangerous path and encourages us to compound faulty beliefs with faulty thinking about those beliefs. Because we are automatically focusing on what feels in alignment with what we already believe, this process has the added strength of "feeling right," even when it is demonstrably and disastrously wrong.

When focus goes awry, it can also result in what Buddhist teachers often refer to as the "Monkey Mind." If you've ever seen a troupe of monkeys at a zoo or in the wild, you have a fair concept of what the Monkey Mind looks like. This is the part of our brain that flits around from one subject to the next, unable to focus on any one thing for long and easily distracted by whatever shiny object catches its attention next. The Monkey Mind is always yammering away at us, filling our head with its incessant (and often mindless) chatter.

The biggest problem with the Monkey Mind is that it often zips around chattering about topics you don't really need to think about, and prevents you from focusing on those you do. For example, whenever we need to concentrate on doing a new or unfamiliar task, more often than not, instead of focusing on the job at hand, the Monkey Mind starts distracting us by reminding us about how stupid we'll look if we mess up or how long it's been since we've attempted this activity. The Monkey Mind is our constant companion, and it knows all of our worst fears and secrets. It's the first thing we hear when we get up and the last thing we hear when we go to bed.

This aspect of the Monkey Mind is the voice that keeps reminding you over and over and over again about the light bill being due, even though it's already on your list of things to handle tomorrow. It's the voice that says, "Where are we going next?" the moment you walk in the door. And it's the voice that says, "Why are you even bothering when you know you're going to fail?" when we try to do something new or frightening.

It's enough to drive you bananas!

Learning to quiet, or at least ignore, the Monkey Mind is essential in order for us to function at our best. It's hard to think critically, view evidence dispassionately and make important, but sometimes tough or scary, decisions if we're constantly being harangued, misled and distracted by our fears, doubts, and insecurities.

2.9 The Chicken and the Egg Paradox

Although mankind likes to think of itself as "the thinking animal," a lot of the thinking we do is either wholly or mostly unconscious. Even when we *think* we're consciously thinking about something, what we're usually doing is simply waiting for our minds to get back to us with an answer to a question. How that answer was generated, and why, are subjects that we are often completely in the dark about.

For example, you would think that if I asked you to sit at a table and randomly raise your right hand at will, you obviously would be making the decision to do so consciously. However, in tests where the subjects are wired to an active MRI that allows scientists to view brain in action and then asked to raise their hand at random intervals whenever they chose, the results are clear: In every case, the areas of the brain that control motor function light up fractionally but clearly sooner than the parts of the brain responsible for cognitive function, even though the subjective experience of the participants was the opposite.

In short, your mind and body start the physical process of raising your hand *before* you decide to do so, although to you it will appear as if you decided to lift your arm and then went about lifting it. How and why this is so, and what it means for concepts like free will, are matters that are still in debate. But the fact that it happens is definitively proven.

The same thing happens with abstract thought. Because of the way our brains evolved (as tools designed to determine and implement the most effective action possible in the most efficient and quickest manner possible), our thinking is subject to the shortcuts, instincts, and pattern recognition systems that our brains have created to save time and speed up reactions as they evolved. Almost all of this happens completely beneath our awareness.

We are faced with a problem—say, a threat to our position at work—and before we know it, the solution, or at least a path to a solution, presents itself. What that solution is will depend almost entirely on our past experiences, our personal beliefs, our assumptions, our biases, our temperament, our upbringing, our current state of health, our genetic structure—pretty much everything, that is, except rational and logical thought.

But because of the way our brains work, it will appear to us to be the other way around; it will feel as if we have rationally come to a logical conclusion based on available data. It's a comforting thought, no doubt, but it's not reality.

Chapter Summary

All human beings share some aspects of their thinking and actions in common. These key traits are what make us uniquely human.

- **Plasticity** is the brain's ability to adapt, to learn new things and to reconfigure itself to meet new needs, situations, and requirements. Without this plasticity, we would be incapable of functioning in our ever-changing environment.
- **Emotions** are strong, instinctual motivators, often stemming directly from our Lizard Brain. These powerful feelings can, indeed, be very useful for navigating social relationships and acting as an early warning system for danger or other problems. But if allowed to rule our actions, they can also lead us into behaviors that are inappropriate, harmful, or even dangerous.
- **Pattern Recognition** is a vital part of our survival toolkit that allows us to recognize familiar people, places, and situations based on prior experience. It is also very easily tricked by random coincidences and superficial similarities. Because it is such a deeply embedded part of our nature, however, it can be very hard to think ourselves out of what our senses tell us to believe.
- **Biases** are the brain's shortcuts. They save us time and effort by enabling us to jump to reasonable conclusions on very little evidence, relying mainly on a combination of pattern recognition and primitive instincts. However, biases can get in the way of critical thinking and can get us into a lot of trouble by making up our minds for us without sufficient information to do so accurately and appropriately. Unfortunately, biases are so deeply ingrained in our psyches, we are rarely aware of their existence, even when we are deeply under their influence.
- **Mindsets** are aggregations of biases and assumptions that collect around a particular aspect of life, such as relationships and work. These mindsets offer us a framework for dealing with reality without having to rethink every situation from scratch every time we come across it.

Sometimes, however, inaccurate information or interpretations create faulty mindsets that cause us much trouble and pain. Unfortunately, like the biases and patterns they are made of, mindsets are notoriously invisible against the background of our thoughts. We are often led by them without ever realizing they are there.

- **The Need to Know** is a key motivator in humans. When faced with uncertainty, we crave answers. This has led to good things, like science and religion. But when our need to know exceeds our ability to know, it also leads to such problems as willful ignorance and superstitions.
- **Focus** is the ability to home in on what is important to us while ignoring everything else. This enables us to recognize the signals of danger in a noisy environment and concentrate on a task while ignoring distractions. However, it also allows us to lose ourselves in pointless and sometimes dangerous pursuits while ignoring information that could prove useful and even lifesaving.

As much as we all share these traits in common, the traits themselves have a common center, i.e., many of them happen well below our conscious level of awareness. This means that before we can even begin to guide, mold, or harness our mental abilities for our own use, we first have to be able to find them, a task made more difficult by the fact that often the expression of the very traits we're seeking to find renders them invisible to our searching eyes.

CHAPTER 3

The Problem: Thinking On Autopilot

"Bias and prejudice are attitudes to be kept in hand, not attitudes to be avoided."
—Charles Curtis

"To increase your effectiveness, make your emotions subordinate to your commitments."
—Brian Koslow

3.1 Mind Games and MindFields: When Good Traits Go Bad

Your mind plays games with you, whether you realize it or not.

Believe it or not, our brains weren't designed to think. They were designed to react, and to store a record of successful reactions so as to speed up the process next time. Thinking is just a pleasant (or sometimes not so pleasant) side effect of excess computing power, much in the same way that the ability to play very complicated and detailed games on your computer is a side effect of bigger, faster, and better computers, which were originally built to handle the slogging drudgery of productive work.

These days, however, we tend to do less reacting and more thinking. Civilization has allowed us to free our minds from tiger and food patrol in order to concentrate on things like project management, philosophy, and fantasy football teams. The problem is that our brains are optimized to pursue quick-and-dirty "good enough" results over rational observation and logical thinking. This is great if you're being chased by something that's trying to eat you. But it's not so great when you're trying to navigate a relationship or negotiate a contract.

Most people attempt to solve problems by playing around with the issues at hand and then making decisions based on faulty logic, biases, emotions, cognitive dissonance resolution and other shortcuts. We may rationalize our decisions afterward, but in reality our solutions are based almost entirely on gut feelings, emotional reactions, and hidden biases. As a result, our solutions tend to be no more valid than the architectural designs built by a child playing with blocks.

Unfortunately, most of our thinking tends to happen well below the level of our awareness. And since we don't know what's going on, we often arrive at conclusions believing we have done so via a process of logical, consistent analysis, when in fact it has been almost entirely an intuitive, gut-reaction response.

We would get much better results if we were to consciously structure our problem solving by applying basic cognitive tools, determining and dealing with any underlying biases and other subconscious issues that could cause problems and then coming to a conclusion based on solid critical thinking. But all of that runs contrary to our innate programming. We resist doing it because it feels unnatural and often involves a lot of hard work, whereas our normal way of doing things is easy and comfortable.

There are MindFields, mindsets and blind spots in play constantly as we think. This section will help people understand the three hazardous areas.

3.2 Navigating Your MindFields

For you, as a project manager, the key to successful problem solving and decision-making is engaged thinking. By engaged thinking, I mean paying attention to your brain's natural tendencies toward pattern recognition, susceptibility to bias and the powerful influence of emotions, and not letting these unconscious habits control your thoughts.

I call these gifts of evolution *The Three MindFields* because, like actual minefields, patterns, biases and emotions are hidden traps that lie beneath the surface of your awareness, and encounters with them can be very destructive. Additionally, as with a real minefield, you usually don't know that you stepped on one until it has blown up in your face.

Unfortunately, since these traits were designed to function automatically in an environment almost none of us currently inhabit, chances are good that the results are not as we would wish them to be. The problem is that unless you find a way to outsmart evolution, you are probably not getting the most out of your short time on this planet.

In order to truly understand these MindFields, it might help to visualize each of them as relating to the future, the present, and the past. *Pattern recognition* is literally your brain identifying what your next step should be in the future, based on the patterns to which it has already been exposed. Emotions live in the present and influence how you interpret things right now in ways that can be both positive and negative. Your biases have a history, and they reinforce and feed off their mental ancestors. They originate in the past.

3.3 The Future Orientation—The Impact of Pattern Recognition

Finding patterns in the stream of events is a deeply hardwired human instinct. When we encounter situations that seem familiar, we recognize the pattern and automatically retrieve a pre-recorded template of expected behavior. This enables us to save a lot of time and energy that we would otherwise spend making it up as we went. But while this instinct goes a long way toward assuring our survival in the wild, and takes a lot of the work out of our day-to-day activities, it can cause serious problems when we are faced with situations that require careful analysis.

Much of project management is a "thinking" activity—planning, analysis, investigation, initial design, proposal generation, specification, business decisions and, last but not least, risk management. Proactively coaching and teaching your project Stakeholders to recognize the difference between beneficial pattern recognition versus destructive pattern recognition is a very good investment.

Remember that the brain is continually trying to expand its network of patterns and will continually seek to create mental shortcuts especially tailored to your use in the future. The idea is to harness this tendency by instilling a pattern of conscious thought and critical analysis in reaction to a problem or a decision.

Pattern Recognition and Association

Our brain is programmed through association. When something is repeated frequently enough, our brain recognizes it as a pattern. Once a pattern is recognized, our brain tries to associate it with something that is occurring alongside this pattern. This can be a feeling, a reaction or a biological response. Part of this is what we call the learning process, which serves as a safety mechanism as well as an educational device.

For example, when a child touches a hot iron for the first time, he does not know what to expect. There is no pattern registered in his brain yet. If it continues to happen, the brain starts to see the pattern. The brain associates iron to the feeling of heat and pain, and it will trigger a response. In this case, the child will try to avoid the iron, even though the iron might not even be turned on. Of course, over time the brain will further detect another pattern—the iron is hot only when the power indicator light is on. Thus, a new association is created.

What our brain learns is registered to both the conscious and subconscious parts of our mind. When we are children, both our conscious and subconscious minds are very flexible. As we grow older, our brains become more and more inflexible. At some point, those things that exist in our mind (consciously or subconsciously) are solidified and become what we are. We start to resist any further change, and habits (good or bad) have formed around repeated behaviors. This is why changing behaviors and bad habits is next to impossible for many people.

In the context of evolutionary psychology, this is a good thing. Survival would have been all but impossible for our ancestors if they had to continually redevelop effective patterns and habits from scratch. In the context of the modern world, however, where our changing environment has far outpaced our behavioral development, it creates problems when the patterns we recognized and the habits we developed as a child are no longer valid or useful in our adult lives.

Language

Although we rarely realize it, the language we use is among the most important mechanisms involved in the association process. This language-thought connection is so deeply embedded in our minds, studies show that even when we think silently to ourselves, we still form sentences in our mind to represent what we are thinking.

If I say the phrase "red apple," what do you see, feel, smell and taste in your mind? Even before you start to consciously think about it, your brain is already associating the phrase "red apple" with specific memories, emotions, and reactions. Even though the apple is not physically there in front of you, you still can visualize it, feel it, taste it and smell it in your mind.

Your brain further associates this phrase with emotions, assuming there are any events in the past relating to red apples that you feel strongly about. For example, when I smell a certain type of soap, it always takes me back to when I was in boarding school; obviously, this smell is in some way related to that location in my mind, no doubt because the soap was commonly used there. In turn, the smell triggers emotions making me very happy, as those times were among the best of my life.

The key difference is that actual stimulus is the real thing—what you smell and see are really there, whereas language is only an abstract concept of a thing, sounds and written symbols we associate with something concrete. In the mind, however, words and language are as real, if not more so, than the original object. To speak it is to think it, and thus to experience it as if it were really happening.

Habit

Habits are formed when we repeat certain actions frequently enough to establish an automatic pattern of behavior. This happens because of the way our brains engage in pattern recognition and association.

Since this process of repeatedly associating a particular action to a particular situation is how a habit is formed, then in order to get rid of a habit we need to retrain our brains to associate the stimuli that trigger our habit to a different pattern of behavior. Off course, we all know this is easier said than done. We can feel the power of patterns by virtue of how hard it is to get rid of an unwanted habit.

Our minds are programmed through interaction with language as well as with our senses. This is why the use of language, in the form of recorded suggestions, hypnosis sessions or autosuggestions, can be successful when used to associate new ideas, concepts, and beliefs to create healthy new behaviors. Along with the use of language, there are other technologies that use our senses, such as snapping rubber bands on our wrists or rewarding preferred behavior with treats, to access the subconscious mind and reprogram our minds to rid ourselves of bad habits.

3.4 The Past Orientation—The Impact of Bias

Biases run our lives. They enable us to process new information very quickly by taking the mental shortcuts created by pattern recognition—we expect that the sun will rise today because it has always risen, and we expect that turning the key in our car's ignition will start the car, because that is what has always happened in the past.

The speed of this process, and the fact that it is unconscious (and therefore uncontrollable), has the effect of strengthening and validating our biases, sometimes at the expense of the truth. For example, if we assume our spouse will react negatively to a suggestion of seeing a horror movie, we will continue to view horror movies as "off the menu" even if our partner's preferences have changed. (It's also possible that our partner never actually expressed distaste for horror movies but merely disliked the one we saw together, and we simply assumed his or her distaste applied more broadly than it did.)

In addition, we tend to give a lot of traction to new information that is consistent with our biases. Conversely, new information that is not consistent with our biases is given low value or is rejected outright. For example, we may miss hints that our partner would like to see a horror movie because this doesn't fit in with our understanding of reality. Either way, if your thinking is stuck on autopilot, it's a powerful "MindField."

How Biases Impact You

If you were going out for a row in a canoe, you would probably want to know about any holes in the boat before you started paddling, right? Well, biases are like holes in your reasoning abilities that can sink your thinking process with poor judgment, faulty assumptions, and misinterpreted evidence.

Of course, simply *noticing* these holes isn't enough to prevent your canoe, or your thinking processes, from sinking. However, by being aware of the holes in your thinking, you can devise methods to plug them up and prevent them from being a problem.

Biases can cause problems for project managers in a number of areas:

- **Decision making**. Any number of biases can distort decision-making. Confirmation bias can lead you to discount information that opposes existing theories, while anchoring can throw off negotiations by forcing you to stand your ground on an arbitrary issue.
- **Problem solving**. Biases can impede your creativity when solving problems. A framing bias can cause you to look at a problem too narrowly. And the illusion of control bias can cause you to overestimate the extent to which your actions influence results.
- **Learning**. Thinking errors can also impact how you learn. The Von Restorff effect can cause you to overemphasize some information compared to the whole. Clustering illusions can also trick you into thinking you've learned more than you actually have.

Let's take a look at some of the more common types of bias.

Confirmation Bias

As we noted earlier, confirmation bias is a tendency to seek information to prove, rather than disprove, a theory. Like many biases, it is strongly intertwined with cognitive dissonance. (Cognitive dissonance is the tension and discomfort we feel when our thoughts and our actions don't align.) In this case, confirmation bias seeks to avoid cognitive dissonance by searching out only that evidence which supports an established point of view, and ignoring or devaluing evidence that opposes it.

Hindsight Bias

Known more commonly under "hindsight is 20/20" rule, this bias causes people to see past results as appearing more likely than they did beforehand. For example, many anti-terrorism tactics, such as limiting liquids at airports, are grounded in hindsight bias. "Well, obviously," we say, "if you can take a large amount of liquid on a plane, it's easy to smuggle explosive chemicals in and combine them to make a bomb." That only became obvious to everyone after someone tried to do it. Before then, we never considered bottles of shampoo to present a threat.

Clustering Illusion

This is the tendency to see patterns where none actually exist. Although this may be a necessary byproduct of our ability to detect patterns, it can create problems when it happens inappropriately. Clustering illusions can also result in things like "cargo cults" and faulty stock market predictions based on completely coincidental "patterns" or associations.

Recency Effect

The recency effect is the tendency to give more weight to recent data. People remember near-past events as being more important than events further back in time. The existence of this bias makes it important to gather enough long-term data, so that the daily ups and downs that loom so largely in our minds don't lead to bad decisions.

Anchoring Bias

Anchoring is a well-known problem in negotiations. It involves stating a position that then becomes an "anchor" around which the rest of the negotiation will form. For example, the first person to state a price will usually force the other person to give a new price based on the first price stated, rather than on other important data such as actual value or demand. This can cause problems when one party winds up defending a position that, in all actuality, doesn't mean that much to her and detracts from her ability to compromise and get what she wants out of a negotiation.

Overconfidence Effect

This has also been called "Lake Wobegon Syndrome," from that show's tagline, "Where all the men are strong, all the women good looking and all the children above average." Almost everyone ranks themselves as being within the top third of all humans for positive traits and skills. At the same time, people tend to imagine the exact opposite in relation to negative traits, with almost everyone placing themselves in the bottom 30% of those exhibiting unpopular or unfavorable traits.

Fundamental Attribution Error

This is the tendency to confuse actions made as a result of external pressures as personal traits or personality. For example, we may conclude that our manager is a tight-fisted jerk when he cuts our budget when, in fact, his actions are the result of decisions made higher up the corporate ladder in which he had no say. Even in situations when we know a person is advocating a particular position based on the luck of the draw (as happens during a debate team competition), we still tend to form a personal dislike for those who are instructed to argue against our own personal beliefs.

For a more complete list of biases and their explanations,
see Appendix 1—Common Biases

Studies have shown that it is difficult to out-think these cognitive biases. Even when participants in different studies were warned about bias beforehand, this knowledge had little impact on their ability to see past them.

What an understanding of biases *can* do, however, is allow you to design decision-making methods and procedures in such a way that biases can be circumvented, in the same way that researchers use double-blind studies to prevent bias from contaminating laboratory results. By making adjustments to your decision-making, problem solving, and learning patterns, you can reduce the effects of any biases that might come into play.

3.5 The Present Orientation—The Impact of Emotions

The mental trait with the greatest influence over our thinking is emotion. As Daniel Goleman wrote in *Emotional Intelligence: Why It Can Matter More Than IQ*, "emotion is a strong link that hijacks or overwhelms our power to reason." Our ancestors relied on their emotions to survive. But, these days, we tend to use our emotions more often for making lifestyle decisions than for staying alive.

Emotions are a basic, gut-level response to a situation or stimulus. Everything we do, encounter or think about triggers emotions, and emotions affect the way we think, feel and act in response to these trigger events. Every level of thinking is based on and colored by emotion. It is the foundation of thought.

Despite how we might view this reality, it's actually quite useful. Emotions trigger instinctive reactions that help us get ourselves out of trouble without having to think things through. Unfortunately, they can also cause us to do other things without thinking them through as well, which is not always so helpful. The trick is to learn when to let emotions guide your thinking, and when it's more appropriate to let thinking take the lead instead.

In addition to saving our skins, emotions help us form and navigate relationships by promoting empathy and being able to experience love, kindness, joy and other positive feelings. In turn, these feelings provoke us to actions, such as holding someone's hand, helping him up from a fall or sharing our food, that can strengthen and secure our bonds with those around us.

The role emotions play in shaping thinking may account for a large part of why we see a failure of good thinking in our team members. When our expectations for higher-order thinking don't translate into our team members using the critical and creative-thinking skills we know they have, it may be because their initial emotional reactions are carrying the day. It is not enough to teach thinking skills. We must also pay attention to the emotions that underlie the thinking process.

Intuition and gut feelings are a large part of the decision-making process and are based on emotion. The most basic of these gut emotions are fear and anger, both of which are generated in the amygdala, which then triggers the hypothalamus to release hormones via the endocrine system, creating what we call the *fight-or-flight response*. When this happens, our bodies go on autopilot and we will act without thinking and without hesitation, often to our complete and utter dismay.

A lot of this happens because of something called the *Reticular Activating System*. This is a sort of master override switch that shuts down your higher functioning in response to the fight-or-flight reaction. At that point, we are operating completely on autopilot, running off of instincts and adrenaline. This is what happens when a spider lands on our head or we reach into a dark crevice and touch something icky. All of a sudden we go from "Master of the Known Universe and All We Survey" to a gibbering monkey, screeching at the top of our lungs and jerking around like we've stepped on a live wire.

Once the threat is past, the RAS flicks the switch again and—Presto Change-O!—we're actually back in control of our bodies and able to think like normal human beings. Of course, by now all of our friends are rolling on the ground and laughing at our perfor mance. But hey, at least that slimy rock mold didn't get a chance to bite our fingers off.

Why We Have Emotions

Emotions serve several very useful purposes. They warn us of things going on that we should be aware of. They tell us how we're doing in social situations. They prime the body for encounters like conflicts and falling in love. They get us moving and inspire us to take action. They enable us to exist in social groups and help us communicate with one another in ways we can all understand. They can guide us toward and away from situations that we need to take part in or avoid.

In short, emotions are like external sensors for our minds. They help us pick up on subtle changes in the body language and speech of others, take in cues from our environments and help us react quickly and decisively once we've compared these inputs with patterns we have experienced in the past. Without these emotions, we would just stand in front of a charging elephant without fear and alienate those around us without realizing it. As a result, we probably wouldn't live long enough to pass on such a maladaptive system in the first place.

Primary and Secondary Emotions

There are two types of emotions, primary emotions and secondary emotions. Primary emotions are what we consider to be the core or basic emotions. Some primary emotions include: love, anger, sadness, happiness or joy, surprise, curiosity, and fear. Although there's no absolute consensus on how many primary emotions there are and what constitutes a primary emotion, the idea is that a primary emotion is what we feel, whereas a secondary emotion is the result of how we feel about that feeling. We feel angry about feeling angry, or angry about feeling sad, etc.

As an example, let's take a look at the emotion "anger." If a friend agrees to do something for us, then decides not to do it, we may feel anger. Because of this anger, we may feel several secondary emotions, such as betrayal (How dare he!) or insecurity (Is he really my friend?) or even guilt (Did I ask too much?).

Secondary emotions are not always useful or helpful. They can provoke us into acting inappropriately toward others, encourage us to suppress or downplay our feelings and drive us to acts that are dangerous or self-destructive.

Most secondary emotions are habits that we learn from those around us. We may be feeling guilty and betrayed about a friend's forgotten promise, and we internalize these emotions as appropriate reactions to these situations. Later on, if one of our friends forgets a promise, we recognize this pattern and react by feeling betrayed at his forgetfulness and guilty for our own imposition at asking him.

Sometimes we even layer additional secondary emotions on top of the original ones, and more on top of those. In the end, we can wind up feeling guilty about feeling betrayed and feeling embarrassed about feeling guilty about being betrayed, and so on. After a few rounds of this, it all becomes very, very complicated and we soon find ourselves experiencing emotions in reaction to situations for which we have no easy explanation, like bursting into tears and running away when our friend throws us a surprise birthday party. That's when we end up on some psychiatrist's couch, funding his next trip to Tahiti while we spend the next few months untangling all these emotional threads.

Generally speaking, secondary emotions are considered to be maladaptive, which means they don't contribute to our survival and may even hinder it. Unfortunately, they are also so deeply grounded in our emotional systems that they can be almost if not entirely impossible to eradicate. In most cases, the best we can do is learn to recognize them and understand that they are not "real" emotions and that we don't have to act on them just because we feel them—and indeed, we can even chose to replace them with something entirely different and more in alignment with our goals if we work at it hard enough.

Biology and Emotion

Your emotions are part of your brain's basic hardwiring. You can't separate the two. Each experience with emotion affects and alters the brain by creating associations and biases around certain events. Likewise, existing biases and associations, plus the way your brain handles and distributes cortisol, serotonin, endorphins and other brain chemicals, affects and alters your emotional state.

Too much cortisol, for example, can cause high blood pressure and raise your blood sugar, which can make you feel tired and anxious and give you a headache. In turn, this may make you easier to anger and leave you feeling irritable and grumpy. Of course, those around you will respond poorly to this behavior and fire back, which will increase your stress level and produce more cortisol, and so on.

If you fail to realize that the reason you feel angry is because you're over-stressed and not eating well, you may assume that these emotions are a legitimate response to a perceived threat and act accordingly. Since this is not the case, your lack of awareness about your own brain patterns will cause harm to you and those around you.

On top of all that, both your thinking and your emotions are shaped by your diet, your health, how much sleep you got last night, the weather and so on. These factors are called
vulnerabilities.

Vulnerabilities

Vulnerabilities are things that can accentuate or deaden emotional response. They include things like not getting enough sleep, personal or professional setbacks, stress, poor nutrition, illness, injury and so on.

These factors create a poor environment for critical thinking. They affect your judgment, increase the likelihood of experiencing negative secondary emotions, lead you to making inappropriate decisions and encourage destructive behaviors.

Being Mindful of Emotions

Mindfulness is the practice of being consciously aware of everything in your life. It means actively taking a part in living your life rather than passively letting life happen to you. Through mindfulness, you learn to inhabit your life fully rather than operating on autopilot.

Mindfulness relies on two key principles: attention and intention. Attention is the result of awareness, of focusing in on what's important in an active and purposeful manner. Intention is purposefulness. It's having a clear understanding of what you want and in what manner you're prepared to go after it. Intention without attention creates a bull in a china shop. Attention without intention provides all those pavers on the road to Hell.

It's about detaching your emotions from your observations so that you can objectively see how you feel about something without getting wrapped up in the feeling. That doesn't mean it's about being emotionless or unfeeling, just that you take a step back and view all that emotional hubbub from outside the feeling, so you can more easily separate those feelings from their triggers.

Mindfulness is about awareness and being in the now. It's about living life fully and keeping your full attention on where you are, and not somewhere else. It's not about chilling out, zoning out or just plain dropping out, however; that's mindlessness, not mindfulness.

Mindfulness is also about seeing what is, rather than what you think it is. It's about looking past all your preexisting concepts and ideas about what something should be or will be and just seeing what it's really like.

Mindfulness is about living. It's about being one with your experiences and not missing out on life because you're too busy worrying about things that aren't happening to enjoy what is.

Dealing With the Effects of Emotion: Judgment and Self Talk

We all have basic assumptions about how things are supposed to be and how they're supposed to work. We have a sense of right and wrong, and we know that we want to be treated in a certain way. Problems arise when our thought patterns on these issues become inflexible or rigid. This is called dichotomous thinking, and it can be described as "either/or" or "all-or-nothing" thinking.

If you hold a belief about how you should be treated, but others around you don't treat you that way, you may feel angry, sad, or afraid. Of course, it isn't wrong to want to be treated in a certain way. But if you stubbornly cling to your expectations without accepting the fact that someone is treating you differently and that you are always going to be treated that way unless you act to change your situation, you'll experience unnecessary emotional suffering as a result.

As we noted earlier, thoughts can trigger emotions as well. And even after the thought that triggered the emotion has passed, subsequent thoughts can keep triggering the same emotion or can trigger secondary emotional responses. (Under this heading of "thought," in addition to conscious thought we also include automatic thoughts, beliefs, giving philosophies, self-talk, or what is sometimes referred to as tapes that have been recorded into our brains.) Whatever we call them, all these aspects of thought affect our emotions.

These types of emotions can manifest themselves as "self-talk," which is the way we talk to ourselves inside our heads about what's going on around us. Failing to deal with negative or inappropriate emotions can result in self-talk like, "I'm so stupid" or "I never learn." As we mentioned in the previous section on language, continual repetition of self-talk can shape our thinking and our behaviors so that we become what we say.

On the other hand, replacing our negative self-talk—"I'm so stupid for asking him out when he's already dating Julie"—with positive self-talk—"I'm not stupid, I just didn't have all the information I needed"—can redirect our energies and emotions into pathways that are useful and supportive and replace our self-criticism with self-assurance.

It is wise to spend some time learning to be aware of these patterns of thought and the emotions they trigger so that you can be prepared for them when they occur. Otherwise, your life becomes like an abandoned raft being dragged down a river by a capricious current—lurching forward and slowing down without warning, getting stuck in endlessly spiraling eddies and then sucked back out into the stream, and spinning around willy-nilly because there is no one there to anticipate these hazards and steer the raft away from them. In the end, unless someone takes the rudder, it will wind up going wherever the current takes it with no intention or purpose. Assuming it doesn't fetch up on a rock and sink first, of course.

To improve your ability to name and recognize the range of the emotions in play at any given time, you can self-check against a set of five core feelings: happiness, sadness, anger, fear, and shame.

Review the range of emotions in the following table:

Intensity of Feelings	Happy	Sad	Angry	Afraid	Ashamed
HIGH	Elated Excited Overjoyed Thrilled Exuberant Ecstatic Fired Up Delighted	Depressed Disappointed Alone Hurt Dejected Hopeless Sorrowful Miserable	Furious Enraged Outraged Aggravated Irate Seething	Terrified Horrified Scared Stiff Petrified Fearful Panicky	Sorrowful Remorseful Unworthy Worthless Disgraced Dishonored
MEDIUM	Cheerful Up Good Relieved Satisfied	Heartbroken Down Upset Distressed Regretful Melancholy	Upset Mad Hot Frustrated Agitated Disgusted	Scared Frightened Threatened Insecure Uneasy Shocked	Apologetic Defamed Sneaky Guilty
MILD	Glad Contented Pleasant Fine Pleased	Unhappy Moody Blue Lost Bad Dissatisfied	Perturbed Annoyed Uptight Put Out Irritated Touchy	Apprehensive Nervous Worried Timid Unsure Anxious	Embarassed Disappointed Let Down

Establishing a high level of self-awareness involves recognizing the sensations you feel and being able to name which emotion is happening. To become more mindful and confident, identify both the emotions you feel most often and which emotions in particular you are feeling in a difficult situation. This will raise your emotional self-awareness and help you determine how to manage these emotions when they surface.

Emotional self-awareness is part of an overall emotional intelligence framework popularized by Daniel Goleman in his groundbreaking book, *Emotional Intelligence.*

Emotional Intelligence and the Project Manager

Emotional intelligence is the product of two key skills: personal and social competence. Personal competence focuses more on you as an individual, and is divided into self-awareness and self-management. Social competence relates to how you behave with other people, and is divided into social awareness and relationship management.

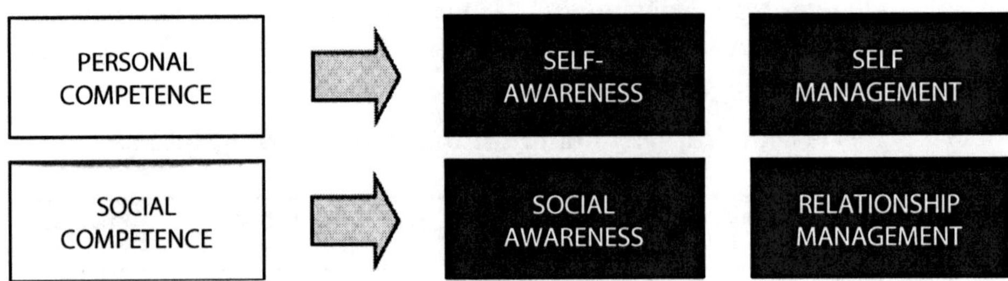

Business-thought leader Peter Drucker says that to better manage oneself, each of us needs to discover our own ignorance. From the perspective of ***Thinking On Purpose***, the key con-cepts for project managers are self-awareness and self-management. Both work together to help you to name the biases, emotions, or habits in play at any given moment, which helps you identify your mindsets.

Research indicates that the biggest obstacle to this process is the desire to avoid the discomfort that comes from increasing your self-awareness. Rather than avoiding these feelings, your goal should be to move toward them, into them and eventually through them. This tactic is commonly referred to "leaning into your discomfort." So, the next situation in which you're aware of an unproductive emotional state, lean into the discomfort and learn from it.

Culture Matters

Your ability to cope with national cultures, corporate cultures, and vocational cultures is often referred to as *Cultural Intelligence.* This is the emerging "must-have" competency for project managers into today's increasingly globalized environment. While it shares many of the properties of Emotional Intelligence, Cultural Intelligence goes a step further by equipping a person to distinguish between behaviors produced by the culture in question and those behaviors that are either unique to particular individuals or found in all human beings.

Because of the increasingly diverse business environment, project managers must be able to successfully navigate through the variety of habits, gestures, and assumptions that are part and parcel of their co-workers' differences. Foreign cultures are no longer found solely in other countries, but also within corporations, vocations, and regions. Interacting with individuals who make up these diverse cultures demands sensitivity and adaptability.

Intercultural difficulties arise when we are unaware of the key features and biases of our own culture. We act on assumptions, cultural references, physical and verbal cues and so on based on our own experiences without realizing that the other person's background assigns an entirely different set of meanings and reactions to these same cues. As a result, we feel threatened, misunderstood or uneasy when interacting with people who are culturally different.

For example, we may not have an overt prejudice against people from other cultures, but we can't help but pick up on the physical and cultural characteristics that make them different from us, which can result in subtle feelings of apprehension, confusion, or alertness. We all find these sorts of differences threatening to some extent, simply because our minds are hardwired to note things that don't "feel right" as potential threats: That dog doesn't seem to be acting normal…it could have rabies. That person appears reluctant to open up…he could be hiding something. That body language doesn't match what I was expecting…there's something going on here that I'm not aware of, and so on.

This hardwiring, however, doesn't take into account cultural differences that may be causing the discrepancies (how can it, if it hasn't been exposed to them?). We have to do that by rejecting autopilot thinking and taking conscious steps to ensure we are aware of all the cultural differences that could be in play—perhaps a cultural taboo against looking superiors in the eye during conversation, or a cultural preference for heated negotiation over quiet compromise as an expression of mutual respect.

The bottom line is that interacting effectively across cultures is now a fundamental requirement in today's global business environment. While it's probably impossible for most of us to engage on a whirlwind world tour in order to learn these cultural differences first hand, there's certainly nothing stopping us from researching those cultures that we're likely to come into contact with until we feel comfortable that we can keep misunderstandings and confusion to a minimum.

3.6 Blind Spots

We all have blind spots in our thinking. A blind spot is simply an inability to see or imagine something, or an inability to think about something in a new or unfamiliar way. These may be a result of biases, patterns, stereotypes or, possibly, even just ignorance of a subject. Blind spots can also be a function of our ability to focus—we may pay so much attention to one thing that we are incapable of seeing anything else.

Blind spots can cause all sorts of problems. For example, up until just recently, stomach ulcers were thought to be caused by stress wearing away at the lining of the stomach. In fact, this was so universally understood to be true that when Dr. J. Robin Warren and Dr. Barry Marshall announced to the world that they had discovered that the stomachs of patients with peptic ulcers showed high levels of the bacterium *Helicobacter pylori*, and theorized that perhaps this microbe was actually the cause of the ulcers, the medical community replied with laughter and derision.

So sure were the two doctors that these bacteria were indeed the cause that Dr. Marshall even swallowed a solution of *H. pylori*. When he subsequently began suffering from an ulcer and gastritis and then cured himself with a round of antibiotics, they were convinced. Still, the blind spot in the medical community to this possibility was so strong that it took nearly a decade for this discovery to become accepted as reality.

In the end, though, the two doctors had the last laugh. They were awarded the Nobel Peace Prize for Medicine in 2005 as a result of their medical breakthrough, and today, treating peptic ulcers with antibiotics is routine, standard medical procedure.

Blind spots occur for many reasons, but primarily they are a result of calcified thinking processes. We get so attached to a particular point of view that we are simply incapable of seeing things another way. By virtue of confirmation bias and other such MindFields, we wrap our inaccurate assumptions in a protective layer of "common knowledge" that supports our beliefs, and dismiss anything that disagrees with our viewpoints.

In the end, we wind up hoisted on our own petard as our blind spots lead us directly into the path of oncoming reality. If we're lucky, we'll get off with just a bruised ego. If we're not, we could wind up ruining relationships, missing out on valuable opportunities, losing our personal and professional reputations and even putting ourselves in real harm's way.

Blind spots are hard to spot, naturally, because we can't see them. But with attention and mindfulness, we can spot how they affect our lives. Like scientists observing invisible cosmic objects by watching the way light is reflected around them, we can use those clues to help us uncover and illuminate those areas that blind us to reality.

3.7 Choosing Your Mindset

A key concept that the rest of this book operates on is that **if you don't take the time to consciously choose your mindsets, they will be chosen for you**.

As we discussed in the previous section, a mindset is an accretion of biases, ideas, concepts, assumptions and other mental shortcuts designed to create a framework for dealing with the world around you. It determines how you will view the world and how you will respond to it.

Mindsets are self-reinforcing. Because you see the world a certain way, you'll react to it as if it were that way. These behaviors will tend to trigger responses in others that play into the way you see things, and thus your mindset is reinforced.

As an example, a project manager who believes that he is a weak negotiator will feel insecure during contract negotiations, and this may manifest as behaviors that put off those with whom he is negotiating. He may even be so convinced of his inability to negotiate that he doesn't bother to prepare properly or keep up with training in this area. As a result of this negative body language, behavior and passive sabotage, the negotiations are likely to go poorly, reinforcing his beliefs.

On the other hand, a project manager who believes she is a strong negotiator will behave confidently, take time to prepare thoroughly and keep up on the latest in negotiation tactics and strategies. As a result, negotiations will probably go smoother and have positive results. *This is true even if the second PM has no more actual innate talent in negotiation than the first.* In each case, the exact same event serves to reinforce two completely different mindsets.

Since mindsets are an automatic construct of our minds, we may not even realize we hold a particular mindset. The opinions and behaviors it creates may simply seem to us to be obvious or common sense. It's only when we're taken out of our familiar environment—say, downtown New York City—and placed in an unfamiliar one—like the Australian Outback—that we realize just how much we operate on the basis of these assumptions and biases, and how environmentally and culturally specific our "universally understood common sense" really is.

Because of this transparency, unearthing and altering our mindsets is very difficult. Fortunately for us, the mind is, to a great extent, a self-changing system. (Note that I said "self-changing," not "self-correcting.") The correctness of a mindset is determined entirely by the culture in which it exists. Given new information, the mind will change the bias or biases that make up the mindset to fit the new reality.

For example, if we are forced by circumstances to collaborate on a project with someone we have always disliked, we may find out that the reasons we disliked him were incorrect or exaggerated, and we may end up liking that person. Many people who grew up in racially discriminatory cultures have had their bigoted mindsets completely demolished and rebuilt from the ground up by the simple virtue of getting to know those whom they were taught to hate. Some have even gone so far as to leave their original culture and assume that of those whom they previously discriminated against.

Creating mindsets is something the brain does automatically, whether you're paying attention or not. You can either actively respond to situations and your environment (and in this way take an active role in the development of mindsets that works for you), or you can passively react to life and allow your brain to create your mindsets without your input. Either way, those mindsets will be created.

However, like concrete, mindsets may be easy and quick to form, but removing them once they have set takes a great deal of work. It is far easier to "set your mind" in the shape you want it to be, than to uncover and break up an already solidified mindset. It's up to you to ensure that the mindsets you end up with are the ones that will benefit, rather than detract, from your success.

Fixed and Growth Mindsets

The difference between having a fixed mindset and a growth mindset can play a significant role in how you develop as a project manager.

Project managers with a fixed mindset believe that there is an upper bound on achievement, improvement, talent or other attributes. Because of this, they tend to avoid things that they believe are "beyond them" and stick to things they know they will do well. Because they don't believe that they can be any better than they actually are, they don't bother to try.

Interestingly enough, this can severely limit the success of even extremely talented people. Because they believe that their talent or skill is innate, they see no reason to practice or push themselves. In fact, they may even feel that participating in such activities implies that they aren't as talented or skilled (or implies that they doubt their talents), since only those without their level of expertise require practice. For project managers with a fixed mindset, it's more important to appear secure in their talents and skills than to actually improve them, and when faced with a failure of these abilities, they will lie and use misdirection or projection in order to protect their image.

A growth mindset, on the other hand, is one that holds that improvement is always possible. It may take lots of work and a long time, but if you keep practicing and trying you will eventually succeed. Project managers with growth mindsets enjoy challenges and will pursue difficult tasks and activities that are well beyond their current skill level. Failure doesn't provoke defensiveness, but rather encourages even greater effort.

It is not unusual for someone with less innate talent, but who has a growth mindset about that talent, to eventually outperform someone who was born with a high degree of skill but hampered by a fixed mindset about that skill. This is the classic case of the tortoise and the hare—the tortoise believes that steady effort can result in success, while the hare is so convinced of his own superior speed he loses the race by failing to even participate.

Luckily for us, a fixed mindset can be replaced with a growth mindset. In order to do so, you have to accept the fact that growth can indeed be achieved. This is the hard part—because you already have a fixed mindset, making this leap of faith can be very difficult. However, it might help to know that science has proven over and over again that the belief that growth is always possible is indeed so. Studies show repeatedly that when people can be convinced that working at a problem will result in improvement, they improve, even if they previously held fixed mindset beliefs about their ability to do that task.

Many fixed mindsets are culturally created. Here in America, it is assumed that physics is a difficult subject to learn, and that only a few very talented people have the ability to learn it. But, as was noted in an article on mindsets by Marina Krakovsky, "A college physics teacher recently wrote to Dweck that in India, where she was educated, there was no notion that you had to be a genius or even particularly smart to learn physics. 'The assumption was that everyone could do it, and, for the most part, they did.'" Obviously, physics is not harder in America than it is in India. The only difference is the belief concerning who does and who doesn't have the ability to learn it.

Perception and Reality

Our perception of reality is neither objective nor accurate. What we see and know as "reality" is really an interpretation of that reality as filtered through our brains. Because of the nature of our brains, we are constantly deleting and distorting bits of reality as we process it.

This happens in a three-stage process. First, our brains take in stimuli and input and **interpret** them before compiling them into information we can use. This involves a whole process of physical and mental gymnastics involving our senses, our cognitive abilities and so on. After it goes through all of these convoluted processes, our brain then "tells" us what we see, hear, feel, etc. In many cases, this is a subjective rather than an objective truth. To use a common example, our brains will color-correct what we see based on lighting conditions, so that leaves still look green even when the setting sun has made them distinctly red.

Second, we **evaluate** what we observe based on our values, biases and so on. For example, if we have a bias that tells us that the designs of firm A are better than those of firm B, we will probably rank a design from A as being better than one from B, even when it turns out that by objective measures such as structural integrity, materials, costs and so on, the reverse is actually true.

Third, **we establish rules** about this experience. Let's say we choose design A for our project and the decision results in cost overruns. Because we have (falsely) evaluated design A to be superior to the alternative, we may blame the contractors instead of the design for the extra expense. If we are not presented with evidence to the contrary (or fail to accept such evidence), we will establish a rule that says, "That contractor can't stay on a budget." The next time we need a design and a contractor, our reliance on that rule may result in our choosing an inferior design and ignoring a perfectly good contractor.

During this process, information gets deleted and distorted from its true nature. As a result, no two people see the same reality in the same way, and our own views will change as well as our experiences and biases change over time.

The Three Realities

Another factor influencing your mindsets are the three realities.

The first is *external reality*. This is the reality of spreadsheets, gravity, and ice cream sandwiches, and other experiences that can be identified and determined by empirical, objective testing. When you hear people talking about reality, they are often talking about external reality.

The second reality is *social reality*. Social reality is a consensus reality. It is the world of things that are so because we all believe them to be so. In American culture, bribery is against the law and is culturally believed to be a bad thing. Therefore, the reality in America is that bribery is wrong. However, in other countries, bribery is just another business expense, like taxes, fees, and rent. Those who ask for or offer bribes suffer no cultural stigma, and have no intention to do wrong. In those societies, the reality is that bribery is a normal part of doing business.

The third reality is *individual reality*. This reality depends on what you, personally, believe to be true. If the only experience you have with dogs has been friendly and loving, in your reality dogs are friendly animals that make good pets. Someone else who grew up in a neighborhood full of vicious, free-roaming dogs may experience a different reality.

Your mindset is heavily influenced by your individual reality and, to some extent, your social reality. External reality just is, and rarely affects our mindsets one way or the other except in rare cases. Problems can arise when mindsets that were created in one reality are asked to perform in different ones.

To use a previous example: If you were born in a country where bribery was wrong, but then subsequently moved to a culture where it was part of everyday behavior, you might have great difficulty accepting this change. On the other hand, you might simply be able to go with the flow. Much would depend on how strongly held your original mindset is, and how deeply it is tied into other key mindsets pertaining to concepts like honor, integrity, proper business practices, money beliefs, worldliness, and cultural flexibility. One person might be violently opposed to offering bribes despite the cultural reality because she feels it compromises her character, while another might place a higher value on maintaining a "when in Rome, do as the Romans do" laissez-faire attitude.

In any case, it is wise to be aware of how our different realities interact with each other. When realities cross, the results can be quite damaging.

3.8 Moving Forward

When it comes down to the wire, you have a choice. You can sit back and accept everything your brain throws at you as is, and allow yourself to be buffeted by the random winds of fate. Or you can take steps to actively and intentionally direct your thinking patterns and thought processes in a way that allows your brain to work for you, rather than against you.

The key to doing the latter is intention. Most of the problems caused by our thinking processes are the result of autopilot thinking. We simply don't take the time to see what's going on and decide for ourselves if it's in our best interests or not.

Some of the damage has already been done by the time we're even made aware that we have a choice in the matter. Childhood experiences, illness, cultural pressures, the nature of our education and other such influences generate biases, emotions, and habits that we may not even realize we have. It's only after repeated, concentrated effort that we are able to free our lives from these tyrannies of the brain and determine for ourselves how we will choose to think and feel.

You do have a choice. You can either continue to think on autopilot—letting your brain create and maintain your mindsets for you in ways that may or may not offer you the best opportunities for success—or you can make a change and start thinking on purpose.

Chapter Summary

The key message of this book is that you must choose your mindsets—how you think about what you think about—or they will be chosen for you.

If you allow your mindsets to be created by default, your results will almost assuredly be suboptimal. Understanding that your brain does not always work the way you want it to is key to learning how to recognize problems and change your thinking patterns to suit your own needs.

The Three MindFields are hidden obstacles that stand between you and the goal of ***Thinking On Purpose***: **pattern recognition, biases**, and **emotions**.

Pattern Recognition is related to the future, in that it tries to predict the future based on what it has seen in the past. This is a very strong, instinctive drive, and is very difficult to overcome. Language and habits are aspects of pattern recognition and, in turn, can strongly influence our perception of patterns in the world around us.

Biases are related to the past, in that they are mental shortcuts created based on past information in order to help us think and react faster. When we fail to properly interpret information, or are presented with faulty information, biases can form that inhibit our success. Out-thinking these biases can be difficult, but it is necessary for the process of critical thinking.

Emotions are related to the present, in that they are immediate, instinctive reactions to stimuli. Emotions serve as beacons or warnings to alert us to external situations that we may not be aware of. They also help us navigate social situations.

There are two different types of emotions: Primary and Secondary

Primary emotions are our base instinctive reactions, such as anger, surprise, joy, sadness, curiosity, love, and fear.

Secondary emotions are more complicated responses to our primary emotions; they're how we feel about what we feel: feeling angry about feeling sad, or feeling fear about feeling surprised.

Emotions are biological in nature and can, in turn, affect our biological state. Additionally, vulnerabilities such as illness, injury and poor health can alter and intensify our emotional state. Emotions are difficult to control, and they are often primary motivators of our actions, even when we believe ourselves to have been acting rationally and logically.

Emotional Intelligence, the ability to regulate and manage your emotions, is emerging as a signature skill for project managers in today's environment. The same thing goes for Cultural Intelligence. It's not enough to master your own emotions anymore. You must take the time and attention to understand and appropriately react to the emotional and cultural personalities of those around you.

Blind spots are another way that your mind can play games with you. Blind spots are a result of our innate ability to focus on what we feel is important, while ignoring everything else. They are also related to confirmation bias. When applied in inappropriate situations, this ability to focus (and the inability to accept information that is contrary to our beliefs) sometimes prevents us from seeing important realities.

Choosing your mindset is the most important principle of Thinking On Purpose. The proper mindsets will speed your progress, increase your success and allow you to maximize your potential. Poor mindsets will slow or prevent progress, inhibit success and minimize potential.

There are two types of mindsets:

1. **Fixed Mindsets** are the belief that talent and skill are predetermined; you're either a natural or you're not. A fixed mindset feels threatened by challenges and rejects practice, training and coaching because the person feels that he or she can't learn, or feels that he or she doesn't need to, and can rely on his or her innate talent to succeed. A fixed mindset limits growth, success, and achievement.
2. **Growth Mindsets** are the belief that talent and skill can be learned and improved; there may, indeed, be those who are born more naturally talented than others, but anyone can improve with practice and dedication. A growth mindset embraces challenge and believes that continual improvement is always an option. A growth mindset maximizes growth, success, and achievement.

Mindsets are affected by perceptions of reality. In order to process the input from our environment, our brains **interpret** the data, **evaluate** it based on past experience and biases, and then **create rules** for dealing with the situation again in the future. Because of this process, what we perceive to be reality is actually a filtered interpretation of that reality containing many **distortions** and **deletions** of the empirical truth.

There are three realities that can affect your mindset:

1. **External Reality**, or the empirically established reality of the outside world.
2. **Internal Reality**, or the sum of our beliefs about the way things are and should be.
3. **Social Reality**, or your community's consensus beliefs about the way things are and should be.

Your mindset is primarily affected by your internal reality and your social reality. If the two come into conflict, the resulting disconnect can negatively affect your mindset. Conversely, your existing mindsets can affect the way you respond to such conflicts, especially in crosscultural situations. Understanding the nature of these two realities is important as you attempt to identify, change, and guide your mindsets.

SECTION 2

THE SOLUTION

CHAPTER 4

The SOLUTION: THINKING ON PURPOSE

"It isn't that they can't see the solution. It is that they can't see the problem."
—G.K. Chesterton

"You can tell whether a man is clever by his answers.
You can tell whether a man is wise by his questions."
—Naguib Mahfouz

Meet Auto Pilot and Topper

Imagine the forces that cause you to think automatically as embodied in a character called **Auto Pilot**. Auto's reason for being is to generate as much of your behavior as possible at the subconscious level, so you don't have to think about it. Additionally, he oversees all the bodily functions that you don't have to pay attention to or think about, such as keeping your heart beating, running your metabolism and closing your eyes when a bit of dust suddenly gets blown into your face.

Auto is like a simple robot guided by a simple computer mind with a few basic but highly adaptable programs. These programs allow him to quickly learn from any given situation so that next time, he can recognize similar situations and quickly call up subroutines for reacting to and behaving in these situations. His raison d'Ítre is to REPEAT programs.

For Auto, things like biases, instincts, and mindsets are a feature, not a bug, because they speed things up and allow him to do many things at once with little time and energy. However, as with every such device, the GIGO principle—Garbage In, Garbage Out—is clearly in force. And also like a computer, old programs can become corrupted or simply obsolete over time. If you fail to upgrade or repair these programs as needed, their effect on the smooth running of your life can be substantial.

It's at these times that you need to have a little more say in how things should be than Auto Pilot allows you. To help you do this, imagine that Auto Pilot has a companion, whom we'll call **Topper**, to remind us to Think On Purpose.

Topper embodies all the aspects of our conscious mind—our thinking brain. He's like the guy with the control box that can alter Auto Pilot's actions. He knows when and how far to let Auto run with our automatic thinking, and when to step in and take control.

Normally, Auto Pilot is left to run on his own. For most day-to-day activities, Auto's onboard programming and previous experiences are more than sufficient. However, should Auto Pilot begin to behave in an inappropriate or unsuitable manner, Topper can take manual control and guide Auto back to a more appropriate path. He does this by RESETTING, so that programs are cleared and (hopefully) replaced with more appropriate ones. By doing so, Topper helps train Auto and, over time, can replace bad programming with programming that better fits the needs and requirements of the current situation.

Helping you learn Topper's traits—critical thinking, mindful awareness of your mental state and conscious direction of your mindset, responses, and actions—is the goal of this book. With this goal in mind, we can begin to set up a system for ***Thinking On Purpose*** that will serve you well whether you're doing project management, planning a family vacation or just organizing the garage.

You will see these images from hereon throughout the book. When you see one, you will know to pay special attention to the text, as it is highlighting an example of either Auto Pilot or Topper in action.

Choosing Between APT and OPT

There are two types of thinking you can engage in, APT or OPT:

1. **Autopilot Thinking, or APT:** Thinking on autopilot means letting your brain do all the thinking for you, without conscious input or control. Thinking on autopilot results in poor decision-making, faulty problem solving and wasted time, effort, and money. This is because by relying on our lower brains, we wind up being led astray by the Three MindFields: pattern recognition, emotions, and biases. We jump to conclusions without evidence, react to our gut feelings and make

unwarranted and sometimes dangerous assumptions based on biased thinking.

2. **On Purpose Thinking, or OPT:** Thinking on purpose means taking intentional, conscious control of our thinking processes. It involves uncovering our hidden MindFields and using our higher thinking abilities to help us choose a path that leads to success, based on rational, logical, and critical thinking. In doing so, we avoid the pitfalls of autopilot thinking and are able to come to useful decisions and solutions.

These styles of thinking have very different characteristics, as demonstrated below:

AUTO PILOT THINKING (APT)— "APT" MEANS TO HAVE A TENDENCY	ON PURPOSE THINKING (OPT)— "OPT" MEANS TO CHOOSE
Five Step Comparison:	Five Step Comparison:
1. Assume your purpose	1. Frame your purpose
2. Accept your information	2. Qualify your information
3. Perpetuate your mindsets	3. Identify your mindsets
4. Follow your thinking	4. Structure your thinking
5. Assume your outcome	5. Validate your outcome

Before we go any further, one thing we need to make Clear is that Auto Pilot is not a bad guy. Without him at the controls, we never would have made it to the top of the food chain. In fact, we probably wouldn't even be a part of the food chain anymore. In fact, you'll be at your best when Auto and Topper are working together to keep you at your physical and mental peak. But how do you know when to take the controls and when to let Auto Pilot do his job?

It's simple but not easy. You can't undo what evolution has done (nor would you want to), but you can outsmart it. By that, I mean that you should let Auto Pilot do what he does best—recognize and act on patterns, formulate mindsets and generally allow you to be a smoothly-functioning human being—*but only when it serves your needs.*

What's most important is that you begin to pay attention to your thinking so that you can identify where and how a particular mindset, behavior or instinct is serving or not serving your needs either in the personal or professional domain. And the primary way to do that is to pay attention to your thinking and think on purpose.

Foresight, Insight, and Hindsight

They say that hindsight is 20/20. The problem is, too many people, project managers included, see the world all too clearly because they persist in viewing it almost entirely through hindsight.

Effective project management is 30% insight,

60% foresight, and 10% hindsight.

Unfortunately, while the maxim that, "failing to plan is planning to fail," has been beaten into the head of every project manager's brain from the pyramid builders on down, it is very seldom applied to real-world project management.

The light bulb came on for me many years ago when I first realized that *planning makes foresight as clear as hindsight.*

What I mean by that is that by cultivating foresight (the perception of the significance and nature of events before they have occurred) and insight (the capacity to discern the true nature of a situation, or the act of grasping the inward or hidden nature of things) you can replace hindsight (perception of the significance and nature of events after they have occurred) as your guiding force. (Source: www.thefreedictionary.com)

The problem is, too many people steer their boat, as it were, by floating downstream until they hit a rock or sandbar, at which point their sole goal becomes to steer the boat away from that obstacle and back out into open water. They react (hindsight), instead of responding (insight) or preparing (foresight), and so their journey becomes a series of one jarring collision after another. Granted, they now know where all the rocks and sandbars are, but unfortunately by the time they actually get anywhere, their boat is in pretty rough condition. If they make it at all, that is.

A better alternative would be to learn how rivers flow, and how to detect submerged rocks and sandbars *before* you hit them (insight). But even better would be to simply buy a map of the river or consult an experienced guide to locate potential trouble spots ahead of time, so you can chart the best path, avoid these obstacles altogether and enjoy a smooth, pleasant ride (foresight).

Foresight is an attribute (like vision or hearing), not a skill. But the good news is that all humans have foresight to some degree or another and everyone can learn to maximize this attribute with a little practice and attention, and by using my 5-Step Process for Thinking On Purpose.

Introduction to The Five Step Process for Thinking On Purpose (TOP)

To help you visualize this in your mind's eye, I have created an easy to follow ***Five-Step Process for Thinking On Purpose*** to help guide you:

- **Step 1—Frame Your Purpose** so that you know what your are trying to accomplish
- **Step 2—Qualify Your Information** so that you can distinguish between fact and fiction
- **Step 3—Identify Your Mindsets** so that you can obtain the necessary information to change them
- **Step 4—Structure Your Thinking** so that you can escape the gravitational pull of your current mindsets
- **Step 5—Validate Your Outcome** so that activity and effort are rewarded with achievement of a goal

Each step is required to ensure that you're thinking consciously and intentionally, but not all steps necessarily have to go deep to be successful.

Step 5
Validate Your Outcome

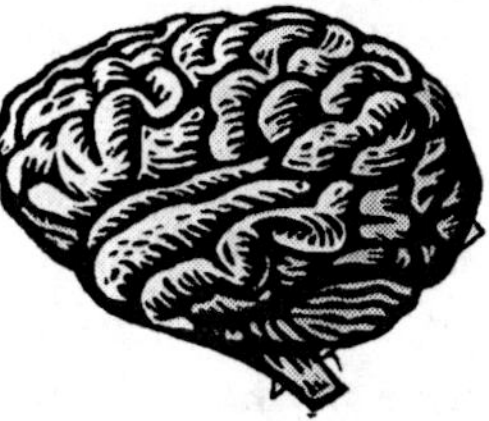

Step 1
Frame Your Purpose

Thinking On Purpose

Paying Attention to Your Thinking and Managing Your MIndsets

Step 4
Structure Your Thinking

Step 2
Qualify Your Information

Step 3
Identify Your Mindsets

4.1 TOP Step 1—Frame Your Purpose

The key to critical thinking and effective problem solving is to know what you want to achieve and how you wish to achieve it. The first step of any problem solving or decision-making process, therefore, should be to *frame your purpose.*

Framing your purpose simply means thinking about the problem as it relates to your goals, desires, needs, and values. This process will focus your energy and your intent, and prevent you from wasting time, money, and effort pursuing non-priority alternatives.

Susan Standing, a British scholar, wrote a book in 1939 on the importance of purpose in thinking. In it, she said, "...to think logically is to think relevantly to the purpose that initiated the thinking: all affected thinking is directed to an end." In other words, we begin problem- solving sessions with a goal or purpose, and then try to figure out what we need to do in order to achieve our goal. Reasoning is the tool we use to come to these decisions using ideas and means. This way of thinking is an integral part of the way we act and take part in the world; we proceed with some end, or purpose, in mind.

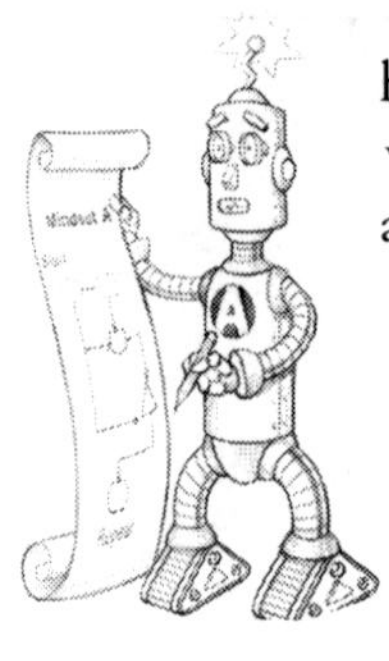

To understand our thinking, we must understand what we hope to achieve and how we hope to achieve it. However, although we always have a purpose in thinking, we are not always fully aware of that purpose, and so we proceed on autopilot, leaving our conscious mind in the dark as to what, precisely, is going on and why. Oh, we may have some vague idea of what our purpose is, or at least think we do, but more often than not, we only have a general idea of what we are trying to accomplish, which may or may not have anything to do with what's really going on beneath the surface.

For example, we might call a meeting to discuss an important issue with our staff; let's say that supplies are coming up missing and we need to stop this petty thievery before it starts eating into the bottom line. Although we know what the issue at hand is—the theft of office supplies—we may not know exactly what we are trying to accomplish in the meeting. Is our main goal to stop the thefts, and not worry about the missing items? Find and punish the thief? Recover the money lost, regardless of whether or not we find who took the supplies? Set up a supply disbursement oversight system? Any of these, or something entirely different, would be a valid purpose.

If everyone comes to the meeting with a different goal in mind, however, and no one takes steps to assure that everyone is working toward the same goals, any time spent in the meeting will probably be wasted, or at least far less productive than it could have been.

Additionally, each person brings personal, unconscious purposes to the table that they may not even be aware of themselves, such as the need to be seen as a strong leader, the desire to shift blame or attention, the urge to be seen as powerful by finding and punishing the offender, fear of having secrets (even unrelated secrets) exposed and so on. As a result of these differing purposes, the discussion and thinking during the meeting may diverge in many unhelpful directions.

Without a clear sense of what we're trying to accomplish, any thinking we do will be unproductive. At the same time, our unconscious goals may be at odds with our conscious goals, and unless we're aware of them, this conflict can cause stalled thinking, self-sabotage, working at cross purposes and other wasteful effort. Obviously, then, raising human goals and desires to the level of conscious realization is an important part of critical thinking.

Humans frequently nurture contradictory purposes. We might want to improve our education, while wanting to avoid intellectual work. We want others to love us, but fail to act in loving ways towards them. We want people to trust us, but behave in ways that undermine trust.

Even more confusing, the purpose we explicitly state may be simply what we would like to believe of ourselves, while our real purpose might be one that we are ashamed to admit, perhaps even to ourselves. For example, we might think we want to pursue a medical career to help and care for people when our actual purpose may be to make a lot of money, gain prestige and status, and be admired by others.

We must be careful, therefore, not to assume that our purposes are consistent with one another or that our announced purposes are actual purposes.

The purposes we pursue additionally influence and are influenced by our point of view, as well as by the way we see the world. Our purposes shape how we see things, and how we see things changes what we see. Each person formulates his or her purpose from a human point of view, determined by the context of his or her own experience. To understand our goals and objectives, then, we should consider the perspectives from which we see the world or some situation in it.

Adopt and "Disciple" a Process

Although there are individuals who naturally think sequentially and will intuitively work through a thinking process in a logical and consistent manner, my experience has been that this group is quite a small minority and that most of us, left to our own devices, tend to make it up as we go along.

The problem is, many of us don't recognize what constitutes a useful and effective thinking process, or believe that using a structured thinking process is either restrictive or stifling. For project managers who are used to working in a process-rich environment, I believe the primary driver is more a matter of simply not recognizing a good process, as opposed to feeling restricted or encumbered.

There's a lot of information about thinking processes on the market today, offered by a wide range of companies. I've worked with several versions myself, and have learned to distinguish between a good process and a poor one. What I've found is that a good process is one that naturally drives sequential, conscious thinking and by doing so eliminates or counteracts many of the MindFields of automatic thought.

By using a situational assessment of the issue at hand, we can easily decide what sort of process will be most useful and most effectively serve our purposes. Adopting a process is the easy part, however, and the only way to get real traction out of your process is to become a disciple of that process.

The definition of a disciple is, "…one who embraces and assists in spreading the teachings of another." The idea of discipling a process is to embrace a sound problem-solving model that will help you and your teams avoid the tyranny of thinking on autopilot.

Without conscious action or intervention, your brain's natural ability to recognize and act on patterns will keep you in a reactive, rather than a responsive, mode. We think that because we've seen problems similar to the one we currently face, that we "just know" how to find the correct solution and therefore we react to it with the same automatic thinking that we have used before.

Unfortunately, we are often sorely mistaken in this belief.

Dealing with pattern recognition in problem solving is similar to dealing with the way gravity affects how we move around on the planet. Just as it takes energy to overcome the force of gravity, so it takes energy to overcome the force of pattern recognition and the autopilot thinking it produces.

Getting a Smart Start

The first thing you can do when presented with a problem or an opportunity is to consciously choose the word "reset" over "repeat." Don't think about the situation or opportunity as being a repeat of something you've done before, even if it is a common occurrence. In reality, every situation is different, if only because the people involved in it have grown and changed since the last time. Instead, bring yourself back to a beginner's mindset, where objectivity and creativity can take hold.

Once you have achieved this mindset, embrace the practice of reframing as a means of gaining new perspective and empowering your team to boldly reject acceptance as the only option.

Finally, and perhaps most importantly, disciple the power of a sequential process to neutralize the hypnotic pull of pattern recognition and automatic thinking. Engage in a process that helps you ask the right questions, facilitates the right answers and protects the right solutions.

Framing Has a Purpose

Framing is a theory popularized by Tversky and Kahneman in 1981. Framing theory suggests that the frame we put around a concept or idea will have a significant bearing on how the concept or idea is perceived. Amos Tversky and Daniel Kahneman conducted an experiment with undergraduate students where they gave different students the same choice. For some, however, the choice was phrased in positive terms, as a choice between a sure gain and an uncertain gamble. In this case, the majority chose the sure gain option, a tendency called "risk aversion." For others, however, the same choices were phrased in negative terms, as a choice between a sure-loss option and the risky gamble. Here the majority chose the risky gamble, a tendency called "risk seeking." Thus the way the options were presented, or "framed," affected the choice people made.

Project managers should keep an eye out, however, for the dark side of framing, called the "Framing Bias." This is the tendency to present facts that are couched in a way that gives an inaccurate impression, or that is skewed toward a certain viewpoint. This bias can get in the way of clear communication when doing project updates or attempting to deliver bad news. To avoid this, you need to make sure that any information you present (or that is presented to you) is free of language or other manipulations that cast the information into either a positive or negative light. Taking a, "Just the facts, please," approach is your best bet here.

On the positive side, though, the fact that communication can be framed means that information can be presented in a way that can improve results and otherwise change a situation for the better. For example, I chose Framing Your Purpose as the first step in the TOP Process because of the impact it has on our thinking. In this first step, when you "frame" a purpose, you are signaling how that purpose should be interpreted or examined. Doing this first sets the tone and direction of your actions and therefore can save you substantial time and energy.

I have chosen five "frames" for beginning the TOP Process within the project management environment:

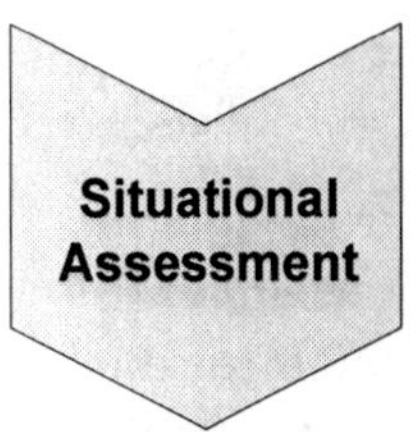

Frame 1—Situational Assessment (SA)

Situational assessment answers the need to examine the situation in its entirety, objectively, before jumping into any specific action. As you learned in Chapter 3, the brain is very good at keeping you out of harm's way by shunting actions and reactions to events happening around you through the subconscious mind. The Situational Assessment frame helps you consciously focus on your purpose by forcing you to slow down and take in the entire picture, and make a rational judgment about what's most important, before taking action.

Too many people believe that failing to solve a problem correctly is the result of arriving at an incorrect answer. However, more often than not they weren't actually solving the right problem in the first place.

Taking the time to identify, anticipate, clarify and prioritize issues in a sequential and logical manner is the foundation of an effective thinking process. It provides a clear and unequivocal answer to the question, "Where do we start?"

The purpose: Identify the problem

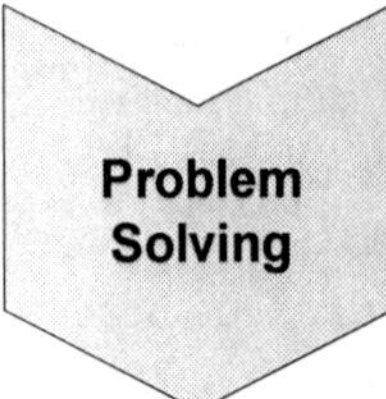

Frame 2—Problem Solving (PS)

Problem solving should be a signature skill for project managers. The key question in problem solving is, "What is the cause?" While the word "solving" implies resolution, the purpose of this frame is totally focused on getting to and confirming the true cause.

The purpose: Determine the cause

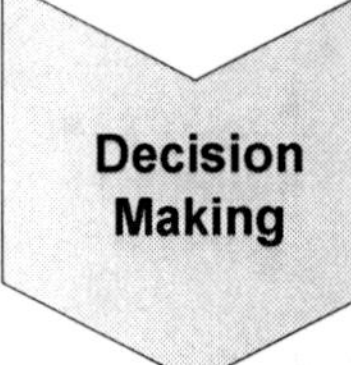

Frame 3—Decision Making (DM)

Paul C. Nutt, reporting on his findings from a nineteen-year study of 356 companies in his book, *Why Decisions Fail*, found that more than 50% of all the decisions tracked either failed, were quickly abandoned, were only partially implemented or were never adopted at all. One of the major decision-making blunders common to most of that 50% had to do with what he termed, "failure-prone practices."

Decision making is a frame designed to help you make a decision in an objective and conscious manner. This frame focuses on making a decision about how to best resolve the true or root causes of an issue. Alternatively, it can be used as a one-off application for addressing concerns such as which contractor or company to select for a specific role in the department.

The purpose: choose a solution

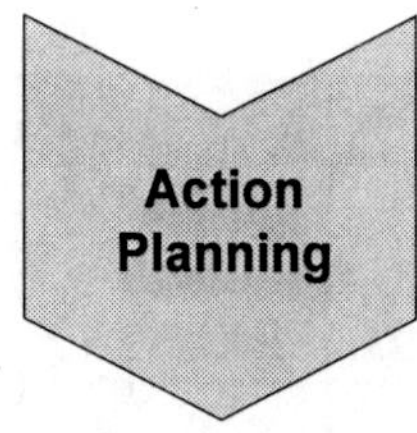

Frame 4—Action Planning (AP)

Action planning is probably one of the most undervalued and overlooked frames. The action-planning frame is designed to pull your brain out of its natural tendency to react without thinking, and redirect that energy into planning out what you are going to do.

Preparation and planning often goes against the way our brains are wired. For project managers, this often manifests in a mindset of, "We don't have time to plan." This frame focuses on instilling the mindset of, "Plan your actions in advance," as opposed to, "Make it up as you go." It works in conjunction with the planning methodology inherent in the project management discipline. For times and situations when you won't be invoking a formal project management planning process for your project (for example, dealing with a small project of low risk), it provides the key minimum questions required to create a useful plan.

Regardless of level of formality, a baseline for measuring progress is a minimum requirement in order to build an understanding of what works and what doesn't. While at first blush, such a baseline would seem to be exclusively oriented toward hindsight, it does serve to galvanize all the project Stakeholders around the concepts of commitment and professional competence in regards to planning.

The purpose: build a plan

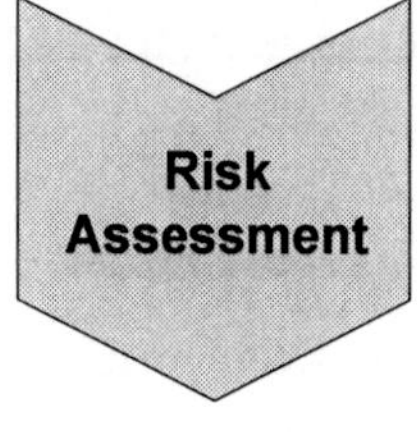

Frame 5—Risk Assessment (RA)

Risk assessment is a frame that brings foresight to the forefront. This frame addresses the need for an accurate assessment of risks, including determining in advance what your planned response will be if the risk does materialize. Risk assessment is another signature skill for project management effectiveness. It is rooted in the concept of *implications thinking*, in which the probable impact of any course of action is thought through to its logical conclusion.

The purpose: protect the plan

The Thinking On Purpose Road Map—Frame Your Purpose

The figure below depicts the relationship between framing your purpose, as mentioned above, and the Five-Step TOP Process. This diagram will build progressively over the remainder of this chapter as relevant information is added for each ***Thinking On Purpose*** step.

Purpose / Thinking Step	The Thinking on Purpose Roadmap: Frame Your Purpose	Qualify Your Information	Identify Your Mindsets	Structure Your Thinking	Validate Your Outcome
Situational Assessment	Identify the Problem				
Problem Solving	Determine the Cause				
Decision Making	Choose a Solution				
Action Planning	Build a Plan				
Risk Assessment	Protect the Plan				

4.2 TOP Step 2—Qualify Your Information

The second step in ***Thinking On Purpose*** is to determine your point of view and the quality of the information that you are dealing with. It is impossible to reason without relying on some set of facts, data, or experience. However, finding trustworthy sources of information and reviewing one's own experiences critically are an important part of thinking on purpose.

We must be vigilant about the sources of our information. We must also be analytically critical of the use we make of our own experience. Experience may be the best teacher, but biased experience supports bias, distorted experience supports distortion and self-deluded experience supports self-delusion. We must not think of our experience as sacred in any way but as simply one factor of thought that must, like all the others, be critically analyzed and assessed.

People often operate on automatic pilot when it comes to using information in their thinking, but when we are thinking on purpose, we are explicitly aware of the importance of that information. As a result, we are much more careful about the information we use and the conclusions it leads us to, and we are more likely to question the information we have, as well as the information that others are using. In short, we realize that our thinking can only be as good as the information we use to come to the conclusion.

Understanding Your Point of View

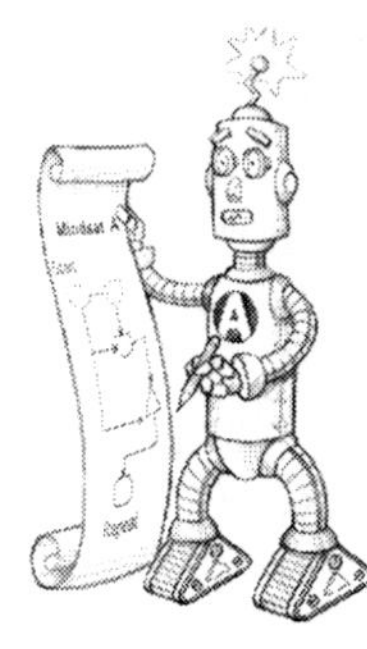

Developing and maintaining awareness about the source and quality of your point of view is one of the most challenging elements of effective thinking to master. On the one hand, we intuitively know that when we think, we think with a point of view. On the other hand, in the midst of thinking something through, when asked to identify or explain our point of view, we are likely to begin expressing anything and everything about what we are thinking. Most people quite simply do not have a clear sense of how their point of view was formed and what it encompasses.

There are many potential sources for our point of view: time, culture, religion, discipline, peers, economic interests, emotional states, social roles, etc. Our dominant point of view as individuals reflects a combination of these factors. Unfortunately, most of us are unaware of the extent to which these factors shape our point of view.

Typically, people do not say, "This is how I see the issue, from a point of view of...." More commonly, we express our views as, "This is the way things are." Our minds tend to absolutize our experience.

Ask yourself the following questions:

1. What is my point of view about this situation?
2. Where did my point of view come from?
3. Is it true?
4. Can it be relied upon?
5. If I take action on this information, what are the risks?

Becoming aware and taking charge of our own point of view is of key importance. The more we recognize when and how our points of view are at work

in our thinking, and in the thinking of others, and the more points of view we understand and are able to think within, the more effectively our thinking will be.

Thinking Critically About Information

Listening, thinking and reading critically—that is, reacting with systematic evaluation to what you've hear and read—requires a distinct set of skills and attitudes. These are built around a series of related critical questions.

Richard Paul and Linda Elder, in their book Critical Thinking: *Tools For Taking Charge of Your Professional and Personal Life*, offer the following standards and questions for judging information (to which I have added one additional entry and repackaged as Information Analysis Standards):

- **Clarity**
  - Could you elaborate?
  - Could you illustrate what you mean?
  - Could you give me an example?
- **Relevance**
  - How does this relate to the problem?
  - How does that bear on the question?
  - How does that help us with the issue?
- **Logic**
  - Does all of this make sense together?
  - Does your first paragraph fit with your last?
  - Does what you say follow from the evidence?
- **Accuracy**
  - How could we check on that?
  - How could we find out if that is true?
  - How could we verify or test that?
- **Depth**
  - What factors make this a difficult problem?
  - What are some of the complexities of this question?
  - What are some of the difficulties we need to deal with?
- **Significance**
  - Is this the most important problem to consider?
  - Is this the central idea to focus on?
  - Which of these facts are the most important?

- **Precision**
  - Could you be more specific?
  - Could you give me more details?
  - Could you be more exact?
- **Breadth**
  - Do we need to look at this from another perspective?
  - Do we need to consider another point of view?
  - Do we need to look at this in other ways?
- **Fairness**
  - Is my thinking justifiable in context?
  - Are my assumptions supported by evidence?
  - Is my purpose fair given the situation?
  - Am I using my concepts in keeping with educated usage or am I distorting them to get what I want?
- **Precedence (Author's addition)**
  - Has somebody in our organization done this before?
  - Do we have a framework or template?
  - Have "lessons learned" been recorded?
  - Who would be "best in class" at doing this?

Thinking carefully is always an unfinished project; a story looking for an ending that will never arrive. Critical questions provide a stimulus and direction for critical thinking. They move us forward toward a continual, ongoing search for better opinions, decisions, or judgments. ***Thinking on purpose*** involves an awareness of this set of interrelated critical questions, plus the ability and willingness to ask and answer them at the appropriate times. A worksheet is included in Appendix 7—TOP 10 Information Analysis Standards

The Sponge and Panning for Gold: Alternative Thinking Styles

Neil Browne and Stuart Keeley, in their book, Asking the Right Questions, refer to the automatic approach to thinking as being similar to the way in which a sponge reacts to water: we absorb whatever we come into contact with. This common approach has a few clear advantages. First, the more information you absorb about the world, the more quickly you become aware of its complexities. Second, the sponge approach to thinking is relatively passive and doesn't require strenuous mental effort. It tends to be rather quick and easy, especially when the material is presented in a clear and interesting fashion.

While absorbing information provides a quick way to acquire knowledge, the sponge approach has a serious disadvantage: It provides no way to filter or sort the information and there's no way to know which opinions to believe and which to reject.

Someone who relies on this method for all or most of their thinking would wind up believing whatever they read or heard. They would be very susceptible to manipulation, and their decisions would become accidents of association instead of reflective judgment.

The alternative approach to thinking is to make educated and conscious choices about what to absorb and what to ignore. To do this, you must view the world around you with a questioning mind. Such a thinking style requires active participation and is sometimes referred to as "panning for gold."

The concept of panning for gold—of carefully sifting through and removing all the dross and filler until you are only left with pure nuggets of high value—provides an excellent model for thinking. It does require some effort, and can occasionally be tedious. Finding the gold in the gravel requires you to ask questions and to think about the answers objectively. But the results are worth it.

To sum it up: The sponge approach emphasizes knowledge acquisition at the expense of quality control; the panning for gold approach stresses quality over quantity.

Weak and Strong Sense Thinking

Everyone has baggage. Our experiences and thoughts about those experiences color our thinking. Additionally, we're attached to our baggage; we tend to get touchy whenever someone questions our biases or argues against our reasoning.

Critical thinking is a valuable tool for examining our beliefs and ideas. But when used incorrectly, it can become a tool for fossilizing and buttressing false information, beliefs, and thoughts. In *Critical Thinking*, Paul and Elder offer two versions of thinking, weak and strong, to describe these actions.

Using critical thinking to defend your beliefs is weak sense thinking. It's weak because it's more concerned with maintaining the status quo than moving toward truth or validity. The purpose of weak critical thinking is to avoid or stifle other opinions or thinking, and to control those who present opposing views.

In contrast, strong sense thinking involves objectively reviewing our opinions and information, and adopting an open stance toward accepting the new information and ideas that prove accurate, even if they disagree with our own. This is a lot harder than it sounds, but enables us to see the real truth of the matter and prevents us from being hoist by the petard of our own insular thought.

The idea behind adopting the "panning for gold" and strong sense approaches to critical thinking is that anything that remains in your mind after all this work is far more likely to be truthful, accurate, and useful. We can be sure that our thoughts, ideas, and opinions are based on an objective review of the facts and are strong, valuable and worthy of our support. At least until new information arrives on the scene to start the process over again.

Inert Information, Activated Ignorance and Activated Knowledge

Paul and Elder also distinguish between three types of information: inert information, activated ignorance, and activated knowledge.

They describe "Inert Information" as information we absorb, but do not actually understand (even though we may think we do). This information is often the result of ritual or rote memorization. A common example of this is children who learn the Pledge of Allegiance in school and can repeat it perfectly, word for word, but have little understanding—if any—about what the words actually mean. Most of us have vast tracts of inert information in our heads that we know, but cannot explain or properly understand.

"Activated ignorance" is what happens when we accept and act on information that, unknown to us, is false or inaccurate. For example, acting on the false information that people of other races were less than fully human or deserved fewer rights has resulted in many instances of human suffering and misery.

Activated ignorance is one of the most dangerous human tendencies there is. Because of this it is vitally important that we review our information objectively and dispassionately before putting it into action, especially when others could be harmed as a result.

"Activated knowledge" involves seeking and applying information that is both truthful and useful. Activated knowledge leads naturally to more knowledge, improved awareness, and greater understanding. The scientific method is a perfect example of activated knowledge. It offers methods to test the scientists' information, conclusions, and predictions, and provides safeguards to prevent abuse and misuse. When used correctly and conscientiously, the scientific method allows scientists to progress quickly and with assurance toward a greater and greater understanding of the world around them, and enables them to clearly and effectively identify and resolve conflicting results and faulty thinking.

Sifting the Gold from the Dross

As Paul and Elder point out, "...An educated person is one who has learned that information almost always turns out to be at best incomplete and very often false, misleading, fictitious and mendacious—that is, information is often just dead wrong."

They also offer several questions that can help us differentiate between true and false information, which I have paraphrased and expanded upon below:

1. Is this information testable through direct experience? How would I go about seeing for myself if this is true?
2. Is this information consistent with my own beliefs and understandings about how the world works? Remember that because of confirmation bias, a yes answer here isn't necessarily an assurance of validity or even reasonability.
3. Does the person giving me this information have verifiable evidence to support it? How do I know?
4. Is there some existing and reliable method for testing this information?
5. Does the person offering this information have ulterior motives for me to accept it? What do they stand to gain if I do? What do they stand to lose if I don't?
6. Does the person offering this information get upset or evasive when I question them? If so, why? Is it a sign that they aware the information is false, or are they just unprepared to answer in greater detail?

As the authors note, however, these questions are just a starting point. They can't ensure we are getting accurate information, but they can help us begin to make that determination ourselves.

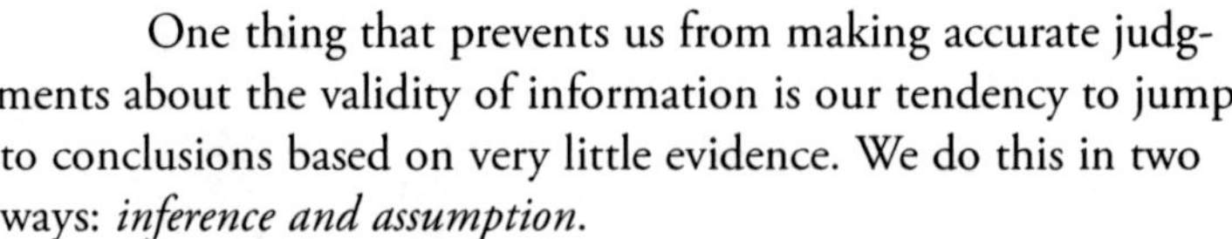

One thing that prevents us from making accurate judgments about the validity of information is our tendency to jump to conclusions based on very little evidence. We do this in two ways: *inference and assumption.*

Inference is what we do when we come to a conclusion about something based on our own biases, without evidence to back it up. For example, if you saw someone ordering food in a restaurant at lunchtime, you might reasonably infer that they intended to eat lunch at that restaurant. Of course, you could be wrong. They could be picking up lunch for someone else.

They could be ordering food to go, and will be eating it elsewhere. They might even be simply talking to the wait staff and not ordering anything at all.

Assumptions are things we "know," (not necessarily correctly) and therefore do not think about. We assume something is true because we believe that it to be so. For example, if you believe that all management is made up of "pointy-haired bosses" who are incompetent and malicious, you will assume that your boss is both stupid and out to get you, when that may not be the case. (Of course, it could be true. But assuming it and verifying that assumption are two different things.)

These two actions are related in that assumptions often lead to inferences. You assume someone is your friend, so you infer positive intent in his or her actions. You assume that dogs bite, so you infer aggression when one approaches you. We do this all the time, every day. It's part of our automatic survival system. But unless we are consciously aware of what's going on behind these thoughts, they can easily lead us astray and get us into trouble.

Thinking on purpose involves examining our assumptions and the inferences they create in an objective, mindful manner. We must learn to distinguish the pure information we receive from our thoughts, assumptions, and inferences about that information. Over time, we realize that these assumptions and inferences are the foundations of our points of view, and this recognition will enable us to broaden our horizons, open our minds and become better, more critical thinkers.

Fact or Fallacy?

The first step in determining whether or not you are being given accurate information is to examine the assertions for questionable assumptions, faulty logic, or deceptive reasoning (called fallacies).

The three most common fallacies you should be aware of are:

1. The information relies on reasoning that involves false or incorrect assumptions.
2. The person is trying to distract us by insinuating that certain information is—relevant or important when it is not.
3. The person is using circular logic, or offering evidence to support a conclusion that depends on that conclusion being true.

There are many logical fallacies that you should be aware of.

See Appendix 2—Common Fallacies for a listing of some of the more common fallacies that people use in everyday thinking and discussion.

Learning about these fallacies can sensitize you to faulty and deceptive reasoning in general, and will also provide you with the language you need to respond to someone who is using these fallacies, whether they realize it or not.

Is It a Fact, or Is It Just an Assertion?

In addition to logical fallacies, almost all reasoning we encounter includes beliefs about the way the world is, was, or is going to be that the communicator wants us to accept as facts. These beliefs can be conclusions, reasons, or assumptions. We refer to such beliefs as *factual claims.*

There are several questions you should ask about any factual claim. First, ask yourself why you should believe their claim. Do you trust this person? Are they credible? Does the information make sense?

If the answer to these questions is yes, the next question is, is there any evidence to support it? If not, the claim is simply an *assertion* and not fact at all, and can be dismissed. If, however, there is some evidence to back up this claim, you then need to question how good is the evidence is.

There are plenty of assertions that have a lot of reasonable-sounding, but faulty, inaccurate or even deceptive evidence to support them, such as the idea that we never landed on the moon or that 9/11 was a government plot. It is up to you to check the sources and evidence of any factual claims you receive. Blindly accepting such claims—because they fit in with your beliefs, because you want them to be true, because they seem true, because you believe or trust the person telling you or for any of the millions of reasons we give ourselves—is simply poor thinking, and relying on such faulty judgment is bound to get you into trouble somewhere along the line.

Do I Have All the Information I Need?

The final question you'll need to ask yourself is not, "Is all of my information correct?" but rather, "Do I have all the information I need?"

Verifying your information is easy; you have the information on hand, all you have to do is make sure it is valid and up to date. It is far harder to ensure that you have all the information you need, because if you don't have it, you may not realize that you need it.

One way to check is to ask yourself, "In a worst-case scenario, what could possibly go wrong?" at every stage and sub-stage of your plan. For each potential failure point, try to come up with a plan for handling or preventing that failure. It will quickly become evident where you are missing pieces—those will be the spots where you can't come up with a "fix" because you don't have some vital bit or bits of information about the original plan or its constituent factors.

For example, in designing and building a college campus, one worst-case scenario might be, "A natural disaster could sweep through and destroy the project." When coming up with a plan to prevent or alleviate this concern, you might realize you don't have all the information concerning the sorts of natural disasters that are common in the area, how often they occur and to what magnitude. This constitutes missing information you will need in order to ensure your design and the resulting structures are suitable for their environment.

Another way to determine if you have all the information you need is to give your information to someone else, and see if they come to the same conclusions. If not, or if they have trouble reaching any conclusion at all, then you are probably relying on assumptions or prior beliefs to cover some logical gap or gaps. Go through the information and note where you and the other person diverge. This will be where information is either missing, or unclear.

Information comes from many sources, but those sources can be broken down into four types:

1. **Simplistic:** This type of question has only one answer. For example, "How many people work at this company? Qualifying this information is usually fairly simple and straightforward.
2. **Deterministic:** This type of problem only has one answer, as well, but it requires a formula to determine it. For example, "What is the current ROI of this company's stock option?" This information can be trickier to qualify. The difficulty lies in ensuring that both the formula and its solution are accurate.
3. **Random:** This problem has several different answers, but all answers can be identified. For example, "What are the names of the people working at the company?" Like our first example, this information is often easy to qualify, if perhaps more time consuming.
4. **Indeterminate:** This problem has several different answers, not all of which can be known. For example, "Where will this company be in terms of profit and market share after five years?" This is the most difficult information to qualify, since there is no way to get all of the input or factors required to create an accurate answer. Qualifying this sort of information relies heavily on ensuring that the sources of your answers are as accurate as possible, and that only conclusions that are actually supportable by that evidence are drawn.

Facilitation as a Signature Skill

Richard G. Weaver and John D. Farrell, in their book, *Managers as Facilitators: A Practical Guide to Getting the Work Done in a Changing Workplace*, define facilitation as, "a process through which a person helps others complete their work and improve the way they work together." What I like about this definition is that it is not "framed" around just a meeting or discussion context, but rather in an overall process management context.

Highly developed facilitation skills are a must for all project managers. When you think about Weaver and Farrell's definition, it's obvious that what they're describing is, essentially, project management in a nutshell. Your job as a project manager is to help others do the work they're assigned and get them to work together as a team. The best way to do this is by facilitation, rather than brute force, manipulation or any other low-level management alternative.

Therefore, it is necessary to recognize the value of facilitation and take steps to increase not only your own skills and abilities in this arena, but to encourage those on your team to do so as well. By doing so, not only will you improve your own abilities and standing as a project manager, but you will also enable your team to continue these best practices in your absence.

The *Thinking On Purpose* Road Map—Qualify Your Information

This chart shows the addition of the
Qualify Your Information details to the TOP Road Map

Purpose / Thinking Step	The Thinking on Purpose Roadmap				
	Frame Your Purpose	Qualify Your Information	Identify Your Mindsets	Structure Your Thinking	Validate Your Outcome
Situational Assessment	Identify the Problem	• Identify your POV • Confirm fact or fallacy • Confirm needed information is available			
Problem Solving	Determine the Cause	• Identify your POV • Confirm fact or fallacy • Confirm needed information is available			
Decision Making	Choose a Solution	• Identify your POV • Confirm fact or fallacy • Confirm needed information is available • Test information			
Action Planning	Build a Plan	• Identify your POV • Confirm fact or fallacy • Confirm needed information is available • Test information			
Risk Assessment	Protect the Plan	• Identify your POV • Confirm fact or fallacy • Confirm needed information is available • Test information			

4.3 TOP Step 3—Identify Your Mindsets

It is important that you identify any mindsets you might have that could affect the outcome of your problem-solving or decision-making. There are three ways to identify your mindsets. The first is to Sweep for MindFields. The second is to Expand Your Point of View. And the third is to Reframe Your Thinking.

Sweeping for MindFields

Like sweeping the mine fields of a military battlefield, sweeping your thinking for bias, emotions, and habits that might be lurking underneath your thinking processes will help prevent you from inadvertently letting a bias, emotion, or habit blow up in your problem-solving or decision-making situation.

The essence of determining which mindsets, emotions, and habits are in play in your situation is asking the right questions:

Question 1: Biases

Regarding the past, ask yourself, *"What potential biases might be in play that could affect my thinking?"*

The best approach is to play a simple mind game of "Name That Bias," either from your own perspective or from that of your team members. Also remember in this process to be very sensitive to other team members' perspectives and personalities. It is much less intrusive to say, "To me, it looks like confirmation bias is heavily influencing this situation. What do you think?" as opposed to, "I can see you are clearly being swayed by confirmation bias."

Here is list of the common biases exhibited by project managers, to assist in this process:

- **Confirmation Bias**—As we noted earlier, confirmation bias is a tendency to seek out information that supports a theory and to ignore contrary information. Like many biases, it is strongly intertwined with cognitive dissonance. (Cognitive dissonance is the tension and discomfort we feel when our thoughts and our actions don't align.) In this case, confirmation bias seeks to avoid cognitive dissonance by searching out only that evidence which supports the point of view, and ignoring or devaluing evidence that opposes it.
- **Hindsight Bias**—This bias is the tendency for events in the past to seem more obvious or likely than they really were. For example, many anti-terrorism tactics such as limiting liquids at airports are grounded in hindsight bias. "Well, obviously," we say, "if you can take a large

amount of liquid on a plane, it's easy to smuggle explosive chemicals in and combine them to make a bomb." That only became obvious to everyone, however, after someone tried to do it. Before then, we never considered bottles of shampoo to present a threat.

- **Clustering Illusion**—This is the tendency to look for and find patterns in events, sequences, or conditions that aren't actually there. Although this may be a necessary byproduct of our ability to detect patterns, it can create problems when it happens inappropriately. Clustering illusions can also result in things like "cargo cults" and faulty stock market predictions based on completely coincidental "patterns" or associations.
- **Recency Effect**—This is the tendency to give greater weight to recent events or information than to those further in the past. Also, people remember near-past events as being more important than events further back in time. The existence of this bias makes it important to gather enough long-term data so that the daily ups and downs that loom so large in our minds don't encourage us to make bad decisions.
- **Anchoring Bias**—Anchoring involves stating a position that then becomes an "anchor" around which the rest of the negotiation will form. For example, the first person to state a price will usually force the other person to give a new price based on the first price stated, rather than on other important data such as actual value or demand. This can cause problems when one party winds up defending a position that, in all actuality, doesn't mean that much to them and detracts from their ability to compromise and get what they want out of a negotiation.
- **Overconfidence Effect**—This has also been called "Lake Wobegon Syndrome," from that show's tagline, "Where all the men are strong, all the women good looking and all the children above average." Almost everyone ranks themselves as being within the top third of all humans for positive traits and skills. At the same time, people tend to imagine the exact opposite in relation to negative traits, with almost everyone placing themselves in the bottom 30% of those exhibiting unpopular or unfavorable traits.
- **Fundamental Attribution Error**—This is the tendency to confuse actions made as a result of external pressures with personal traits or personality. For example, if a person cuts us off on the way to work, we think he's a jerk rather than assuming he didn't see us. On the other hand, we tend to view our own actions as primarily caused by external events, rather than by flaws in our own character (we tell ourselves we cut someone off because we didn't see them, when instead the truth is that we weren't looking carefully enough). Even in situations when we

know a person is advocating a particular position based on the luck of the draw (as happens during a debate team competition), we will still tend to form a personal dislike for those who are instructed to argue against our own personal beliefs.

Question 2: Emotions

Regarding the present, ask yourself, *"What emotions am I feeling right now and how could they be affecting my thinking?"*

In much the same way you identified your biases in the previous section, using the mind game called, "Name That Emotion," can help you identify emotions that could be causing problems. To improve your ability to name and recognize the range of emotions in play at any given time, self-check against a set of five core feelings: happiness, sadness, anger, fear, and shame.

Review the range of emotions in the following table:

Intensity of Feelings	Happy	Sad	Angry	Afraid	Ashamed
HIGH	Elated Excited Overjoyed Thrilled Exuberant Ecstatic Fired Up Delighted	Depressed Disappointed Alone Hurt Dejected Hopeless Sorrowful Miserable	Furious Enraged Outraged Aggravated Irate Seething	Terrified Horrified Scared Stiff Petrified Fearful Panicky	Sorrowful Remorseful Unworthy Worthless Disgraced Dishonored
MEDIUM	Cheerful Up Good Relieved Satisfied	Heartbroken Down Upset Distressed Regretful Melancholy	Upset Mad Hot Frustrated Agitated Disgusted	Scared Frightened Threatened Insecure Uneasy Shocked	Apologetic Defamed Sneaky Guilty
MILD	Glad Contented Pleasant Fine Pleased	Unhappy Moody Blue Lost Bad Dissatisfied	Perturbed Annoyed Uptight Put Out Irritated Touchy	Apprehensive Nervous Worried Timid Unsure Anxious	Embarassed Disappointed Let Down

For example, imagine you have just received an email from one of your development leads on a major project, advising you at the last minute of a forecasted slippage that is a significant surprise to you. Your "lizard brain" reacts predictably, and mobilizes you for fight (certainly not flight). You are enraged and clearly in the high intensity range for "Angry" using the chart above.

Twenty seconds later, you take phone call from another team member who needs help with a matter you consider to be routine. Chances are your reaction to this phone call is going to be heavily influenced by the intensity of your current emotional state unless you consciously move to a more appropriate state.

Question 3: Habits

Regarding the future, ask yourself, *"Which habits could I be falling into that could affect my thinking?"*

Horace Mann, an early leader in education, offers one of the absolute best metaphors for visualizing habits: "Habit is a cable; we weave a thread of it each day, and at last we cannot break it."

The neural pathways we discussed Chapter 3 are the actual creators of these patterns of thought. Once these pathways are created, like paths worn through a thicket, the same thoughts and thought processes are likely to be repeated, rather than new ones created. This is because repetition of a thought decreases the biochemical resistance to that thought happening again. Therefore, the connections between the brain cells on these neural pathways become stronger; every time you think a thought, the resistance to thinking that thought again is reduced, increasing the likelihood of you having that thought again. This is how the "cable of habit" is formed, and why it is vitally important that you monitor this tendency in your thinking.

While there are an almost infinite number of habits that you could have formed over time as a result of biases and emotions altering the way you think, the following habits comprise a fair encapsulation of the most common bad habits we tend to fall into. Reviewing these—and checking to see if they're present in your current thinking processes—would be a solid place to start the game of "Naming That Habit":

- **Not Being Persistent**—Not persevering to see a task through to completion. Not looking for ways to reach your goal when stuck. Literally, giving up.
- **Not Managing Impulsivity**—Not thinking before acting nor remaining calm, thoughtful, and deliberate in the face of adversity.
- **Not Listening with Empathy and Understanding**—Not devoting mental energy to understanding another person's thoughts and ideas. Not making an effort to consider other points of view.
- **Not Thinking Flexibly**—Not changing perspectives or generating alternatives or considering options.
- **Not Paying Attention to Your Thinking**—Not being aware of your own thoughts and feelings, or of how your actions affect others.

- **Not Striving for Accuracy**—Not setting high standards, not checking your results and not looking for ways to improve.
- **Not Applying Knowledge**—Not using what you learn. Not applying knowledge beyond the situation in which it was learned.
- **Not Questioning or Posing Problems**—Not having a questioning attitude or figuring out what data is needed to solve a problem. Not asking, "How do I know?"
- **Not Thinking or Communicating with Clarity and Precision**—Not striving to be accurate in both written and oral communication.
- **Not Gathering Data Through All Senses**—Not paying attention to the world around you nor gathering information using all senses—taste, touch, smell, hearing, and sight.
- **Not Creating, Imagining and Innovating**—Not trying different ways of doing things, nor generating new and novel ideas.
- **Not Responding with Passion**—Not having fun dealing with challenges and issues inherent in ***Thinking On Purpose*** and in managing projects.
- **Not Taking Responsible Risks**—Not venturing out and being adventuresome; staying too close to your comfort zone and not straying from the middle ground of your competence.
- **Not Finding Humor**—Not being able to laugh, especially at yourself.
- **Not Thinking Interdependently**—Not working together; not being able to work with and learn from others in reciprocal situations.
- **Not Remaining Open to Continuous Learning**—Not learning from your experiences. Not having humility and being able to admit you don't know something.

(Adapted from http://www.habits-of-mind.net/)

By dint of careful observation and attentive work, each one of these habits of mind can be, to use Mann's metaphor, untwisted and recabled to create a positive, energizing and meaningful thinking process. The first step is to be aware, followed by a careful laying down of new "cables" of habit one strand at a time.

Expanding Your Point of View

Almost all situations you will encounter will require you to operate with, around or in opposition to other people. Therefore, you will need to learn to view the situations, problems, and solutions from other points of view than your own.

Other people's views (OPV) will by definition be foreign to your own. Because of OPV, people will see different factors, envision or prefer different consequences, and have different objectives and priorities.

Different people obtain their viewpoints by exposure to different backgrounds, positions, knowledge, interest, values, experiences, needs and so on. It is important that you learn to view the situations, objectives, consequences and priorities of any decision-making or problem-solving process from the points of view of everyone involved. Otherwise, you are sure to be blindsided by problems, failures, bottlenecks and other issues that you would have otherwise been able to foresee.

The problem is that rank, social order, personality differences and other cultural and personal bias often prohibit people from expressing their views. Many people, for example, feel that lower level workers should never make suggestions to executives. And in some groups, women may be less upfront and aggressive about expressing negative views than their male counterparts. This means that you will have to work harder to discover what they are.

A good way to test whether you are doing this is to try to accurately articulate the other person or persons points of view in your own words. Seek confirmation from them directly, if possible, and from the most credible source regarding them if you cannot deal directly with them (for example, a competitor).

The other side to expanding your point of view is exposing yourself to new and unfamiliar experiences, information, and stimuli. A fun way to do this is to spend some time in a large bookstore reading magazines on subjects you rarely or never consider. Another way is to make a point of going to places you don't ordinarily go and talking to people with whom you don't ordinarily talk. Subscribing to foreign news feeds, reading books on subjects you don't normally read and so on are also ways you can expand your point of view to encompass that of others.

Reframe Your Thinking

The final way you can identify your mindset is by reframing your thoughts. You do this by consciously taking a different stand or looking at your thoughts from another point of view. This can open up all sorts of avenues for change and give you a clearer picture of your hidden mindsets.

Too often, a problem is improperly solved because people are too caught up in their normal way of thinking about the problem or situation to see the right solution (or, for that matter, the real problem). For example, the discovery of a cure for ulcers depended on a pair of researchers being able to reframe the traditional thinking about ulcer treatment.

Instead of thinking, "How can we treat this ulcer based on what we know?" they began by thinking, "Are we sure we know what causes ulcers, or are we just assuming that we do?" In this way, they were able to step outside of decades of assumptions and "common knowledge" and were able to discover that, indeed, ulcers are caused by a bacterial infection and not stress, thus leading to a simple and inexpensive cure for a condition that was previously thought to only be treatable (but not permanently cured) by expensive medications and drastic lifestyle changes.

The power of reframing really came to life for me as I studied the incredible life of Alexander the Great. As a young boy, Alexander was tutored by Aristotle—one of the finest minds the world has ever known. Very early on, he taught Alexander the power of reframing a situation to change what people pay attention to or deem important.

This is perfectily illustrated in the events of 320 B.C., during Alexander's push to conquer Persia from Darius III. The reputation of Darius was so intimidating that Alexander burned all his ships when he first arrived on the shores of Asia Minor so that his troops had nowhere to go but forward. However, in doing so, he left himself with another, apparently unsolvable, problem: He could no longer use those ships to protect his supply lines from depredation by the Persian navy.

So how did he solve this problem? By reframing.

Instead of looking at how he could defeat the Persian navy on the water, an obvious—and, at this point, fruitless—line of thought, Alexander reframed the issue to, "How can I defeat the Persian *navy on the land*?"

This reframe—and his solution—was so brilliant that it's studied today in every naval war college on the planet. By carefully gathering and analyzing information about his enemy, he found their ultimate weakness: the need to maintain a steady supply of fresh water. Armed with this knowledge, he directed his generals to secure all the fresh water ports within a two-day rowing time (since a two-day supply was all the water an average warship could carry). As a result of this strategy, the pride of the Persian war machine was brought to its knees.

For project managers, the first move when confronted with a seemingly unsolvable problem or opportunity is to reset your thinking. Ask yourself, "How could I achieve my core interest through alternative actions?" The next move is to test for point of view (make sure you're not overlooking or eliminating alternatives because of inflexible thinking or framing) and finally, to reframe your problem statement in a way that helps you and your team change your approach as required.

This is a simple (but not easy) concept. However, mastering it significantly increases your probability of success. Once you have reset your approach to how you are thinking about your supposedly unsolvable problem, the next move is to reframe the problem to make it solvable.

Thinking On Purpose Road Map—Identify Your Mindsets

Below, see the addition of the Identify Your Mindset details to the TOP Road Map.

Purpose / Thinking Step	The Thinking on Purpose Roadmap: Frame Your Purpose	Qualify Your Information	Identify Your Mindsets	Structure Your Thinking	Validate Your Outcome
Situational Assessment	Identify the Problem	• Identify your POV • Confirm fact or fallacy • Confirm needed information is available	• Expand your POV • Sweep for MindFields • Reframe your thinking • Choose your mindset		
Problem Solving	Determine the Cause	• Identify your POV • Confirm fact or fallacy • Confirm needed information is available	• Expand your POV • Sweep for MindFields • Reframe your thinking • Choose your mindset		
Decision Making	Choose a Solution	• Identify your POV • Confirm fact or fallacy • Confirm needed information is available • Test information	• Expand your POV • Sweep for MindFields • Reframe your thinking • Choose your mindset		
Action Planning	Build a Plan	• Identify your POV • Confirm fact or fallacy • Confirm needed information is available • Test information	• Expand your POV • Sweep for MindFields • Reframe your thinking • Choose your mindset		
Risk Assessment	Protect the Plan	• Identify your POV • Confirm fact or fallacy • Confirm needed information is available • Test information	• Expand your POV • Sweep for MindFields • Reframe your thinking • Choose your mindset		

4.4 TOP Step 4—Structure Your Thinking

Structured thinking is a logical framework for focusing and staying focused on key points, and for ensuring that each element and factor of a problem is analyzed separately, systematically, and sufficiently.

Why is structure so important? When it comes to problem solving, we humans tend to be poor analysts. We poorly analyze the facts we do have, make suppositions and assumptions about the facts we don't have, come up with a solution that "feels" right and hope it solves the problem. If it doesn't, we repeat the process until we either solve the problem or resolve to live with it. We call this process trial and error—and believe me, there are plenty of both involved in this type of thinking.

As we discussed in Chapter 2, structuring our analysis is fundamentally at odds with the way the human mind naturally works: When it comes to problem solving, our programming is not necessarily our best friend.

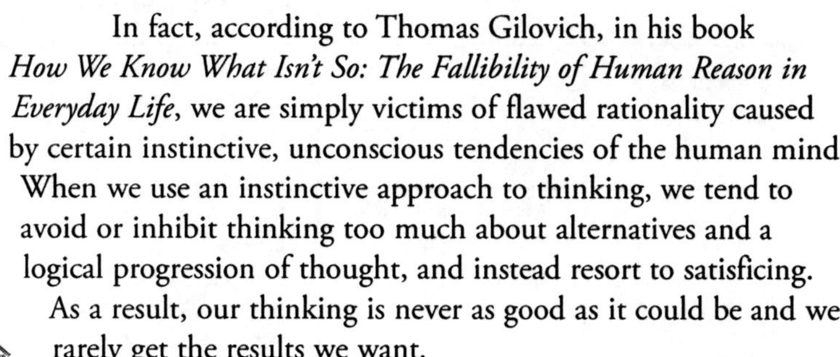

In fact, according to Thomas Gilovich, in his book *How We Know What Isn't So: The Fallibility of Human Reason in Everyday Life*, we are simply victims of flawed rationality caused by certain instinctive, unconscious tendencies of the human mind. When we use an instinctive approach to thinking, we tend to avoid or inhibit thinking too much about alternatives and a logical progression of thought, and instead resort to satisficing. As a result, our thinking is never as good as it could be and we rarely get the results we want.

On the other hand, using a structured thinking process automatically encourages you to look at situations in a systematic and deliberate manner, examining each factor and aspect individually and applying logic, foresight, and insight to the solution creation process. As a result, your solutions are more accurate, effective, and productive than with an intuitive approach.

An example of structured thinking that we're all familiar with is mathematical equations. If I were to ask you to divide two large numbers, you would start by drawing a vertical and horizontal line connected together in the top left-hand corner, then proceed by placing the number to be divided by on the outside left, and the number to be divided into at the inside right, of the figure. You probably learned this structured approach to the division process in your early school years as a manual way of working through the mathematical calculation on paper.

Think of this fourth step, Structure Your Thinking, as the same sort of thing—the application of some process, technique, tool, or template to help you neutralize the natural tendencies of the human brain—e.g. viewing the world around us in patterns, instantaneously and unconsciously.

Each step in the thinking process is summarized below, along with a set of key questions to help guide you in finding and organizing the required information and context. However, each step is vulnerable to certain pitfalls or hidden hazards. Where appropriate, I have recorded a possible best practice or TOP Tool* reference that will either help you spot the pitfall in advance (foresight), or prevent it from becoming a factor at all.

*The detailed listing of the *40 TOP Tools* is available in Chapter 7.

Situational Assessment Frame—*(See TOP Tool #36 for detailed description)*

	Process/Key Questions	Potential Pitfall	Best Practices/ Tools
Situational Assessment	• What are the issues, what is the priority and is the root cause known?	• Not documenting information assembled in the process	• Follow template as outlined in *TOP Tool #35: Situational Assessment*
Identify Issues	• What is happening? • What could happen in the future?	• Not including the right people • Trying to analyze potential issues while in the process of identifying them • Information lacking integrity	• Use project stakeholders list as starting point • Facilitate session using brainstorming rules • Use *TOP Tool #20: Informational Analysis Standards*
Clarify Issues	• What evidence do you have?	• Not testing validity of the evidence • Not drilling down ot precise issue	• Use *TOP Tool #20: Informational Analysis Standards* • Use *TOP Tool #4: Ask "Why" Five Times*
Prioritize Issues	• How important is the issue? • How urgent is the issue?	• Not defining prioritization criteria • No team involvement	• Use *TOP Tool #35: Situational Assessment* to identify prioritization approach • Use *TOP Tool #16: Facilitation* to ensure team involvement
Assess Root Causes	• Do you know the root cause?	• Believing thinking situations can be neatly reduced to one key issue to be addressed	• Use *TOP Tool #17: Force Field Analysis* to flush out driving forces and sustaining forces

Problem Solving Frame—*(See TOP Tool #32 for detailed description)*

	Process/Key Questions	Potential Pitfall	Best Practices/ Tools
Problem Solving	• What is the root cause of the issue?	• Not documenting information assembled in the process	• Follow template as outlined in *TOP Tool #31: Problem Solving*
Describe Problem	• What is happening? • Where is it happening or not happening? • When is it happening or not happening?	• Problem not well defined • Jumping to solution before cause is known	• Use *TOP Tool #30: Problem Restatement* to further define • Use *TOP Tool #4: Ask "Why" Five Times* to drill down
Generate Causes	• What could be causing the problem? • What has caused similar problems in the past?	• Not generating a complete list of possible causes	• Use *TOP Tool #6: Cause and Effect Diagram* to enable thoroughness
Test Causes	• If this cause is the true cause, how does it explain the IS and IS NOT data? • What assumptions need to be verified?	• Jumping to conclusions without factual evidence	• Use *TOP Tool #20: Information Analysis Standards* to help validate evidence • Use *TOP Tool #6: Cause and Effect Diagram* to widen possibilities
Confirm Cause	• How can the cause be confirmed?	• Not having evidence to support proposed true cause	• Use *TOP Tool #20: Information Analysis Standards* to help validate evidence • Use *TOP Tool #19: Hypothesis Testing* to confirm cause

Decision Making Frame—*(See TOP Tool #13 for detailed description)*

	Process/Key Questions	Potential Pitfall	Best Practices/ Tools
Decision Making	• What is the best alternative? • What is the decision statement?	• Not documenting information assembled in the process	• Follow template as outlined in *TOP Tool #12: Decision Making*
Identify Objectives	• What results do you want, need, or expect? • What resources can you spend or do you want to conserve? • What constraints limit your choices?	• Not identifying enough objectives to facilitate a good comparison of alternatives • Not retaining objectives created for other decision points	• Use *TOP Tool #5: Brainstorming* to flush out potentials • Use *TOP Tool #9: Debrief* to review lessons learned and items to be considered for carryover to other decisions
Generate Alternatives	• How have you accomplished these objectives in the past? • How could these objectives be accomplished in a new, innovative or creative way?	• Not generating a "full" set of alternatives to solving the decision question	• Use *TOP Tool #5 Brainstorming* • Use *TOP Tool #13: Divergent and Convergent Thinking* and *TOP Tool #36: Six Thinking Hats* to expand the field
Evaluate Alternatives	• Which alternatives pass the MUST objectives? • Which alternatives best satisfy the WANT objectives? • What are the risks?	• Not assembling the necessary data to compare alternatives both qualitatively and quantitatively	• Use *TOP Tool #40: Weighted Ranking* to help validate evidence
Choose Solution	• Which is the best alternative? • Who needs to support, approve, or implement this decision?	• Not having a "smell test" to help confirm that the best decision has been made • Not considering where buy-in is required	• Use *TOP Tool #27: IPMI — Plus, Minus, Interesting* to quickly confirm • Use *TOP Tool #37: Stakeholder Assessment* to determine needs

Action Planning Frame—*(See TOP Tool #1 for detailed description)*

	Process/Key Questions	Potential Pitfall	Best Practices/ Tools
Action Planning	• Build a plan of action to reach the goal	• Not documenting information assembled in the process	• Follow template as outlined in *TOP Tool #1: Action Planning*
Draft Plan	• What are the objectives to be achieved? • What action steps are required to meet your objectives? • When must each step be completed? • Who will be responsible for each step?	• Don't know where to start • Not having the right people in the room • Not making action planning a team game	• Use *TOP Tool #5: Brainstorming, #23: Mind Mapping,* and *#3 Affinity Analysis* to structure your thinking • Use *TOP Tool #37: Stakeholder Assessment* to validate the who and the why
Anticipate Changes	• What dependency or sequence is likely to change?	• Not expecting change	• Use *TOP Tool #17: Force Field Analysis* to identify drivers and restrainers of change
Revise Plan	• Are logic and flow still intact?	• Not choosing the appropriate planning support tool • Not using "network logic" at all	• The case for using PM Planning software rests squarely in its ability to help you make changes quickly and easily in the plan
Set Baseline	• Which is the dominant driver — time, cost, or scope?	• Not being clear with the client or sponsor which dimension is dominant • Fear of baselines	• Use *TOP Tool #33: Reframing Matrix* to force a change of view • Use *TOP Tool #4: Ask "Why" Five Times* to get to the bottom of the fear

Risk Assessment Frame—(*See TOP Tool #35 for detailed description)*

	Process/Key Questions	Potential Pitfall	Best Practices/ Tools
Risk Assessment	• Protect the plan	• Not documenting information assembled in the process • Not making this process a team game	• Follow template as outlined in *TOP Tool #34: Risk Assessment*
Identify Risks	• What could go wrong?	• Focusing on threats and ignoring opportunities • Not casting the identification net wide enough	• Develop two risk registers — one for threats and one for opportunities • Use *TOP Tool #16: Facilitation* • Use *TOP Tool #36: Six Thinking Hats* to expand the net
Qualify Risks	• What is the probability? • What is the impact?	• Not systematically assessing cause and effect • Misreading the impact	• Use *TOP Tool #6: Cause and Effect Diagram, #29 Probability Tree,* and *#32: Process Mapping*
Plan Response	• What can be done to reduce the probability? • What can be done to reduce the impact?	• Not identifying creative options for responding to the risks	• Use *TOP Tool #5: Brainstorming, #30: Problem Restatement,* and *#33: Reframing Matrix*
Monitor & Control	• How frequently will the risks be monitored and who will do it?	• Not staying focused on the need to monitor probability for each risk	• Identify your current mindset using *TOP Tool #4: Ask "Why" Five Times* to determine its origin • Identify the required mindset to properly monitor fluctuations in probability • Apply changed POV, name it, or reframe to help lock in as a new mindset

4.5 TOP Step 5—Validate Your Outcome

Validating your outcome is really about follow-through and follow-up, or what I call F&F. As you have probably guessed, the Monkey Mind—with its attention span of a caffeine-addled gnat—is not your friend when it comes to F&F.

Pattern recognition drives us to believe that since we started out in the right direction, we will automatically end up at our proper destination, and as a result we tend to develop a mindset of ignoring or dismissing the need to follow up and follow through. Alas, pattern recognition is a very naÔve force, and we heed its advice to our extreme detriment.

Thinking On Purpose is all about paying attention to your thinking and managing your mindsets. You can use it to change a "No time or interest in follow-up" mindset into something more practical and functional by reframing follow-up and follow-through.

As mentioned earlier, reframing is the ability to change your perspective or point of view about certain data or information in order to facilitate new patterns of thought or insights. To illustrate, let's reframe F&F differently. Instead of looking at it as a necessary evil (and really, who wants to do evil, necessary or otherwise?), reframe F&F as a wonderful opportunity to review your actions, improve your process and validate your decisions (and, if you did well, it also allows you to take a moment to bask in the sunshine of a job well done).

HERE'S HOW THE PROCESS OF FOLLOW-UP AND FOLLOW-THROUGH PLAYS OUT IN THIS REFRAME:

- Circling back to make sure the framed purpose has been achieved legitimizes the original purpose. If the original purpose was not valuable, why did we approach it in the first place?
- Circling back to the framed purpose sends the message to the team that measuring success against a target or baseline is a valid and expected part of the thinking process, and is just as important as doing the same thing for the elements of the triple constraint of time, cost, and scope.
- Circling back to the framed purpose provides an opportunity to make this aspect of TOP a T.E.A.M game:
    - **T**EACH IT: Teach your team both the mindset and the value proposition of proper follow-through and follow-up (F&F).
    - **E**XPECT IT: Expect each of your team to circle back and confirm assumptions.

- o **A**NCHOR IT: Provide your team with job aids, reminders, and other mental anchors that show how this process and TOP overall should work.
- o **M**ODEL IT: Demonstrate your commitment by modeling F&F and, in particular, validating your purpose.

- Circling back on the framed purpose, especially for decision making, facilitates measuring your success *after* the decision has been put into practice. Many a hastily conceived decision ends up being reversed after implementation, often without any accountability for the person who made the decision. Circling back enables you to determine your real "hit rate" on decisions. There is often a big difference between making the right decision and making the decision right.
- The Debrief (TOP Tool #9) is a key enabler of this step and can be done either in a small group setting or with the full team.

Adopt a follow-through and follow-up mindset for every purpose, every time.

Putting It All Together

With each of the five TOP steps now in place, we can now fully populate a TOP Purpose one-page job aid depicting the continuous cycling that occurs throughout the TOP Process.

The TOP steps need to be applied and reapplied for each purpose to neutralize the "impacts of evolution," or the way a situation—and its resolution—changes as time goes by. The following chart describes the desired outcome of each purpose and how the TOP steps should be applied.

Thinking On Purpose Road Map—Validate your Outcome

This chart adds the Validate Your Outcome details to the TOP Road Map.

Purpose / Thinking Step	The Thinking on Purpose Roadmap: Frame Your Purpose	Qualify Your Information	Identify Your Mindsets	Structure Your Thinking	Validate Your Outcome
Situational Assessment	Identify the Problem	• Identify your POV • Confirm fact or fallacy • Confirm needed information is available	• Expand your POV • Sweep for MindFields • Reframe your thinking • Choose your mindset	• Identify the issues • Clarify the issues • Prioritize the issues • Establish if cause is known	• Problem identified?
Problem Solving	Determine the Cause	• Identify your POV • Confirm fact or fallacy • Confirm needed information is available	• Expand your POV • Sweep for MindFields • Reframe your thinking • Choose your mindset	• Describe the problem • List possible causes • Test possible causes • Confirm root cause	• True cause determined?
Decision Making	Choose a Solution	• Identify your POV • Confirm fact or fallacy • Confirm needed information is available • Test information	• Expand your POV • Sweep for MindFields • Reframe your thinking • Choose your mindset	• Identify objectives • Generate alternatives • Evaluate alternatives • Choose solution	• Best solution chosen?
Action Planning	Build a Plan	• Identify your POV • Confirm fact or fallacy • Confirm needed information is available • Test information	• Expand your POV • Sweep for MindFields • Reframe your thinking • Choose your mindset	• Draft a plan • Anticipate changes • Revise the plan • Set a baseline	• Most realistic plan built?
Risk Assessment	Protect the Plan	• Identify your POV • Confirm fact or fallacy • Confirm needed information is available • Test information	• Expand your POV • Sweep for MindFields • Reframe your thinking • Choose your mindset	• Identify the risks • Qualify the risks • Plan responses • Monitor and control	• Plan well protected?

Chapter Summary

We have a choice when it comes to thinking. We can Think On Autopilot or we can Think On Purpose. Autopilot thinking (APT) is the result of relying on our lower brains to do all the work for us, and following wherever that leads. On purpose thinking (OPT) is the process of using your thinking brain to harness the lower brains to serve your needs.

It is also critical to remember the rule that effective project management is 30% insight, 60% foresight, and 10% hindsight. By developing insight and foresight, and relying less on hindsight, project managers can give their projects a clear path to success.

There are Five Steps to Thinking On Purpose:

Step 1—Frame Your Purpose

Framing our purpose ensures that all subsequent activity is aimed at a single goal or set of goals. We do this by adopting and discipling a structured method of thinking.

There are 5 parts to framing your purpose

- Assess a situation
- Solve a problem
- Make a decision
- Build an action plan
- Do a risk assessment

Step 2—Qualify Your Information

This step is based on the maxim of "Garbage In, Garbage Out." You can't create a useful solution with inaccurate or insufficient information.

There are 2 METHODS OF TAKING IN INFORMATION:

- **The Sponge Method** involves absorbing everything that comes your way indiscriminately. The result is a hodge-podge of accurate, inaccurate and deceptive information with no way to determine one variety from the other.
- **Panning for Gold** involves using critical thinking skills to validate information, and then accepting only that information that passes these tests, and only for as long as it continues to stand up to scrutiny.

There are three types of knowledge that affect our decisision-making

- **Inert Information**, which is information that we have passively absorbed but don't really understand in anything other than a superficial way.

- **Activated Ignorance**, which is when we accept and act on inaccurate information.
- **Activated Knowledge** is when we seek out and act on accurate information.

Other keys to assembling quality information are:

- Recognizing and understanding **assumptions** and **inferences.**
- Being aware of logical **fallacies** and false arguments.
- Determining the difference between **facts** and **assertions.**

It is also vital to make sure that not only is your information good, but that you have all the information you need to make an accurate decision or create a useful solution.

Step 3—Identify Your Mindsets

Your mindsets determine how you think and act in a given situation. Becoming aware of mindsets that may be hidden to your conscious awareness is vital before change can begin.

The three ways to identify your mindsets are:

- **Sweep for MindFields** by asking yourself which emotions, biases, or habits may be in play.
- **Expand your point of view** by exposing yourself to other people's viewpoints and to new ways of thinking.
- **Reframe your thoughts** by challenging your preconceived assumptions.

Step 4—Structure Your Thinking

Thinking On Purpose is defined by critical, structured thinking. Relying on our natural habits, biases, and emotions to define our thinking puts us at the mercy of thought patterns, conclusions, assumptions, reactions and potentially faulty information we may not even be aware of.

By using the tools, templates, and structured processes of ***Thinking On Purpose***, you can eliminate the mistakes and wasted time inherent in autopilot thinking and optimize your problem solving and decision making.

Step 5—Validate Your Outcome

Validating Your Outcome involves a process of Follow-Through and Follow-Up, or F&F. By validating your outcome each and every time, you build an understanding of how the TOP Process can improve your decision making and problem solving, and you get a better feel for what works and what doesn't.

Validating Your Outcome is all about objectively reviewing actual results through a process of circling back and checking how those results played out, both during and after the decision-making and problem-solving process, using the T.E.A.M. approach:

TEACH IT

EXPECT IT

ANCHOR IT

MODEL IT

CHAPTER FIVE

Personal Evolution

"The older I get, the more wisdom I find in the ancient rule of taking first things first—a process which often reduces the most complex human problems to manageable proportions." —Dwight Eisenhower

"Nothing can stop the man with the right mental attitude from achieving his goal; nothing on earth can help the man with the wrong mental attitude." —Thomas Jefferson

In the beginning of this book, I positioned my "pay attention to your thinking" message in the context of human evolution, and how we as human beings have evolved into our present state over time. I went on to say that mindsets drive behavior, and behavior drives performance, and performance drives results. Therefore, poor mindsets lead to poor results. In this final chapter, I want to address your own personal evolution, both personally and professionally, in one of the finest professions on the planet.

While our evolution as species has taken place over millions of years, your evolution as an individual will take place over a mere seventy to one hundred years, if you're lucky. There is a high probability that, if my demographics are right, you're are at least a third of the way through your time on this planet already. So my question is: How will your remaining time on the planet unfold, and how might this book affect how that happens. Also, if evolution is defined as a gradual process during which something changes into a different and usually more complex or improved form, how will you evolve throughout your remaining time, and what influences will shape those changes?

5.1 It Really Is All in Your Mind

Primarily, the key catalyst for change is going to be your mindset. In Chapter 3, I talked about the difference between a fixed mindset and a growth mindset, as laid out in the book, *Mindset: The New Psychology for Success*, written by world-renowned psychologist Carol S. Dweck, Ph.D.

Dweck describes the fixed mindset as the belief that your qualities, talents, skills, and abilities are carved in stone, immutable and unimprovable—you're either smart or dumb, talented or untalented, and there's nothing you can do about it except play the hand you're dealt and hope you got a royal flush instead of a pair of tens. Because this mindset is predicated on the belief that you only have a certain allotment of traits to carry you from birth to death, you constantly feel the need to prove that you were dealt a winning hand and to bluff about or cover up any perceived lack. It's a stressful, fearful and insecure way to live, and not at all conducive to rational thought and critical thinking.

On the other side of the spectrum, Dweck describe the growth mindset as the belief that your attributes and characteristics can be built up, improved and even gained from scratch. The key difference is that in the growth mindset is the understanding that the hand you're dealt is just a *starting point* for development.

Dweck writes that individuals with a growth mindset believe that their basic qualities are traits that they can cultivate through their own efforts, and that although we all differ in terms of initial talents, aptitudes, interests, etc., everyone can change and grow through education, application, and experience.

A fixed mindset is perpetuated by Auto Pilot Thinking (APT). When using APT thinking, you literally accept the mindsets in play today as the determination of your destiny. Your biases, emotions, and habits go unnamed (that's just the way things are) and therefore outside your conscious awareness.

As a result, all that you know about project management, general management and your field overall (as well as your personal life) will continue to be filtered through your current fixed mindset.

A growth mindset, on the other hand, is enabled by On ***Purpose Thinkin***g (OPT), and supported by using the Thinking On Purpose Process:

- Challenges are embraced, because through them you can achieve greater success and personal development. Using the TOP process provides the confidence, methodology and toolset for thinking through any situation. Project managers and teams who adopt a growth mindset are willing to embrace challenges and conflict when they believe there is no problem or issue they cannot solve.
- Effort is maximized through the TOP process because of the tools available to assist with the "mental heavy lifting," and because of a

sense of confidence brought about by knowing where to start in any situation.

- Criticism is framed more positively, because it implies an opportunity for learning. The TOP process provides a context for understanding the intent and point of view of the source of the feedback, and a means of making sure that emotional reactions are monitored and regulated in keeping with the situation.
- Success of others is framed in terms of risk and reward. TOP provides a basis to clarify and appreciate what others either risked or did to achieve their success. In addition to acknowledging that accomplishment, the discipline of expanding one's point of view through the use of TOP creates a more positive and useful frame of reference.
- Reaching higher levels of achievement is rooted in the desire to view success as a result of learning, not because you did something in a flawless manner. TOP is a learning orientation whereby you are able to free yourself from the gravitational pull of autopilot by dint of effort and attention. You are much less fearful of making mistakes, because you have the means to identify the cause and take appropriate corrective action, which is what learning is all about.

Below is a table showing the two types of mindsets and their tendencies, as adapted from Dweck.

Fixed Mindset Intelligence is static	**Growth Mindset** Intelligence can be developed	
Leads to a desire to appear masterful or gifted, and therefore a tendency to...	Leads to a desire to learn, and therefore a tendency to...	
Challenges	avoid	embrace
Obstacles	get defensive or give up easily	persist in the face of setbacks
Effort	see effort as fruitless or worse	see effort as the path to mastery
Criticism	ignore useful negative feedback	learn from criticism
Success of Others	feel threatened by the success of others	find inspiration in the success of others
As a Result	they may plateau early or achieve less than their potential	reach ever higher levels of achievement

Thinking On Purpose is very closely aligned with a growth mindset. A growth mindset is absolutely critical to being successful in developing and using the insight, foresight and hindsight traits that every project manager needs to be successful.

5.2 TOP Ten "Nuggets"

Thinking On Purpose is a continuous journey. My experience and observation has shown that the gravitational pull of autopilot thinking is relentless, powerful, and unforgiving. And although I would like to be with you all the time to offer my experience and insights, I can't. However, I can offer you this book, and the following summary of the bare minimum you absolutely need to take with you out of it:

Nugget 1

The 30/60/10 Rule—Remember, planning makes foresight as clear as hindsight. Successful project management is 30 percent insight, 60 percent foresight, and 10 percent hindsight. This rule demonstrates the need for the project manager to cease relying on hindsight as the basis of his or her planning process, and develop his or her powers of foresight and insight.

Nugget 2

Auto Pilot and Topper—The concept of Auto Pilot is a double-edged sword that can cut the hand of the person that holds it as readily as the hand of their foe. Auto Pilot is depicted as a robot to represent its repetitive, programmed nature. His mantra is to "REPEAT" a program over and over again. Without Auto Pilot, we would not have survived to be the incredibly powerful species that we are today. However, the shortcuts and patterns that facilitate our day-to-day existence can also cause serious problems when they are applied in situations that require rational, measured and critical thinking.

Topper, on the other hand, is very much aware of the hypnotic pull of pattern recognition and the built-in mental shortcuts referred to as biases, and he has strategies for dealing with them so that they don't interfere with the smooth and effective running of day-to-day affairs. Topper really is all about mindfulness and staying awake to or aware of what is happening, what has happened, and what is likely to happen. His mantra is "RESET."

Topper and Auto Pilot should be viewed as a team, rather than adversaries. They are, in the final reckoning, symbiotic—interdependent on one another to create a successful and secure life for the humans they reside in.

Nugget 3

Follow-through and Follow-up (F&F)—Following through and following up are vital aspects of project and general management, as well as a basic life skill. However, this activity is a prime target for Auto Pilot. It's easy to get into a habit of not following up or following through on plans, especially if there are never any serious consequences. Once this happens, pattern recognition kicks in with its hypnotic pull, and you become inclined to dispense with F&F altogether.

In practice, what happens is that the MindField of "habit" kicks in, and pretty soon you find yourself not following up or following through because, "it's always been fine before, it'll be fine this time." The templates built into each of the processes of Thinking On Purpose—Situational Assessment, Problem Solving, Decision Making, Action Planning, and Risk Assessment—function as a sort of manual override for resisting these Auto Pilot habits.

Nugget 4

Mindsets—Mindsets are an accumulation of biases that have been formed over time as a result of your environment and experiences. These mindsets in turn dictate to a large degree how we see and act within the world around us and, to a great extent, determine the nature of our lives.

A key rule to remember regarding mindsets is that if you don't choose your mindset, it will be chosen for you. The point here is to acknowledge that mindsets will develop with
or without your input. Your mind will settle on a certain positions or viewpoints that will override other thinking processes unless you consciously intervene.

There are three key strategies for identifying your mindsets. 1) Sweep for the MindFields of bias, emotions, and habits on a constant basis. 2) Consciously expand your point of view to facilitate new and greater perspectives. 3) Reframe your thinking to prevent autopilot reactions and approaches to decision making and problem solving.

Nugget 5

Emotions and Thoughts Are Connected—Remember the expression from Daniel Goleman's book, *Emotional Intelligence*, referring to the "amygdala highjack?" Goleman was talking about how, under certain stressful or emotional situations, the amygdala (the small walnut-sized part of the brain considered to be the seat of human emotion) will "highjack" the rational parts of your brain (the frontal lobes) and create an overwhelming fight-or-flight response. This process takes only fractions of a second to occur, but it can have a long-lasting impact on your rational thinking. It is part of the process involved in the creation of phobias, flashbacks, Post-Traumatic Stress Disorder, and other debilitating emotional issues.

In project management, as in any situation where you interact with people, not paying attention to this evolutionary trait can create interpersonal difficulties. For example, if you grew up in a home where speaking up as a child led to physical punishment, you might get "hijacked" in a situation that requires you to take a stand against another person. Or, if you have had issues in the past of being bullied by older individuals, you might be "hijacked" into responding aggressively and inappropriately to older superiors, clients, or colleagues.

Amygdala hijacking is just one of the many potential issues that our emotions can create for us. Emotional responses are deeply-seated brain reactions, and their impact is both severe and primary, in the sense that the body and mind tend to give emotional responses the lead when it comes to determining our actions and thoughts. Only a habit of careful and conscious recognition, acknowledgement, and control of your emotions will allow you to rely on critical thinking rather than animal reaction in emotionally charged situations.

Nugget 6

Thinking On Purpose is a T.E.A.M Game—As a project manager, you have the unique opportunity of being in a leadership role, either by virtue of the organization chart or by professional expertise. And while it may be a surprise, just because you are the project manager doesn't mean you are the smartest person in the room, or that you have the most insight into a particular situation.

However, being the project manager does mean that you have an obligation to teach your team how to think on purpose, holding them to the standard of doing so as a part of their normal activities, anchoring the process in different ways and, most importantly, "walking the talk."

Just imagine the power of a team that believed there was no problem it could not solve!

Nugget 7

Tools and Templates Do Not Replace Thinking—In Chapter 2, we defined *thinking* as the process of perceiving and modeling the world around us in a way that allows us to interact with it so that it makes sense to us. When ***Thinking On Purpose***, you perceive and model the project management world fully aware of the mindset and emotional filters affecting your perception, and consciously directing how you respond to the situation.

Tools, like the set included in this book, provide a structure to help you expand your point of view and reframe the information at hand to gain leverage or traction in order to reach the best possible conclusion or direction. Some tools, like Brainstorming, provide a means for more effective divergent thinking—generating as many ideas, concepts or options as possible. Other tools, like Affinity Diagrams, provide a means for more effective convergent thinking—processing as much information as possible about a situation and using the information to create a solution.

Either way, however, the tools can only provide the framework and a way to organize the data. You must provide the brainpower to process that data within the framework effectively. Being fully aware of how hidden mindsets, biases, habits, and other pitfalls can significantly affect the results by virtue of Thinking On Purpose is what allows that to happen.

Nugget 8

"Naming" Is the First Step in Mitigating the Impact of Biases and Emotions— When sweeping for MindFields—biases, emotions, and habits—the first step is to simply name the bias, emotion or habit in play at the particular moment. The quicker you name it or become aware of it, the quicker you can avoid APT (autopilot thinking).

For example, let's say you need to participate in a situational assessment session on a problem regarding the lead vendor on your project that, one month away from the first conversion, has advised you of an unexpected two-week delay. Unfortunately, it isn't until you get to the third TOP step, Identify Your Mindsets, that you first realize that, in your reaction to this statement, you are being heavily influenced by the confirmation bias—the tendency to accept information or evidence that supports your preconceived beliefs.

Initially, the fact that the vendor is reporting this information so close to the implementation date validated your preexisting belief that vendors in general cannot manage their schedules effectively. However, in reviewing the typical biases that come into play into these situations (namely, confirmation bias), you begin to open up to the possibility that perhaps the delay isn't caused by vendor at all. This open-mindedness can then lead you to discover the true cause of the delay: Your testing team delivered the required test cases to the vendor one week late.

Without being aware of, and then capable of naming, the biases that are affecting your judgment and actions, such realizations might never take place, therefore setting the scene for a continuing cycle of repeated mistakes, problems, and poor reactions.

Nugget 9

Make Asking the Right Question a Signature Skill—The first step in making *asking the right question* a signature skill is learning the distinction between *having the right answers* and *answering the right questions.*

In school, there is generally an emphasis on being able to answer all the questions put to you, in order to demonstrate your grasp of the information. In the world of work, however, there is a need to come up with answers to questions that, unlike in school, are not laid out on paper. (Granted, as you move into college and university, case studies are used as a means of getting closer to real-world situations. Unfortunately, in most case studies, the questions are also provided and so you never get to practice making sure you're actually asking the right questions.)

A companion technique to asking the right questions is *reframing*, as discussed in Chapter 4. By reframing, you consciously change your point of view of the problem in order to see it a different way. Reframing is a power tool for ferreting out and validating questions, as well. Note the difference in the two viewpoints below, and how the solution could be achieved in significantly different ways:

> Original question: How can I get this task done?
>
> Reframed question: What is the optimal configuration of resources to get this done in the most appropriate and accurate fashion?

The first question, basically APT in action, automatically orients the mind of the questioner toward getting the job done using only themselves as a resource. The reframed question, coming from a more OPT viewpoint, orients the mind of the questioner toward determining how this task can be best accomplished by using available team members, existing support structures and other available resources, and then organizing and mobilizing these resources toward a workable solution. The reframed question provides a framework that is much more conducive to teamwork and resource optimization.

So, how do you get to better questions? Start by considering a simple concept called OPV, or Other People's View. Your team, your company, your colleagues, and your support systems are all valuable sources of reframing and assistance—as you are for them. In fact, I believe the most important question a project manager needs to learn to ask skillfully and often is, "What do you need from me?"

Nugget 10

Get the OPTICS Right—OPTICS is an acronym that stands for Opportunity, Problem, Team, Influence, Change, and Stress. These six elements are like a window into the soul of project managers. The way they play out in action depends on whether you are using APT or OPT.

Opportunity is defined as a combination of circumstances favorable for the purpose. In reality, security and opportunity cannot co-exist. Whenever you move on an opportunity, there is always an element of risk. But like an entrepreneur who sees the opportunity and is willing to manage the risk, OPT will facilitate your leveraging of the opportunity. APT, with its fixed mindset, generally does not even look at opportunities at all, and therefore offers no probability of discovering that "big one" that can make the difference.

Problem is defined as results not meeting expectations. To some experts, problem solving is one of the key competencies of high quality project management. APT, with its susceptibility to jumping to conclusions or solutions based on incomplete data, generally results in problems being Band-Aided and having to be "solved" multiple times. OPT, on the hand, enabled by a conscious, structured approach and an awareness of MindFields, zeroes in on root causes and ultimately leads to solutions that solve the problem for good.

Team is defined by Jon R. Katzenbach and Douglas K. Smith, in The Wisdom of Teams, as a group of people with complementary skills committed to a common purpose and set of specific performance goals. Imagine a team approaching their purpose on APT, and along with it the probability of low energy and a high degrees of apathy. Now imagine this same team, hooked on OPT, and believing that there is no problem they cannot solve. What energy and power they could apply to their situations!

Influence was succinctly described over a hundred years ago by Albert Schweitzer when he said, "Example is not the main thing in influencing others. It is the only thing." Helping your Stakeholders think more effectively and more efficiently, by virtue of OPT, sends a very clear message that collaboration and joint problem-solving is in the interest of the greater good and is a signature of your style. Not being mindful of the greater good is competitive and short term focused. Ultimately, you will get what you model.

Change, or more precisely how you manage change, will play a big part in defining you as a project management professional. Poor change control is often cited by experts as the root cause for every project manager's nightmare—scope creep. A project manager and his or her team, functioning through APT, will undoubtedly experience repeated instances of "unmanaged change" and the repercussions that come with it. The same PM and team, functioning through OPT have a much better chance of being ahead of the change curve, and having the discipline to manage how change happens.

Stress, according to Richard Saunders, is clearly a bad thing: "Brain cells create ideas. Stress kills brain cells. Stress is not a good idea." Stress is often generally described as either bad or good. Bad stress is caused when people feel frustrated or trapped, like the feeling of an individual or team who can't seem to make any headway despite their good intentions and hard work. APT literally lets the environment and your mindsets guide the fortunes of you and your team, thereby creating substantial bad stress. Good stress, on the other hand, is created when the problems may be difficult, but the team believes they are capable of solving them and that there is a functional is a way to address the problem. OPT gives the team both the confidence and systems required to tackle difficult problems and still have fun working hard, and thus alleviating bad stress and replacing it with good.

5.3 Where Do I Go from Here?

The first part of any journey, be it physical or intellectual, is to determine where you are in comparison to where you want to be. The same thing applies to the Thinking On Purpose process. You need to know where you stand on a spectrum of APT (Auto Pilot Thinking) to OPT (On Purpose Thinking) before you can determine the best way to proceed.

The first step, then, is to complete the self-assessment in Appendix 3. Then take a look at your score and what the scoring system tells you about the results:

Novice

Your Tendencies and Vulnerabilities

Scoring 5-9 on the assessment puts you in the TOP Novice range. This means that you are very much at the mercy of your emotions, habits, and biases. Your decisions are heavily swayed by your emotional state, your existing beliefs and your gut feelings, and you almost never take a structured, objective approach to checking these decisions against relevant, qualified information.

In fact, because you don't habitually attack problems in a structured and linear way, you often go too fast, get ahead of yourself and/or try to do too much at once, and wind up getting overwhelmed by all the details and processes involved in the situation at hand. As a result, you tend to resist methodically examining and prioritizing all of the data and required actions because of the confusion it creates. Instead, once you hit that wall you tend to just go whatever "feels right," rather than trying to work your way through the confusion.

Your Strategy

Your goal as a Novice is to get rid of the habit of going with your feelings, and to find a way to avoid being overwhelmed by the data in any decision. Since you are probably starting more or less from scratch, my suggestion is that you use this book literally as a workbook and a template for problem solving.

Whenever you are faced with a decision or problem, copy out the tables, matrices and tools in this book to create a step-by-step checklist/plan that you can follow. By doing this, you're taking the process out of the realm of your head and heart (which are currently too likely to be influenced by autopilot thinking) and putting it on paper so you can see what steps are coming up, and where you're tempted to skip them. Since everything is right there in front of you in black and white, it is difficult to be led astray by autopilot thinking without it becoming obvious.

Over time, you will begin to absorb the TOP principles and processes to the point that they become habitual and automatic, thereby replacing older and less functional habits. Until then, however, it's important for you to make a point of checking and double-checking your progress against the TOP charts and tables at every step to ensure you remain on track with the process from start to finish.

Apprentice

Your Tendencies and Vulnerabilities

Scoring 10-14 puts you in the Apprentice range. (Unfortunately, a job with Donald Trump is not forthcoming with this particular distinction. Our apologies.) This ranking indicates that you have internalized at least a few of the concepts of structured problem solving, and are functionally using them. However, you still have some way to go to achieve complete competence.

If you've ever heard the maxim that a little knowledge is a dangerous thing, you can see the dangers present at the Apprentice level. It's easy to assume you're thinking critically and in a structured manner all of the time simply because you're doing it part of the time. This can leave you open to being influenced by autopilot thinking when you think you're thinking critically.

This shows up in action as tendency to move to quickly through the process (often by skipping steps), to make assumptions that feel like critically examined conclusions, to confuse hindsight with insight, to conflate credible sources with qualified information and so on. In short, you know where you want to go, but you have a tendency to take shortcuts getting there—and as we all know, the best way to wind up where you don't want to go is to take jump off the path in order to take a "shortcut."

Your Strategy

The most important piece of advice I can offer a TOP Apprentice is to slow down. Use this book as a guidebook to check your actions against the steps in the ***Thinking On Purpose*** process. After you've completed each phase of your decision making, review TOP and see where you've stayed on track and where you've veered into APT thinking. If you spot missed steps, rushed decisions, leapt-upon conclusions, unsupported assumptions, unqualified information, bias influences and so on, go back and address those lapses.

The only way to advance from functionality to competency to mastery is by proactive planning, engaged practice, and review. Each of these steps is as important as the others, and none of them can be overlooked, bypassed or given "a lick and a promise" if you expect to move beyond your current skills and abilities. Don't let your innate resistance get the better of you. Resist taking shortcuts, even when the direction of the path seems obvious. You'd be surprised how quickly and how far you can be led astray.

Journeyman

Your Tendencies and Vulnerabilities

Scoring 15-20 puts you squarely in the ranking of Journeyman (or Journeywoman, as the case may be). Congratulations! You're almost there. You've moved from functional to competent, but you have yet to achieve mastery.

Since you're using OPT thinking most of the time, you're achieving good results on a fairly consistent basis. This can lead to complacency, however, especially in the few remaining areas where your critical thinking turns into autopilot thinking. You still have a few MindFields in play; hotspots where emotion, habit, bias, hindsight/experience, assumption, and inattention prevent you from making the best choices and decisions. However, if you don't take steps to track these issues down and work to eliminate them, you will never improve.

The key here is the difference between *adequate* and *optimal* results. At this point, you are doing work that is, by all measures, good enough. However, good enough isn't always good enough, especially in situations where that small margin of error can lead to serious repercussions.

Your Strategy

Your best strategy is to use this book as a reference or cookbook, both to guide your planning before you take action and to review your decision-making process after the fact. In this way, you can spot the few remaining places where autopilot thinking is taking over and take steps to correct them. By doing so, you will eventually move from competence to mastery and as a result, make ***Thinking On Purpose*** your default mode of thought.

Master

Your Tendencies and Vulnerabilities

A score of 21-25 places you in the category of Master. Congratulations, sensei. Your decision-making and problem-solving processes are structured, linear and taken in order. Your emotions, habits, and biases no longer rule your actions, nor are your solutions and decisions founded upon assumptions, hindsight, and faulty information. But your work isn't done yet.

Your primary concern at this point is two-fold. First, you need to be on guard against overconfidence. If you get too comfortable with the idea that you will always and automatically do things the right way, it's easy to revert to taking shortcuts. (In case you haven't guessed, falling for your own publicity is a common and dangerous bias, one that can blind you to your own faulty actions.)

Second, you need to be wary of any tendency to keep this information to yourself. Your responsibility, both as a Project Manager and as an ethical person with valuable knowledge, is to share that knowledge with others for the greater good of the project, the team as a whole, and the individual personal development of those around you.

Teaching the TOP process to others is a vital part of maintaining your mastery in other ways, as well. For starters, continually teaching it will serve to reinforce it in your own mind, which will prevent overconfidence in your approach and complacency in your actions. It will also give you a greater understanding of the principles of ***Thinking On Purpose***, since the best way to understand anything is to teach it to others. Finally, if those around you are following the TOP steps, they'll be less likely to let you get away with taking shortcuts, and will be able to catch your and each other's mistakes before they can cause problems.

Your Strategy

Your strategy, then, is to use this book to check that you're actively using the TOP process, and as a textbook to pass on what you've learned with those around you. In this way, not only will your company have the benefit of a TOP Master as their Project Manager, they'll also have an entire team that's working, thinking and acting as clearly and as critically as possible. As a result, the quality of the company's work will increase and your own personal evolution will follow, as well.

Chapter Summary

In the Introduction of this book, I shared my goal of promoting leadership in project management by putting a Thinking On Purpose arrow in the quiver of every project manager on the planet. No matter where you are on the TOP continuum—Novice, Apprentice, Journeyman or Master—your team, your Stakeholders and your organization expect you, above everything else, to lead.

There is no better way to demonstrate your leadership than by building and maintaining the following habits:

- Carefully and rationally determining the best place to start when faced with a wide variety of situations, rather than simply wading into the fray willy-nilly or taking action without planning.
- Learning how to ask the right questions and how to choose the right answers.
- Being willing to lead from the front, by facilitating the acquisition of good data and Stakeholder cooperation in dealing with difficult situations.

- Being mindful of how the brain works and how evolution can be outsmarted through the use of the processes, tools, techniques, and templates indexed in this book
- Recognizing the limits of your knowledge and expertise, and how you can maximize the potential thinking power of your team by unifying them around a common approach to ***Thinking On Purpose***.
- Applying and promoting foresight as a signature skill for all team members, as a means to reduce stress, focus resources and to allow hard work to be fun.
- Taking the growth mindset approach to leveraging your knowledge, expertise, and hard work to lift yourself to the highest level of accomplishment you desire, instead of taking the fixed mindset approach of assuming that you're either a natural or you're not, and resting on your laurels.

I believe that every project manager has the necessary knowledge, skills, and aptitude to progress. But some are held back, in varying degrees, by the gravitational pull of the evolutionary MindFields of mindsets, habits, and emotions. My goal in this book has been to provide all project managers with a new mindset about how the way in which you think affects your success in both your profession and your life.

You don't have to wait until your traits show up in some future generation to make a difference and get the results you deserve. You can start now, by outsmarting evolution and playing a bigger game in this lifetime. Think On Purpose!

SECTION 3

THE APPLICATION

A Brief Intermission

In the previous chapters, I have explored the evolution of the human brain, how this evolutionary development affects your thinking and the pitfalls, and dangers to look out for. I've also introduced the Thinking On Purpose principles and process, providing you with the tools and techniques you need to conquer your Auto Pilot reactions and replace them with a critical and structured thinking process.

These chapters comprise the educational portion of this book—everything you need to know in order to begin Thinking On Purpose can be found in the previous five chapters. However, I have always found that raw data and instruction, without supporting resources and real-world application, is little more than an academic exercise. I can read as many books as I want on blacksmithing, but until I actually get my hands on a hammer and anvil and begin putting my learning into action, I'm no closer to mastering the art of ironworking than I was before.

Likewise, the information and instruction I have given in this book are very useful stuff, if I do say so myself. But unless you know how to apply the TOP process in the real world and have the tools at your disposal to do so, then that knowledge, too, is little more than an academic exercise—interesting, perhaps, and possibly enlightening, but not terribly useful.

To that end, the remainder of this book is devoted to making the information I've given you come alive.

Chapter 6—Thinking On Purpose In Action

Chapter 6 contains the complete versions of the three case study scenarios that I briefly touched on in the introduction. Within each scenario, you will find people just like you working in the project management field and running into the same types of situations and problems you've probably dealt with yourself.

Each scenario explores a different set of characters and problems, each with its own unique solution. At every step in the resolution process, I've cross-referenced the steps taken in the scenario with the relevant TOP principles and processes, as well as the tools taken from the TOP Toolkit, which comprises Chapter 7.

Chapter 7—The TOP Toolkit

In the TOP Toolkit, I've collected forty of the most common and useful tools in the project management field. These have been drawn from a wide variety of sources, and expanded with templates, examples, and suggestions for use. Additionally, each tool is cross-referenced with other tools that can be used to enhance or expand its usage, and the original source is listed for those who would like to pursue more detailed information.

Bibliography and Appendices

Following Chapters 6 and 7 are a comprehensive bibliography of sources that I've called upon in the writing of this book. The curious reader will find more than enough source material here to keep him or her busy for quite some time, should he or she so desire.

I've also included several appendices that reference and expand on the information included in the book, including a rather expansive listing of Biases and Fallacies and the self-assessment tool that accompanies Chapter 5. A summary of the TOP Ten Nuggets, the TOP Road Map and a summary listing of the TOP Toolkit are also included for quick reference.

It is hoped that these additional resources will help you, the reader, maximize your use of the ***Thinking On Purpose*** system.

CHAPTER SIX

THINKING ON PURPOSE in Action: Top Case Studies

"A stupid man's report of what a clever man says is never accurate because he unconsciously translates what he hears into something he can understand." —Bertrand Russell

"The mind is like the stomach. It's not how much you put into it, but how much it digests."—Albert J. Nock

By being aware of the pitfalls of thinking on autopilot, a project manager can take preventative and corrective action and redirect his or her efforts toward ***Thinking On Purpose***. This section brings these concepts and tools into the operational, day-to-day backyard of the project manager through the development of the three hypothetical project management scenarios we introduced you to at the beginning of this book.

Read on to discover how the TOP tools, principles, and critical thinking processes can be applied to these real-world situations.

Scenario One—Red Light, Green Light

George Green had been working on projects in the IT department at First Company for over ten years and in the last five years he was a Project Manager. He really enjoyed doing project management and felt he was really good at it. He was in his comfort zone; he had a lot of experience in IT, he knew most of the Subject Matter Experts (SMEs) in the company, and year after year he had been given bigger and higher-profile projects. He could see his career path leading right up to Vice-President of Project Management.

His current project was a simple application conversion with very little development: In order to move to a new application, they would have to purchase new servers and upgrade the desktops. The project was referred to as Sales Management Upgrade (SMU). So far everything was going very well. He had four teams: Network, Development, Infrastructure (Server & Desktop), and Business.

He was just about to start a regular status meeting that he had actually contemplated canceling because everything was going so well. Every meeting was the same: Network: Green, Development: Green, Infrastructure: Green, and Business: Green. He had a great team and he had completely empowered them. There had been very few changes to manage and everything was on track to meet the deadline a month away. In fact, everything was going so smoothly that George was already starting to think about his next assignment.

As he entered the meeting room, he noticed that the Network guys were in a huddle, talking quietly amongst themselves. They stopped talking as soon as he entered the room and took up their normal seats. He decided to go ahead and get the meeting underway; he knew it would be a fast meeting and he had a presentation for an Executive Steering Committee meeting to prepare.

Development went first and said they were Green, on track. So far, so good. But when it came around to Network, their representative Susan Bowman spoke quietly, saying, "Network is Red and it looks like we won't get our activities completed for another six weeks."

George couldn't believe what he was hearing. There were only four weeks left in the project and there were two more weeks of activities after the Network guys finished their deliverables. When George questioned the Network team about the slippage in the timeline, they said that the timeline was unrealistic and he should be aware that the Development team was behind as well.

Development confirmed that they, also, might not meet the dates they had committed to. The senior developer they had expected to work with on the project wasn't available, and the new developer who joined the project needed training, which took up time, and he worked much slower than the senior developer. Development had done all their estimates based on working with the senior developer. George asked them why they had continually reported Green if these problems had been on the horizon, and they responded that they hadn't actually missed their date yet, and besides, George seemed happy when they reported Green.

George was speechless. He was four weeks away from implementation, and by his calculations the team now needed eight weeks to complete their deliverables. Even after Network and Development completed their tasks, there was still testing to be done. George realized he was going to miss his implementation date by at least eight to ten weeks. He could envision the impact this was going to have on other projects, and he wasn't looking forward to telling his boss about this slippage in the timeline. But what really concerned George the most was that he wasn't sure how this happened; he had thought he had everything under control.

The next day George met with his boss, Ingrid Cameron. She was as concerned as George about the slippage and agreed that they needed to get the project back on track. She told George about the ***Thinking On Purpose*** (TOP) process that she had used before, and that it had been very helpful in coming up with a solution. What she really liked about the process was that it helped you think through the problem objectively and critically, and that when the decision was finally reached everyone felt confident that it was the right decision and all Stakeholders were committed to the decision.

George had heard about the TOP process and he was anxious to see if it could help him and his team reach their objectives. Ingrid had summarized the five steps of TOP on his office whiteboard:

1. Frame your purpose
2. Qualify your information
3. Identify your mindsets
4. Structure your thinking
5. Validate your outcome

Applying the Thinking On Purpose Process

George's boss, Ingrid Cameron, realized that George has some biases that were common to project managers:

- B**eneffectance:** The tendency to believe yourself responsible for positive events, but not for negative ones.
    - o *George felt that the project was going very well and a lot of the credit was due to his project management skills. He attributed the slippage in the timeline to the team and didn't take any responsibility upon himself.*
- **Blind spot:** The tendency to miss important information due to existing biases and beliefs.
    - o *In George's case, his blind spot was that as long as the project was being reported as "on track," he didn't look any further into the details from each of the sub-teams. He felt this was a good project management style and that things couldn't possibly go wrong on his watch.*

- **Confirmation bias:** The tendency to accept information or evidence that supports your preconceived beliefs, while ignoring evidence to the contrary.
    - *George was very happy to be told that things were going well. His own team said they continually reported Green because, "They hadn't actually missed their day yet, and besides George seemed happy when they reported Green." George was focused on bigger and better things—future promotions and his next assignment—so it was easy for him to accept that everything was going well and not dig any deeper.*

Ingrid was anxious to see the outcome of the TOP Process. She knew that George needed to work with the team to structure both his and the entire team's thinking. She felt that George and his team would greatly benefit from following this process together.

George's first step was to assemble his team to complete the "TOP—Situational Assessment Worksheet."

Applying the Thinking On Purpose (TOP) Process to the Red Light, Green Light Scenario—Situational Assessment

TOP—SITUATIONAL ASSESSMENT WORKSHEET

Situational Assessment

Purpose: Identify the problems

Project: Sales Management Upgrade

Situation: Project time line under pressure due to development delays

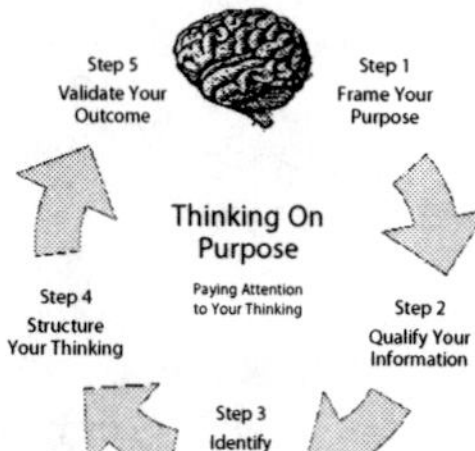

Identify Issues

What is happening?

What could happen in the future?

What is deviating from plan or expectations?

- Project timeline is slipping and the implementation date is in jeopardy
- Ineffective communication
- Ineffective monitoring and control
- Poor estimating

What evidence do you have?

TIMELINE SLIPPAGE

- Ineffective communication
- Development deliverables are also slipping

COMMUNICATION

- Throughout the project each team has indicated that everything wasGreen, there was no mention of issues around the timeline

MONITORING & CONTROL

- Project Manager was caught unaware of issues

POOR ESTIMATING

- Development based their estimates on a specific resource and did not re-estimate when the resource was no longer available.

How important is the issue?

How urgent is the issue?

- Timeline slippage is a high priority issue; it impacts the overall project timeline and has an impact on other projects in the organization
- Communication and Monitoring & Contol are also high priority, because solutions can be put in place to address timeline slippage. But if the communication is not rectified the same issue can happen again
- Poor estimating is medium priority on this project at this point in the project cycle

Assess Root Causes

Do you know the root cause?

- Root cause was not known
- The next step is to move to problem solving

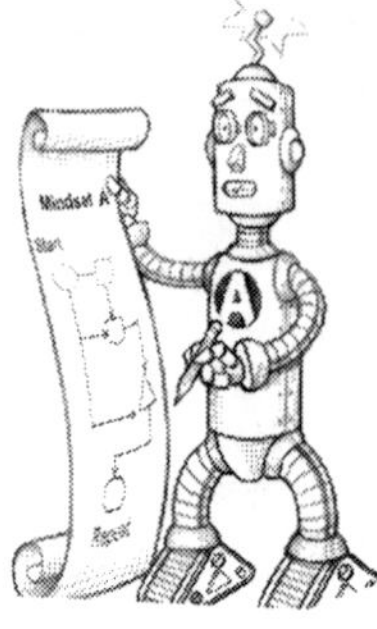

Before working with Ingrid, George had never thought about his mindsets. He never really thought about how they influenced his thinking or how they determined how he thought about the world around him.

He thought about the biases that Ingrid had shared with him, and realized that he had also exhibited some additional biases:

- **Illusion of control:** The belief that we exert some measure of control over situations or events that we clearly do not.
  - *George felt that the project was going well because he was the project manager and that if you have a good, seasoned project manager things go well—mainly because they always had in the past. George realized, after clarifying the issues and prioritizing them, that he was guilty of not monitoring the project closely enough and that if he didn't remedy this issue, he would continue to have problems like this going forward.*
- **Optimism bias:** The tendency to believe that a plan of action will go as intended.
  - *George realized that he had allowed his optimism to carry over to the project in such a way that everyone always told him good news, because that was what he expected.*
- **Hindsight bias:** The tendency to believe that past events were more predictable than they actually were.
  - *Tied into everything was George's knowledge that every project he had worked on had been very successful, so this one would be as well. He now realized his past successes didn't necessarily have anything to do with the current project.*

George also realized that he really didn't know the cause of the current problem, so he and his team proceeded to work through the "TOP—Problem Solving Worksheet."

Applying the Thinking On Purpose (TOP) Process to the Red Light, Green Light Scenario—Problem Solving

TOP—PROBLEM SOLVING WORKSHEET

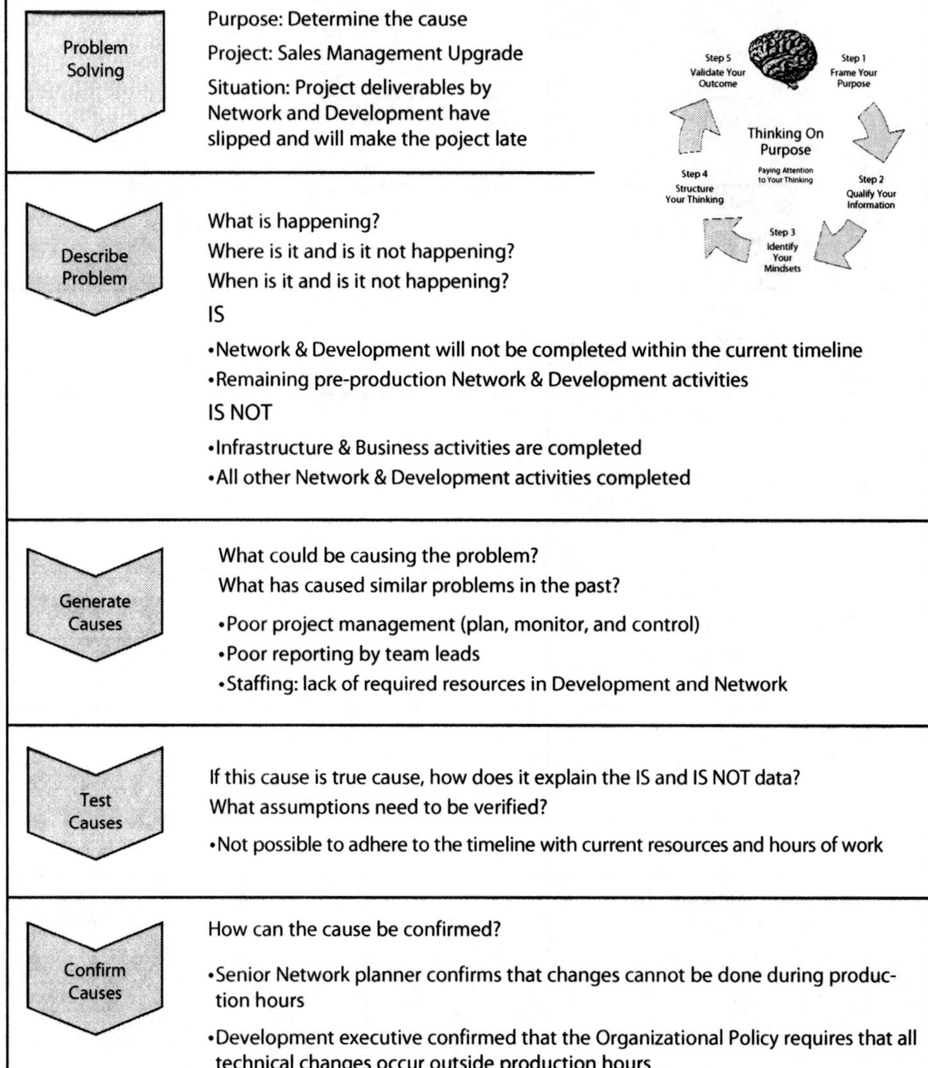

Problem Solving	Purpose: Determine the cause Project: Sales Management Upgrade Situation: Project deliverables by Network and Development have slipped and will make the poject late
Describe Problem	What is happening? Where is it and is it not happening? When is it and is it not happening? IS •Network & Development will not be completed within the current timeline •Remaining pre-production Network & Development activities IS NOT •Infrastructure & Business activities are completed •All other Network & Development activities completed
Generate Causes	What could be causing the problem? What has caused similar problems in the past? •Poor project management (plan, monitor, and control) •Poor reporting by team leads •Staffing: lack of required resources in Development and Network
Test Causes	If this cause is true cause, how does it explain the IS and IS NOT data? What assumptions need to be verified? •Not possible to adhere to the timeline with current resources and hours of work
Confirm Causes	How can the cause be confirmed? •Senior Network planner confirms that changes cannot be done during production hours •Development executive confirmed that the Organizational Policy requires that all technical changes occur outside production hours

George Green used Hypothesis Testing as a way of getting to the bottom of the problem in *Red Light, Green Light.* While the evidence clearly showed that the cause of the problem was lack of staffing in Network and Development, poor project management fundamentals played a big hand in preventing the exposure of these issues earlier in the project life cycle, when there was more time left in the schedule to fix it.

Ref	Evidence	Hypotheses		
		Poor Project Management (Plan, Monitor, Control)	**Poor Reporting by Team Leads**	**Staffing: Lack of required resources, I.e network and Development**
1.	Project activities are slipping	I	I	C
2.	Inaccurate and inconsistent project reporting	C	C	I
3.	Junior developer not able to work at the same speed as senior	I	I	C
4.	Time lines unrealistic given resources	C	I	C
5.	Over-allocated resources	C	I	C
6.	Network staff diverted from project due to support day-to-day production	I	C	C
7.	Late start on project activities due to unexpected training requirements for junior developer	I	I	C
8.	PM "full empowerment" mangement style—minimal followup	C	C	I
9.	PM did not establish exception reporting criteria	C	C	I
10.	Experienced developer not available	I	I	C
11.	Change process stopped all project activities being completed during the day	I	I	C
Legend			**C = Consistent**	**I = Inconsistent**

George realized he had not been vigilant about qualifying the information he received. He had not questioned the information, and therefore it had led him to incorrect conclusions. After the team finished the Problem Solving section of the TOP process, George was completely blown away by the things he heard. For example, he had no idea about the constraints around the timing of putting things into production. He had done many projects in the past and thought he knew the organization pretty well, but this was something he had never heard about.

This brought up a few more biases that had been at play in the problems:

- **Planning fallacy:** The tendency to assume that an activity will take less time than it does.
  - *Both George and the Network and Development teams had assumed that certain activities would take less time than they actually did. There was very little time to work on the activities each day due to the production timeframe constraints.*
  - *The other information that surprised George was learning that the teams working on his project were the same people supporting production every day. He acknowledged that it wasn't possible to work all day and then start working on project deliverables after hours.*
- **Overconfidence effect:** The tendency to overestimate your own skill or ability.
  - *George realized that he had been overconfident, and he also believed he had transmitted that overconfidence to his team members. As a result, they had also overestimated their own abilities.*
- Selective perception: The tendency for you to see what you expect to see.
  - *George realized the bias that had caused him the most grief was "selective perception." He only saw what he expected to see. He didn't dig any deeper, he didn't ask any probing questions and he only saw positive aspects of the project.*

George and his team now proceeded to determine the best way of dealing with the current issue of the timeline slippage by using the "TOP—Decision Making Worksheet".

Applying the Thinking On Purpose (TOP) Process to the Red Light, Green Light Scenario—Decision Making

TOP—DECISION MAKING WORKSHEET

Step 5 Validate Your Outcome
Step 1 Frame Your Purpose
Thinking On Purpose
Paying Attention to Your Thinking
Step 2 Qualify Your Information
Step 3 Identify Your Mindsets
Step 4 Structure Your Thinking

Decision Making

Purpose: Choose a solution

Project: Sales Management Upgrade

Situation: Best way to respond to the projected timeline slippage

Identify Objectives

What results do you want, need or expect?

What resources can you spend or do you want to conserve?

What constraints limit your choices?

MUST

- All activities need to be completed in four weeks (Network, Development, Business & Infrastructure)
- Any activities that affect production must be done outside the production timeframe

WANTS

- Infrastructure & Business activities are completed
- All other Network & Development activities completed

Generate Alternatives

How have you accomplished these objectives in the past?

How could these objectives be accomplished in a new, innovative or creative way?

1. Crash the plan, looking for opportunities which would include:
   - m Non-standard working hours
   - m Activities that can be completed simultaneously
   - m Activities where extra resources will reduce the duration
2. Get an extension on the project timeline
3. Get a new project manager
4. Outsource the Development and Network activities

Choose Solution

Which is the best alternative?

Who needs to support, approve or implement this decision?

- The best alternative is number one, "Crash the plan, looking for opportunities"
- The team needs to support the decision, the Stakeholders, and the Executive Steering Committee

Evaluate Alternatives

Which alternatives pass the MUST objectives?

Which alternatives best satisfy the WANT objectives?

What are the risks?

- #1 could meet all the Musts and most of the Wants
  - m Risk of burnout
  - m Risk that resources may not want or be able to work non-standard working hours
- #2 does not meet all the Musts:
  - m Risk of other projects falling behind; SMEs not available for other projects
- #3 not known if it will address the Musts or Wants:
  - m Risk of the same issues, Project Manager has not been identified as the cause
- #4 could meet all the Must and most of the Wants:
  - m Risk of outsourced resources causing technical issues due to inexperience with environments
  - m Risk of resentment and lack of cooperation from regular staff

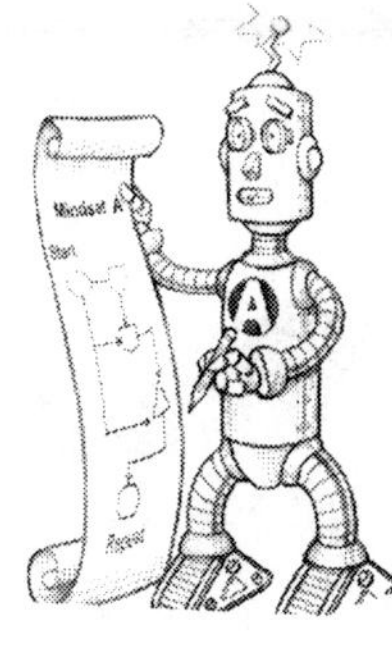

George was quite surprised at the result of the Decision Making step. He had assumed that the outsourcing alternative would logically be the best choice because this is what he had seen done on past projects. Going through the process with the team made him realize that his intuitive approach was not going to get him to the right decision. The structured decision-making process, however, produced a solution that was more effective.

Again, he checked for biases that were at play in this process:

- Mere exposure effect: The tendency for people to prefer something simply because it's familiar.
    - *George realized that by going with the more familiar choice, he would have been jumping to an unfounded conclusion. He was glad that he kept his opinion to himself. The alternative that the team picked was by far the best choice.*

George and his team then proceeded to "crash the plan" with the guidelines that they established in the "TOP—Action Planning Worksheet," and supporting tools.

Applying the Thinking On Purpose (TOP) Process to the Red Light, Green Light Scenario—Action Planning

TOP—ACTION PLANNING WORKSHEET

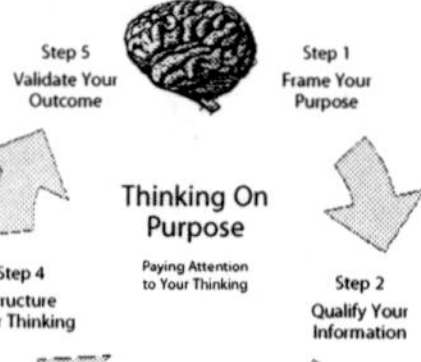

Action Planning

Purpose: Build a plan

Project: Sales Management Upgrade

Plan: Approach for crashing the plan, looking for opportunities, which would include:

- Non-standard working hours
- Activities that can be completed simultaneously
- Activities where extra resources reduce the duration

What are the objectives to be achieved?

What action steps are required to meet your objectives?

When must each step be completed?

Who will be responsible for each step?

Crash the plan in order to meet original launch date:

- Non-standard working hours
- Objectivesmust maintain quality, as per company policies, and contain cost wherever possible (established by Project Manager & Executive Steering Committee).
- Non-standard working hours
- Identify all critical path activities and non-value-added activities (TEAM)
- Focus on critical path activities (flow charts will keep team focused on current and next critical path activities (TEAM)
- Remove delays and non-value-added steps wherever possible (TEAM)
- Review Work Breakdown Structure (WBS) to identify the impact of crashing on each activity (TEAM)

What dependency or sequence is likely to change?

- Establish regular reporting (replace weekly with daily; monthly with weekly) to further control activities and constantly measure progress
- Added supervision around transition to new schedule/plan, especially around over-time, burn out, and rising costs

Are logic and flow still intact?

- Leadership team focuses on roadblocks, communication, monitoring and control, and the level of support required for the accelerated schedule

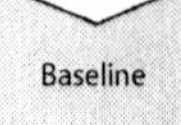

Which is the dominant driver—time, cost or scope?

- Establish new schedule/plan, get team agreement/commitment (Project Manager)

Applying the *Thinking On Purpose* (TOP) Process to the Red Light, Green Light Scenario—Risk Assessment

George emphasized to his team that while the revised plan made sense on paper, it needed to be "protected" with a high quality risk assessment that would include the "TOP—High-Level Risk Assessment," along with the Risk Assessment Plan found in the Toolkit section.

TOP—HIGH-LEVEL RISK ASSESSMENT

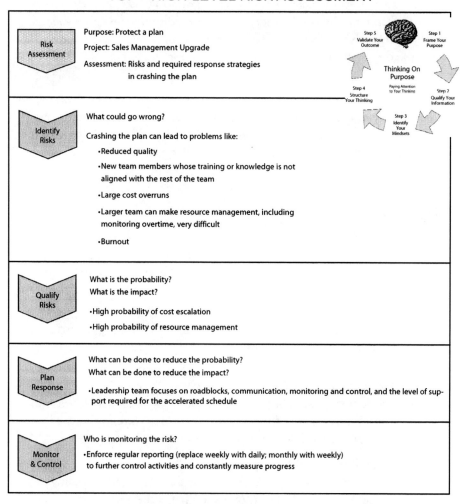

Risk Assessment	Purpose: Protect a plan Project: Sales Management Upgrade Assessment: Risks and required response strategies in crashing the plan
Identify Risks	What could go wrong? Crashing the plan can lead to problems like: •Reduced quality •New team members whose training or knowledge is not aligned with the rest of the team •Large cost overruns •Larger team can make resource management, including monitoring overtime, very difficult •Burnout
Qualify Risks	What is the probability? What is the impact? •High probability of cost escalation •High probability of resource management
Plan Response	What can be done to reduce the probability? What can be done to reduce the impact? •Leadership team focuses on roadblocks, communication, monitoring and control, and the level of support required for the accelerated schedule
Monitor & Control	Who is monitoring the risk? •Enforce regular reporting (replace weekly with daily; monthly with weekly) to further control activities and constantly measure progress

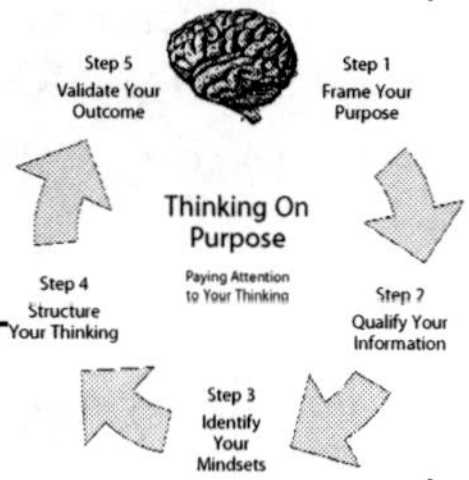

Thinking On Purpose
Paying Attention to Your Thinking
Step 1 Frame Your Purpose
Step 2 Qualify Your Information
Step 3 Identify Your Mindsets
Step 4 Structure Your Thinking
Step 5 Validate Your Outcome

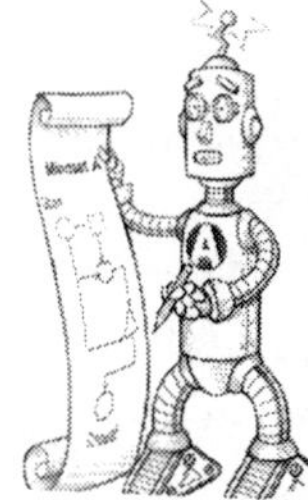

Again, after the Risk Assessment step, George found himself faced with another bias that had contributed to his problems:

- **Attentional bias:** The tendency to ignore or neglect important or relevant data when it is associated with less relevant data that we perceive as threatening or more interesting.
    - o *George realized that in the past, he would have ignored some of the problems that came up as possibilities in the Risk Assessment.*

Applying the Thinking On Purpose (TOP) Process to the Red Light, Green Light Scenario—Conclusion

After following the TOP Process, George now felt completely prepared to go to Ingrid with a good, sound plan going forward. He felt that through using the Situational Assessment, he completely understood the real issues. By using the Problem Solving process, he understood what caused the problems that lead to the timeline slippage. By the end of the Decision Making step the team had all agreed on a solution to address the issues—and most importantly, because they were all part of the solution, the whole team was committed to the new plan. George was convinced that the project team had a good plan because he had done a Risk Assessment and was preparing a mitigation strategy for all the risks that had been raised.

George knew that he would never again discount the impact of biases, nor would he fall prey to the restrictive nature of his "it if worked for me in the past, it will work for me now" mindset. He was committed to being more aware of his biases and, most of all, the critical need to continually qualify the information he used to manage a project.

Scenario Two—All Together Now

Caroline was a seasoned project manager who had worked at Acme for over ten years in the PMO at Acme's regional office on the west coast. She recently transferred to the head office and joined the PMO as Program Manager. In this role, in addition to leading a program, Caroline was expected to provide mentoring and consulting to project managers in the PMO.

Her first assignment was to work on the Regional Notification Program. This program was well underway, but Mike Kelly, the project sponsor, was very concerned that the project was going to miss its deadline. As Vice-President of Operations, Mike had a number of projects on his plate that need to be completed, and if the Regional Notification Program didn't finish on time all of the other projects' dates would slide and some revenue-producing projects would not be completed.

Before Caroline met with the project manager or the any of the project team members she decided to meet with Mike to get a better understanding of his concerns. She asked to meet Mike at his office to discuss the entire project, but he only had thirty minutes to spare and wanted to focus on the timeline.

Caroline's meeting with Mike was not as productive as she had hoped; his assistant and the telephone constantly interrupted him. The only information that she was able to get from him was that A) the program needed to be completed in six weeks, B) he was tired of seeing that tasks were not completed or running behind on the status report he received by email every Monday morning, and C) this was a project that he felt was not being taken very seriously by the team members. Finally, he emphatically stated that this project was very high profile, and that he was going to have to report to the board in six weeks and didn't want to have to tell them that it wasn't complete.

The message was very clear to Caroline: find out what was causing the slippage in tasks, get a stronger commitment from the team members, and find out if it was possible to complete the project within the timeline laid out by Mike.

Caroline went back to her desk, logged onto the project's shared drive and started to review the documentation. She was meeting with the project manager later in the day and she needed a solid understanding the project objectives, the deliverables, and the timelines.

First, Caroline read the project charter. It was a brief document only a few paragraphs in length:

PROJECT CHARTER

Background

The Regional Notification Program (RNP) is an extension of Acme's Emergency Notification Group (ENG). The ENG is the framework Acme uses when there is a need to quickly broadcast a message to the whole company and engage the appropriate recovery teams in emergency situations. The team hasn't needed to invoke the ENG process very often in the last five years. Three years ago, ENG was invoked during a power outage that affected both the main office and one of the larger satellite offices. The ENG team assisted in ensuring that all employees made it home safely and that all the necessary technology was up and running. The last time ENG was invoked was last year, when there was a fire in the Computer Center.

Objectives

The RNP will add regional teams to the ENG framework. These teams will be located in every Acme office building and each team will consist of a facilities person, a business person and a technology person. The RNP will assist in providing two-way communication between the head office and each of the Acme satellite offices.

Deliverables

- RNP manual for each RNP team to follow
- RNP database

- RNP communication tools
- RNP training

Team Members

Business Representative

- Bob Keeling, twenty-three years with Acme and founding member of ENG

Facilities Representative

- Mel Leung, four years with Acme, responsible for facilities in all satellite offices
- Elaine Lucas, fifteen years with Acme, responsible for facilities in the main office and Computer Center

Technology

- Dennis Smith, one year with Acme, Database Technology
- Ron Nixon, eight years with Acme, Communication Technology

Human Resources & Training

- Yvonne Brown, twenty-four years with Acme, head of HR & Training

Project Manager

- Brian Sweet, twelve years with Acme, mostly technology projects

Timeline

- Completed by June 25th

Caroline could not find a Project Work Breakdown Structure (WBS). The only timeline she found had fewer than twenty tasks on it and it was very high-level, with end dates only. She couldn't find listed durations for any of the tasks, specific names of resources, or how tasks linked to each other. It was impossible to see what tasks were prerequisites for other tasks.

Caroline decided to meet with each of the project team members and the project manager individually. The meetings are summarized below:

Bob Keeling—Business

- Bob didn't understand why the RNP was needed, and felt that the ENG was working fine.
- He felt that adding RNP to the ENG framework was adding unnecessary complexity and therefore greater risk.
- He didn't have time to spare and couldn't spare any of his people because they were all busy making money for Acme.
- He didn't like having a timeline dictated to him, as June was right in the middle of his biggest sales period.
- He was unable to make most project meetings because he was always pulled away for higher priority issues.

Mel Leung—Facilities, Satellite Offices

- Mel didn't understand the purpose of RNP.
- He didn't have facilities staff in every satellite office, so he couldn't even commit to RNP.
- He didn't feel that the project manager understood how important his job was and how busy he was; Mel never made his deliverables on time because he was busy keeping the lights on in all the offices.
- Mel didn't think that Mike Kelly, the project sponsor, really supported the faculty, and was only interested in projects that made money.
- He thought the project timeline was fine.

Elaine Lucas—Facilities, Main Office & Computer Center

- Elaine thought that RNP was going to be a fine enhancement to ENG and was really excited about new software that she had seen, which would manage the information of over 5,000 people per location.
- She had already talked to the company and had one of her staff playing with a demo on their PC.
- She didn't always make her deliverables but she was way ahead of the rest of the team on understanding what had to be done to rollout the software to make RNP work.
- Elaine knew that this program was going to give her visibility and the recognition that she deserved.

Dennis Smith—Database Technology

- Dennis didn't understand what RNP was for (as far as he could tell it was being implemented for two-way communication, and he thought that was what phones were for!).

- Dennis felt that the team was asking him to build a database but that none of the information was consistent and nobody could tell him exactly what was required.
- The timeline was crazy; he would never be able to build a database in time because he was on-call for database issues in other areas of Acme.

Ron Nixon—Communication Technology

- Ron wasn't clear on what RNP was delivering; he was always asking what issue was being addressed with RNP and he never got a straight answer.
- Ron still hadn't delivered the communication solution because he was still looking at products.
- The timeline provided to him conflicted with another project he was working on for the business and it would be finished in two weeks so he could devote more time to RNP.

Yvonne Brown—HR & Training

- Yvonne wasn't sure of the value of RNP; since ENG wasn't invoked very often, she wasn't sure why they should add another component.
- She felt that they were providing a big solution for what might be a small problem.
- Yvonne was concerned that the RNP would unnecessarily add work to staff that were already busy, especially in the satellite office.
- Her training budget was slashed this year, so she wasn't sure how she would find money or time to add RNP training to her workload.

Brian Sweet—Project Manager

- The RNP was Brian's first non-technology project, and he wanted to prove to the organization that he could do all kinds of projects, not just technology.
- Brian wasn't happy with the implementation date given to him by the sponsor but he felt that if he worked really hard he could make the timeline work.
- Brian was frustrated by the other team members; he often cancelled the team meetings and met with each member individually.
- Brian had successfully delivered many projects in the past and wasn't sure why the team wasn't engaged.
- Brian had completed most of the project documentation in isolation because the team couldn't always make meetings, but he hadn't had time yet to put it on the shared drive.

- Brian felt he had good team members, but he also felt that they tended to over-commit and then weren't able to meet the dates they agreed to.

Caroline realized that Brian had always been a very successful project manager doing technology projects, and that he was outside his comfort zone and working hard wasn't going to be the solution. Caroline knew that working through the ***Thinking On Purpose*** process could help Brian identify why his team wasn't engaged and turn this project around.

Applying the *Thinking On Purpose* Process

Caroline gathered the whole team together in order to complete the TOP Process. Since there were a large number of people on the team, she opted to use a brainstorming session to get all the ideas and suggestions on the table. She scheduled four hours to complete the process.

Applying the *Thinking On Purpose* (TOP) Process to the All Together Now Scenario—Situational Assessment (via Brainstorming)

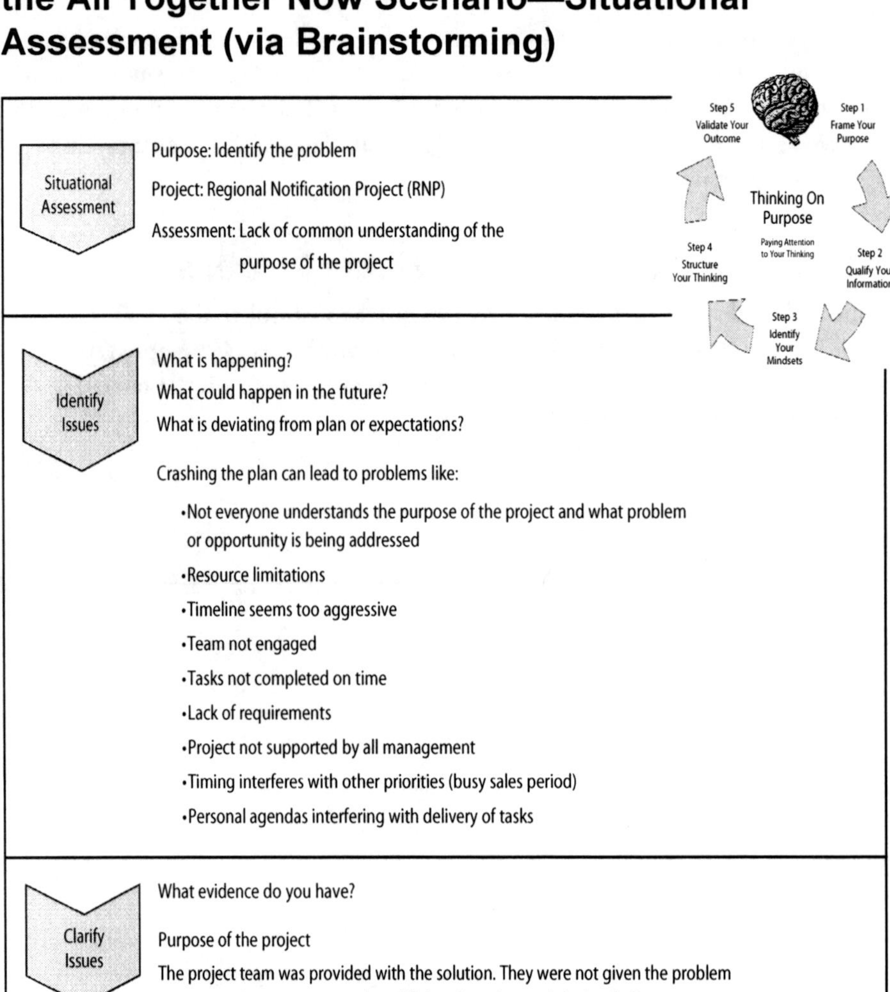

Situational Assessment

Purpose: Identify the problem

Project: Regional Notification Project (RNP)

Assessment: Lack of common understanding of the purpose of the project

Identify Issues

What is happening?
What could happen in the future?
What is deviating from plan or expectations?

Crashing the plan can lead to problems like:

- Not everyone understands the purpose of the project and what problem or opportunity is being addressed
- Resource limitations
- Timeline seems too aggressive
- Team not engaged
- Tasks not completed on time
- Lack of requirements
- Project not supported by all management
- Timing interferes with other priorities (busy sales period)
- Personal agendas interfering with delivery of tasks

Clarify Issues

What evidence do you have?

Purpose of the project

The project team was provided with the solution. They were not given the problem or opportunity statement, so they didn't truly understand the level of importance or how this project fit into the corporate strategy.

Resource limitations

Everyone has other commitments, other projects, and conflicting priorities, and some team members don't have the capacity to work on this project.

Timeline aggressive

Project provided with an end date that was not arrived at by doing a standard. Work Breakdown Structure, followed by building a schedule. There didn't seem to be any correlation between the project deliverables and the end date.

Team not committed

Many of the team members don't understand the purpose of the project. They are missing meetings for this project, but are attending other project meetings where they do understand the value they bring to the table.

Tasks not completed on time

- Not a priority, over committment on other items
- Team members are afraid to say they can't meet the date
- Poor planning, under-estimating time commitment for tasks
- Lax tracking and control, corrective action not taken when a task slips

Lack of requirements

Since the solution was provided while the purpose was unknown, there were no requirements completed

Project not supported

- Doesn't seem to be supported by all senior management
- Doesn't seem to be strategic
- Poorly communicated

Timing interferes with other company priorities

- No evaluation of timing in the business cycle and impact to the business
- No understanding of the reason behind the deadline

Personal Agendas

- Some team members are looking out for individual promotion; "WIFM" (What's in it for me?)
- Some team members are not objective about overall project because some components benefit them directly

How important is the issue?

How urgent is the issue?

1. Purpose of the project is a high priority issue; without the purpose there is little or no direction, understanding, and commitment
2. Resource limitations are a medium priority issue; the skill sets aren't specialized
3. Timeline aggressive is a high priority issue; the real issue is the lack of correlation between the tasks and end date
4. Team not committed is a high priority and relates to #1 above
5. Task not completed on time has a direct relationship to #1 and #3
6. Lack of Requirements is a high priority; the team was given a pre-existing solution, so they didn't do any requirements. The project will try to make everything fit into the solution, right or wrong!
7. Project not supported is high priority, relating to #1
8. Timing interferes with other company priorities is a high priority that can have a detrimental impact on the timeline
9. Personal agendas is a medium issue that can be managed

Assess Root Causes

Do you know the root cause?

Yes, the project was given to the team with a solution, timeline, and deliverables already in place, but with no explanation of purpose, strategic fit, or reason for aggressive end date

It became evident to Caroline, as she proceeded through the TOP process, that the team all had very grave concerns about the project but had never felt they had a forum to voice those concerns. She found many of them quite passionate regarding their lack of understanding of the project's goal and purpose, and how it fit into the organization's strategy.

She realized that they all wanted to make sure that any changes they were making were for the right reasons, and to feel that they made a difference. She decided to continue directly onto the Decision Making part of the TOP Process. (Since everyone was pretty clear on the problem they did not need to complete the Problem Solving Worksheet.)

Applying the *Thinking On Purpose* (TOP) Process to the All Together Now Scenario—Decision Making

TOP—DECISION MAKING WORKSHEET

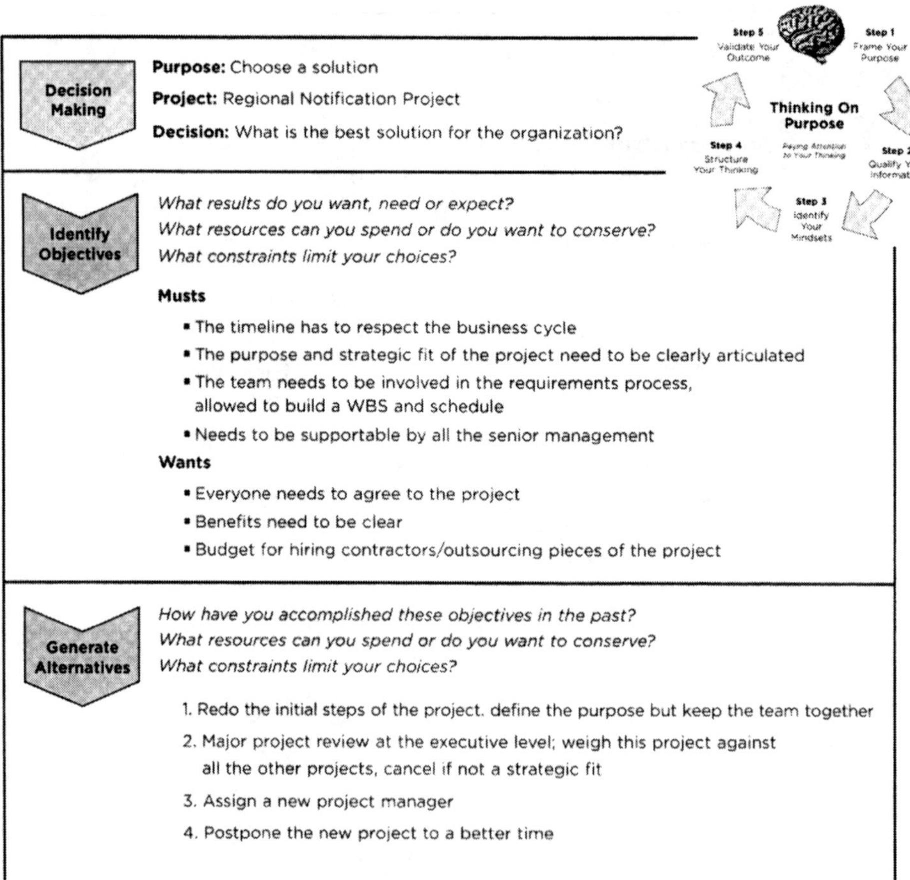

Decision Making

Purpose: Choose a solution

Project: Regional Notification Project

Decision: What is the best solution for the organization?

Identify Objectives

What results do you want, need or expect?
What resources can you spend or do you want to conserve?
What constraints limit your choices?

Musts

- The timeline has to respect the business cycle
- The purpose and strategic fit of the project need to be clearly articulated
- The team needs to be involved in the requirements process, allowed to build a WBS and schedule
- Needs to be supportable by all the senior management

Wants

- Everyone needs to agree to the project
- Benefits need to be clear
- Budget for hiring contractors/outsourcing pieces of the project

Generate Alternatives

How have you accomplished these objectives in the past?
What resources can you spend or do you want to conserve?
What constraints limit your choices?

1. Redo the initial steps of the project. define the purpose but keep the team together
2. Major project review at the executive level; weigh this project against all the other projects, cancel if not a strategic fit
3. Assign a new project manager
4. Postpone the new project to a better time

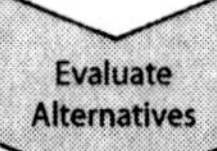

Which alternatives pass the MUST objectives?
Which alternatives best satisfy the WANT objectives?
What are the risks?

- #1 meets two of the four Musts and one Want:
  - The purpose and strategic fit are clearly articulated
  - Team involved in the requirements process, WBS and schedule
  - Benefits need to be clear
- #2 meets most of the Musts and most of the Wants
  - The timeline has to respect the business cycle
  - The purpose and strategic fit are clearly articulated
  - Needs to be supportable by senior management
  - Everyone needs to agree to the project
  - Benefits need to be clear
- #3 doesn't meeet the Musts or Wants
- #4 only meets one Must and does not meet the Wants

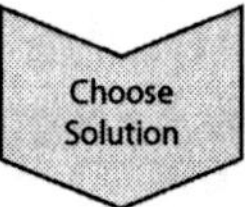

Which is the best alternative?
Who needs to support, approve or implement this decision?

The best alternative is #2, "Major project review at the executive level; weigh this project against all other projects, cancel if not a strategic fit."

Again, Caroline was impressed by the level of passion and commitment the team brought to the Decision Making process. Because they felt that they were working through a process that allowed them to do the appropriate level of due diligence, they weren't complaining. They could look back at the rationalization and feel that all their conclusions were well thought out. Listing their objectives and evaluating their alternatives made them really think about the decision; it had to be good for the organization, not just for a select few.

Satisfied with their results, they moved on to Action Planning.

Applying the *Thinking On Purpose* (TOP) Process to the All Together Now Scenario—Action Planning

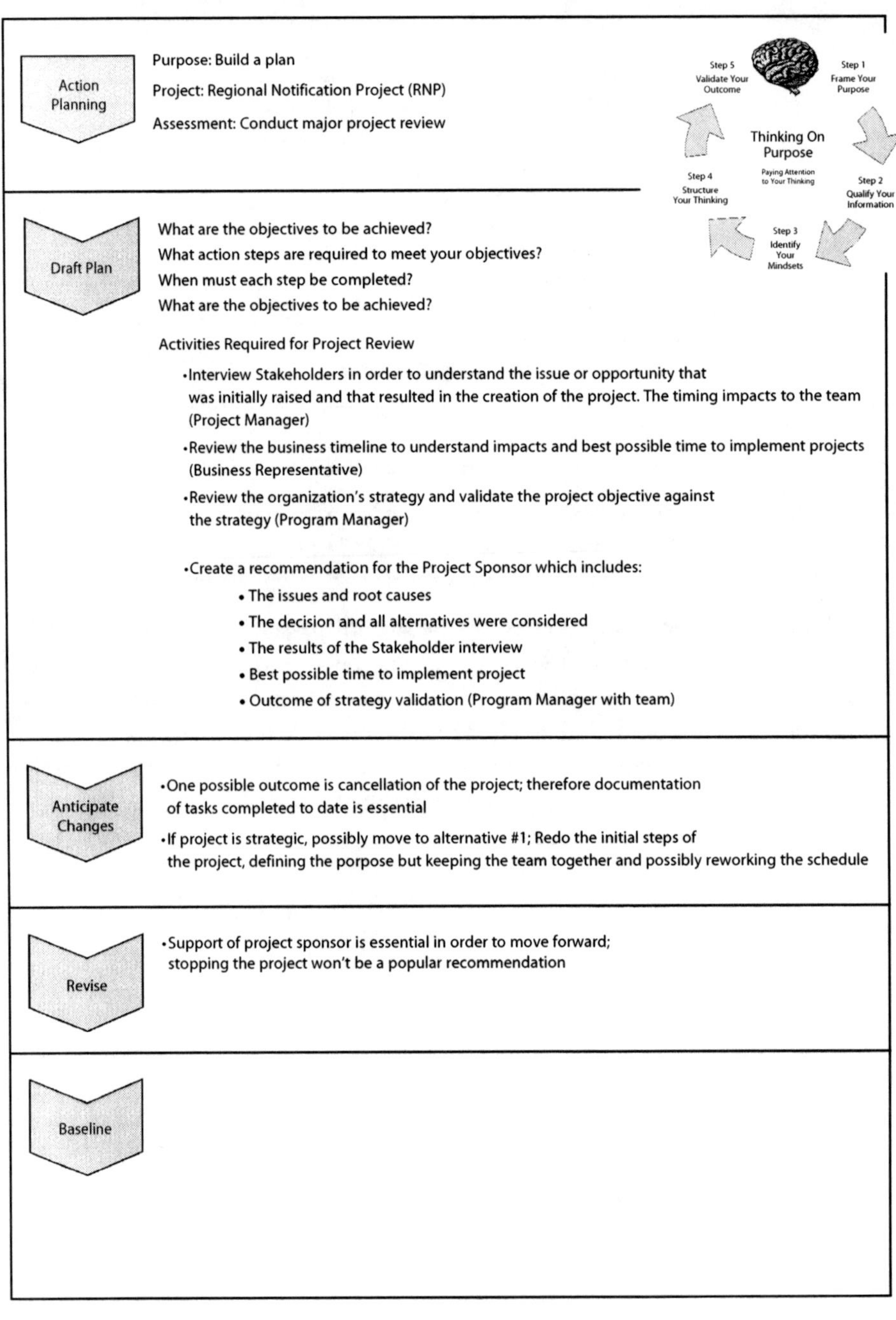

Action Planning
Purpose: Build a plan
Project: Regional Notification Project (RNP)
Assessment: Conduct major project review
Step 5
Validate Your Outcome
Step 1
Frame Your Purpose
Thinking On Purpose
Paying Attention to Your Thinking
Step 4
Structure Your Thinking
Step 2
Qualify Your Information
Step 3
Identify Your Mindsets
Draft Plan
What are the objectives to be achieved?
What action steps are required to meet your objectives?
When must each step be completed?
What are the objectives to be achieved?
Activities Required for Project Review
•Interview Stakeholders in order to understand the issue or opportunity that was initially raised and that resulted in the creation of the project. The timing impacts to the team (Project Manager)
•Review the business timeline to understand impacts and best possible time to implement projects (Business Representative)
•Review the organization's strategy and validate the project objective against the strategy (Program Manager)
•Create a recommendation for the Project Sponsor which includes:
• The issues and root causes
• The decision and all alternatives were considered
• The results of the Stakeholder interview
• Best possible time to implement project
• Outcome of strategy validation (Program Manager with team)
Anticipate Changes
•One possible outcome is cancellation of the project; therefore documentation of tasks completed to date is essential
•If project is strategic, possibly move to alternative #1; Redo the initial steps of the project, defining the porpose but keeping the team together and possibly reworking the schedule
Revise
•Support of project sponsor is essential in order to move forward; stopping the project won't be a popular recommendation
Baseline

Applying the *Thinking On Purpose* (TOP) Process to the All Together Now Scenario—Risk Assessment

Purpose: Protect the plan

Project: Regional Notification Project (RNP)

Assessment: Risk in the major project review

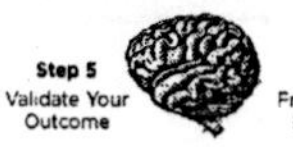

Thinking On Purpose

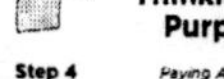

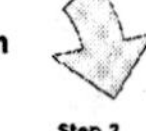

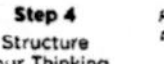

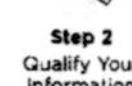

What could go wrong?

1. Strong negative executive reaction
2. Lack of Stakeholder support in preparing the discussion package
3. Loss of team member to other projects while review is underway
4. Loss of funding to other initiatives

What is the probability?
What is the impact?

1. Medium probability: The executive already has an inkling that things aren't going well; he has heard about and it is general knowledge that tasks were not completed or are running behind, and the project is not being taken very seriously by the team members
2. Low probability: The Stakeholders see this as an opportunity to be heard and to do the "right thing" for the organization
3. High probability: If the project review is lengthy, team members may be reassigned
4. Medium probability: Until the outcome of the project review, the funding will probably remain; there is a fair amount of sunk costs and part of the review will look at the financials

What can be done to reduce the probability?
What can be done to reduce the impact?

Quickly prepare a report to provide the appropriate level of information to the review team for making an informed decison

As per standard Risk Management methodology

Applying the *Thinking On Purpose* (TOP) Process to the all Together Now Scenario—Conclusion...

After they completed the TOP Process, Caroline realized that she had enough information and commitment from the team that she could leverage the information collected during the TOP Process to move ahead with preparing an executive briefing.

REGIONAL NOTIFICATION PROGRAM EXECUTIVE SUMMARY

SLIDE #1

Project experiencing delays & running behind

–Team is not committed and project purpose not understood
–Resource limitations—conflicting priorities, limited capacity
–Aggressive timeline
–Tasks not completed on time
–No requirement
–Timing in conflict with other corporate priorities

Root Cause

–The project was given to the team with a solution, timeline and deliverables already in place
–No explanation of purpose, strategic fit, reason for aggressive end-date in the middle of the busiest time for the business

---

SLIDE #2

The best solution for the organization

- Non-negotiable Objectives
  –The timeline has to respect the business cycle
  –Articulation of the purpose and strategic fit with the organization
  –Standard PM methodology needs to be completed
    - Requirements
    - WBS
    - Project Plan etc.
  –Unanimously supported by Senior Management

SLIDE #3

- Alternatives considered
  - –Redo the initial steps of the project:
    - •Keep the team together
    - •Define the purpose
  - –Major project review at executive level:
    - •Weigh it against other projects
    - •Cancel if not a strategic fit
  - –Assign a new Project Manager
- Recommendation
  - –Major project review at executive level:
    - •Weigh it against other projects
    - •Cancel if not a strategic fit

SLIDE #4

Next steps

- –Interview Stakeholders to learn:
  - • Original issue/opportunity which resulted in the project
  - • Timing impacts to the business
- –Review the business timeline looking for best possible implementation date
- –Review the organization's strategy and validate the project objective
- –Facilitate major project review with all Stakeholder Executives
- –Await decision from project review

The fate of the project itself might have been unknown, but one thing was certain—because they were made a part of the process (rather than simply being assigned to a project without sufficient input or information), whatever the final decision turned out to be, the team finally felt engaged and committed, and that they were part of the solution instead of the problem.

Scenario Three—But Wait, There's More!

Tom was three months into the CAMP Project (Corporate Audit Information Management process). He was feeling very good about his performance on the project. It was the first time he had worked on a project that touched all areas of the company. At the beginning of the project, he had found it difficult to get everyone to agree on the scope and requirements—or for that matter even participate in scope and requirements definition. Finally, he had everyone in agreement, albeit some reluctantly, but the project was well underway and tomorrow he was going to give his first update to the Executive Steering Committee.

Tom had put a lot of thought into the presentation. He was going to be able to tell the Executive Steering Committee that although the team had been overworked at times, the hours were becoming more normalized and he even felt that he would come slightly under budget with a little careful monitoring and control. He had recently talked to the head of the PMO and found out that there were two projects that were waiting for the completion of his project to free up two SMEs who were needed on other projects. With all of this activity relying on his project, he was excited and relieved to be able to report that he was on-schedule and anticipated completing his project within budget, and that they were going to meet all the deliverables they had committed to in the charter:

Project objectives

- Develop a process for scheduling, storing and tracking Information for BCD Company's Corporate Audits.
- The system would use technology already in place accessible with standard company desktop.
- Process needed to be in production within six months.

In Scope

Processes for:

- Scheduling Audits
- Storing and retrieval of Audits
- Establish process for destruction of data (number of years)
- Tracking & Reporting

Out of Scope

- New technology or database
- Any other documentation other than Corporate Audits.
- Any new forms for Audits

The Executive Steering Committee consisted of Tom's boss, Dave Moody, who was Vice-President of the PMO; Karen Reid, the sponsor from Corporate Audits; Carrie MacMillan, SVP Operations; and a few Finance and HR representatives. When Tom finally met with them and told them his good news story, they seemed quite pleased. As he completed his presentation, however, Karen Reid, the sponsor, turned to Carrie MacMillan and said she was very pleased with the project, but that adding electronic signature capabilities would make the system really "leading-edge" and would save many hours wasted on chasing down signatures. She went onto say that she would like to add "Sox" Audits as well as the regular Corporate Audits. Carrie MacMillan said she thought the additions were a great idea. She then turned to Tom and said, "Make it happen!"

Tom was taken aback by the request. It was clearly out of scope, but he didn't want to push back in front of the sponsor. He decided to go talk to his boss and see if he could help him find a way to convince both Carrie and Karen that adding the new functionality and additional processes would cause a great deal of difficulty.

When Tom met with his boss the next day, he was really worried about the implications of the new deliverables that had been assigned to him. Tom knew that scope creep would cause a cascade of problems on the project, such as extending the timeline, straining team members who were already overworked, going over budget and cross-impacting other projects.

Dave Moody agreed that adding the extra features could cause all the issues that Tom had expressed, but he also noted that it was a delicate matter and they should take the time to thoroughly explore the all aspects of the decision. They would need to be able get the entire team's participation and be able to show how they made their decision and why it was the right decision. Dave told Tom that he would like Tom to use the TOP Process to arrive at the decision.

Applying the *Thinking On Purpose* (TOP) Process to the But Wait, There's More! Scenario—Situational Assessment

TOP—SITUATIONAL ASSESSMENT WORKSHEET

Situational Assessment

Purpose: Identify the problem

Project: Corporate Audit Information Management

Assessment: Problems and opportunity

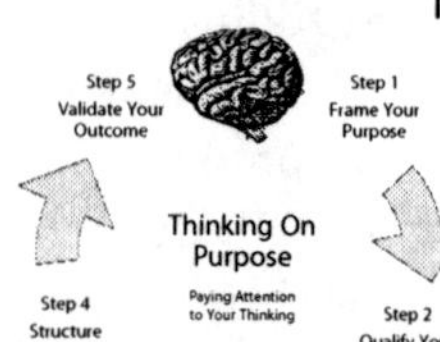

Identify Issues

What is happening?
What could happen in the future?
What is deviating from plan or expectation?

- The project sponsor wants to add new functionality to the project, which is well underway

Possible Impacts

- Extended timeline
- Straining team members who were already overworked
- Going over budget
- Cross-impacts on other projects
- New team members

What evidence do you have?

Extended timeline & over budget

- The timeline was already ambitious; up to this point in the project, the team had been overworked to meet all their deliverables
- The team would not be able to commit to more functionality without extending the timeline, or at the very least increasing the budget
- Project financial report indicates that the project will come in under budget by 1.5%; this is not enough to cover the cost of the hardware, application, and resource costs, which can't be met under the current budget

Straining team—overwork

Due to overworking the team in the beginning of the project, the team would not be receptive to adding new functionality, which would greatly increase their already heavy workload. There is a risk of burnout.

Cross-impacts on other projects

The new functionality would impact projects that were already waiting for two SMEs from this project; it would put them behind schedule and there could be a domino effect.

New team members

- Since there was originally no new technology required in the existing project, new team members would have to be added to the project that weren't originally part of the resource pool. This will increase costs and they may require training in order to align new members with the original team.
- Current sponsor confirmed that they do not have responsibility for SOX Audits; therefore a new sponsor would be added to the team.

How important is the issue?
How urgent is the issue?

- *Timeline slippage* is a high priority issue: it impacts the overall project timeline and has an impact on other projects in the organization
- *Going over budget* is a medium to low priority issue: presumably the sponsor would be receptive to providing more funds for increased functionality
- *Straining team*—overwork is a high priority issue; burnouts would impact both this project as well as other projects in the organization
- *Cross impact on other projects* is a low priority issue for this project but could be a medium to high priority for the organization
- *New team members* is a medium priority issue: can be remedied by adding a budget for the appropriate number of resources as well as training

Do you know the root cause?

Yes, project sponsor has requested unplanned change to scope, which means the next required step is Decision Making

Tom was very impressed with the team response to the TOP Process. He often found it difficult to get team members to attend Post-Implementation Reviews, and here they were giving up half of their day to work through this activity.

When Tom raised the point, the team agreed that they felt they were involved in the change rather than having it forced upon them. Whatever the decision turned out to be, at least their ideas and opinions would be heard. They moved onto Decision Making.

Applying the *Thinking On Purpose* (TOP) Process to the But Wait, There's More! Scenario—Decision Making

TOP—DECISION MAKING WORKSHEET

Decision Making

Purpose: Choose a solution

Project: CAMP

Assessment: Best way to respond to the sponsor's request for unplanned change

Step 5 Validate Your Outcome
Step 1 Frame Your Purpose
Thinking On Purpose
Paying Attention to Your Thinking
Step 4 Structure Your Thinking
Step 2 Qualify Your Information
Step 3 Identify Your Mindsets

Identify Objectives

What results do you want, need or expect?

What resources can you spend or do you want to conserve?

What constraints limit your choices?

Musts

- The recommendation must ensure that the team is not overworked in order to meet the goals
- The recommendation must ensure that the original deliverables are met within current timeline
- Maintain quality as per company policies

Wants

- Closely managed incremental costs
- No impact to other projects in the organziation
- New team members familiar with project and new technology
- New team members familiar with additional audits
- New sponsor agreeable to work with existing processes

Generate Alternatives

How have you accomplished these objectives in the past?

How could these objectives be accomplished in a new, innovative or creative way?

1. Add new functionality and re-plan the project
2. Complete the first project. Start up a new project to deliver the new functionality
3. Keep the team together; establish a phased protocol
4. Add new functionality and squeeze the new functionality not the current schedule and budget
5. Stop the project and restart the project, including new functionality

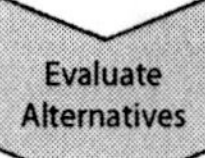

Which alternatives pass the MUST objectives?
Which alternatives best satisfy the WANT objectives?
What are the risks?

- #1 does not meet the Musts:
    - Risk of team burnout from overwork
- #2 does not meet the Musts:
    - Starting a new project after the first one is completed would allow it to be planned in such a way that the appropriate team members could be added. It can be like any new project, fitting into the organizational strategy and timelines.
    - There is a risk that the second project won't be completed if it doesn't fit into the organizational strategy.
- #3 meets all the must and some of the wants:
    - Keeping the team together could impact other projects
    - Risk that new team members may not be of the quality desired due to current job assignment
- #4 does not meet the Musts:
    - Risk of poor quality
    - Risk of team burnout from overwork
    - Risk of not meeting the original deliverables
- #5 does not meet the Musts:
    - Risk of not meeting the original deliverables in the current timeline

Which is the best alternative?
Who needs to support, approve or implement this decision?

- The best alternative is #2, "Complete the first project. Start up a new project to deliver the new functionality."
- The team supports the decision; Tom needs the support of the Executive Steering Committee. Tom needs Dave's support because this may not be a popular decision with the sponsor and the SVP Operations.

Note: Where alternatives are numerous and complex, decision analysis can be enabled by the use of the Weighted Ranking approach. Refer to TOP Tool #40: Weighted Ranking.

Applying the *Thinking On Purpose* (TOP) Process to the But Wait, There's More! Scenario—Action Planning

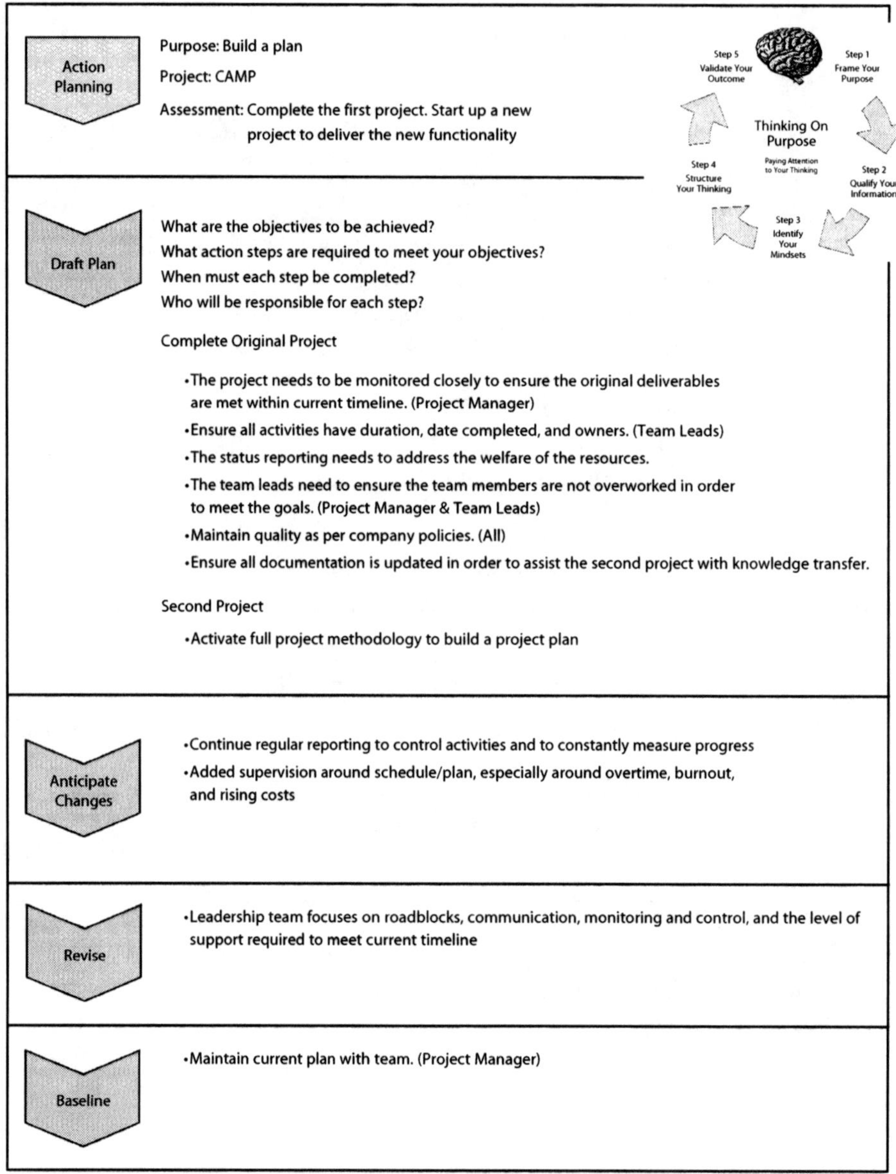

Action Planning

Purpose: Build a plan

Project: CAMP

Assessment: Complete the first project. Start up a new project to deliver the new functionality

Draft Plan

What are the objectives to be achieved?
What action steps are required to meet your objectives?
When must each step be completed?
Who will be responsible for each step?

Complete Original Project

- The project needs to be monitored closely to ensure the original deliverables are met within current timeline. (Project Manager)
- Ensure all activities have duration, date completed, and owners. (Team Leads)
- The status reporting needs to address the welfare of the resources.
- The team leads need to ensure the team members are not overworked in order to meet the goals. (Project Manager & Team Leads)
- Maintain quality as per company policies. (All)
- Ensure all documentation is updated in order to assist the second project with knowledge transfer.

Second Project

- Activate full project methodology to build a project plan

Anticipate Changes

- Continue regular reporting to control activities and to constantly measure progress
- Added supervision around schedule/plan, especially around overtime, burnout, and rising costs

Revise

- Leadership team focuses on roadblocks, communication, monitoring and control, and the level of support required to meet current timeline

Baseline

- Maintain current plan with team. (Project Manager)

Applying the *Thinking On Purpose* (TOP) Process to the But Wait, There's More! Scenario—Risk Assessment

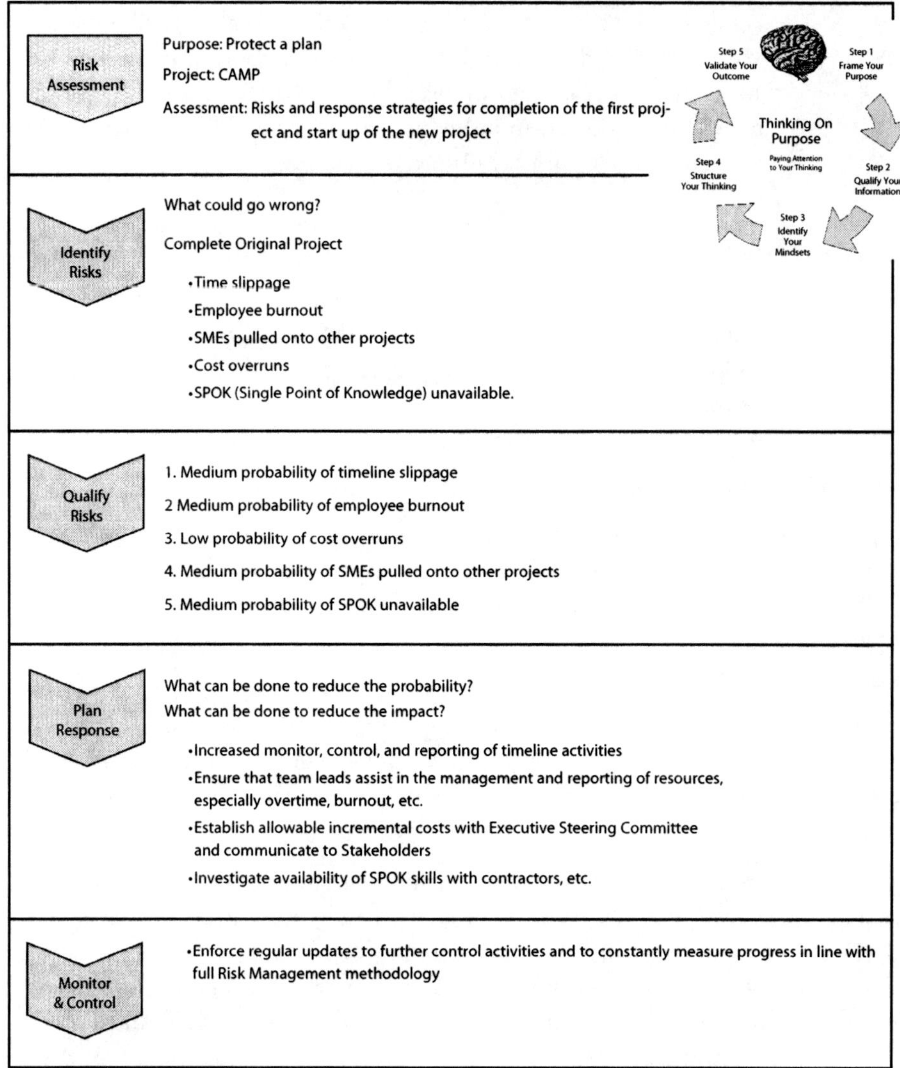

Risk Assessment
Purpose: Protect a plan
Project: CAMP
Assessment: Risks and response strategies for completion of the first project and start up of the new project
Step 5
Validate Your Outcome
Step 1
Frame Your Purpose
Thinking On Purpose
Paying Attention to Your Thinking
Step 2
Qualify Your Information
Step 3
Identify Your Mindsets
Step 4
Structure Your Thinking
Identify Risks
What could go wrong?
Complete Original Project
•Time slippage
•Employee burnout
•SMEs pulled onto other projects
•Cost overruns
•SPOK (Single Point of Knowledge) unavailable.
Qualify Risks
1. Medium probability of timeline slippage
2 Medium probability of employee burnout
3. Low probability of cost overruns
4. Medium probability of SMEs pulled onto other projects
5. Medium probability of SPOK unavailable
Plan Response
What can be done to reduce the probability?
What can be done to reduce the impact?
•Increased monitor, control, and reporting of timeline activities
•Ensure that team leads assist in the management and reporting of resources, especially overtime, burnout, etc.
•Establish allowable incremental costs with Executive Steering Committee and communicate to Stakeholders
•Investigate availability of SPOK skills with contractors, etc.
Monitor & Control
•Enforce regular updates to further control activities and to constantly measure progress in line with full Risk Management methodology

Applying the *Thinking On Purpose* (TOP) Process to the But Wait, There's More! Scenario—Conclusion

In the end, Tom had enough material from the TOP Process to convincingly present a proposal to set the additional requests aside for the time being, and package them as a separate project, with its own budget, timeline, and resources. By applying the TOP Process to his situation, Tom was able to find a solution that avoided encroaching scope creep in his current project, while still addressing the needs and concerns of his project sponsors.

Chapter Summary

It's one thing to theorize a process, it's another to show how that process works in real life. In the three scenarios, I have taken you step by step through the process of applying the principles of ***Thinking On Purpose*** in real-world settings dealing with real-world project management issues.

Red Light, Green Light

George was the very picture of optimism as a project manager. He was managing a basic changeover of technology to update his company's software application, and all of his teams were green-lit, putting the project on track for a successful completion.

Until it all fell apart, that is. During a weekly status meeting, George got the unwelcome news that two of his teams had gone from "Green" to "Red" seemingly overnight, for reasons which seemed to come out of nowhere. Suddenly, George was facing a looming crisis and was left wondering why he never saw it coming.

Fortunately, George's boss requested that he use the TOP Process to see if he could determine the nature of the breakdown and get his project back on track. During this Process, George discovered that several biases were at the root of the issue, namely his tendency to substitute blind optimism and past successes for objective measurements and foresight. He also learned that there were time constraints and production policies in place that hampered timely completion of the project. By using this information, George and his team were able to reconstruct a workable plan that accounted for all the vital criteria and built in strategies for dealing with potential issues and other contingencies.

By using the TOP Process, George now has a deeper understanding of his tendency to see and hear what he wants to see and hear, and his tendency to let overconfidence lead his actions. He now knows how to make and protect a plan that accounts for these biases and tendencies. Such a plan also keeps him and his team honest and helps them pinpoint potential problems and make plans for dealing with them before they become showstoppers.

All Together Now

In this scenario, we dealt with applying TOP to a team that was both disengaged and disenfranchised. The team members were not well informed about their project, nor did they have the resources or belief in the project to commit to it wholeheartedly.

By working through the TOP Process, the project leader Caroline was able to engage the team in the Process and discover where the project had run aground—the fact that By the end of the TOP Process, Caroline succeeded in engaging the team and creating a workable next step—taking the project back to the executive committee for review. Although the fate of the project was still unresolved, the team was now more cohesive and involved, and they felt as if their input actually mattered.

But Wait, There's More!

Tom was faced with an all-too-familiar project management bugbear—scope creep. After having a difficult time reaching a consensus on scope during the initial project planning sessions, Tom thought he was home free—his project was coming in on time and under budget.

But during his first status meeting with the Executive Steering Committee, Tom was blindsided by a request to add new and unnecessary functions and features, additions which could very well scuttle the entire project. Tom took his concerns to his boss, who shared his reasoning but wisely advised Tom to use the TOP Process to make sure his arguments for containing the project scope were sound, objective, and well-supported by evidence.

As a result, Tom was able to create a proposal that met all of his and the team's needs and wants, plus those of the project sponsor—to complete the project as it stood, and add the additional functionality and features as a second project after the first was complete. Assuming he could get the support of the Executive Steering Committee, he had a workable plan that included the new requests while avoiding team burnout, cost overruns, and timeline slippage.

CHAPTER 7

The Thinking on Purpose Toolkit

For each aspect of the process of Framing Your Purpose—situational assessment, problem solving, decision making, action planning and risk assessment—I have researched, described and catalogued a set of common tools for you use that will help you complete these tasks.

Like a carpenter's toolbox, this Toolkit contains tools and techniques that may have only one specific purpose. In this toolbox, for example, the Devil's Advocate concept is exclusively used in seeking complementary or contradictory evidence to challenge the validity of a particular viewpoint. On the other hand, there are some tools that have multiple uses. The Weighted Ranking tool, for instance, can be used in problem solving, decision-making, and risk assessments.

I have gathered these tools from a number of sources, which are noted both in the write-up of the tool and in the bibliography. My goal for this Toolkit is to provide a comprehensive catalogue of decision making and problem solving tools, a source point where you can get more in-depth information about the concepts and their application and, where appropriate, what templates exist to fast track that application in the everyday project management environment.

The forty tools in this section are recorded in the matrix below, in alphabetical order, along with an indication of the most appropriate "purpose frame": SA—Situational Assessment, PS—Problem Solving, DM—Decision Making, AP—Action Planning and RA—Risk Assessment.

Ref.	Tool or Technique	SA	PS	DM	AP	RA
1	Action Planning				X	
2	Affinity Diagram	X	X			
3	Appreciation	X				
4	Ask "Why" Five Times	X				
5	Brainstorming	X	X	X	X	X
6	Cause and Effect Diagram	X				
7	Concept Fan	X	X	X		
8	Consensus			X		
9	Debrief	X	X	X	X	X
10	Decision/Event Tree		X			
11	Devil's Advocacy	X				
12	Decision Making			X		
13	Divergent/Convergent Thinking		X	X	X	X
14	DO IT		X			
15	Drill Down		X			
16	Facilitation	X	X	X	X	X
17	Force Field Analysis	X				
18	Gap Analysis				X	X
19	Hypothesis Testing	X	X			
20	Information Analysis Standards	X	X	X		
21	Ladder of Inference					
22	Matrix and Grids		X	X		
23	Mind Mapping	X	X	X	X	X
24	Multi-Voting	X				
25	Paired Comparison Analysis			X		
26	Pareto Analysis			X		
27	PMI — Plus/Minus/Interesting			X		
28	Provocation					
29	Probability Tree			X		X
30	Problem Re-Statement		X			X
31	Problem Solving		X			
32	Process Mapping		X			
33	Reframing Matrix	X	X	X	X	X
34	Risk Assessment					X
35	Situational Assessment	X				
36	Six Thinking Hats			X		

Ref.	Tool or Technique	SA	PS	DM	AP	RA
37	Stakeholder Assessment		X			
38	SWOT Analysis		X			
39	Utility Tree/Matrix			X		
40	Weighted Ranking			X		

7.1 Getting The Most Out of Your Tools

Use the guide below to help you choose the tool or structure that best meets the needs of your situation, as follows:

Need 1: Getting Started

The four tools in this grouping provide a way for you to find the best starting point and direction of action for any situation:

Ref No.	Tool Description	Snapshot
18	Gap Analysis	How do we get where we want to go?
35	Situational Assessment	What is really happening?
37	Stakeholder Assessment	Getting the right people involved
38	SWOT Analysis	How do we get where we want to go?

Need 2: Establishing Connections

The three tools in this grouping will help you make sense of large volumes of information (issues, opportunities, etc.):

Ref No.	Tool Description	Snapshot
18	Gap Analysis	How do we get where we want to go?
35	Situational Assessment	What is really happening?
37	Stakeholder Assessment	Getting the right people involved

Need 3: Expanding Possibilities

The eight tools in this grouping are aimed at using structure to increase your creativity. By forcing your brain to challenge APT, options and alternatives previously outside your sphere of attention or consideration suddenly come into clearer focus and become ultimately more actionable.

Ref No.	Tool Description	Snapshot
5	Brainstorming	Generating Ideas
7	Concept Fan	Complex to simple
11	Devil's Advocacy	Intentional opposing view
13	Divergent and Convergent Thinking	Focused generation of ideas
28	Provocation	Stimulating thinking outside of the box
30	Problem Restatement	Achieving problem clarity
33	Reframing Matrix	Leveraging other points of view
36	Six Thinking Hats	Structuring thinking outside of the box

Need 4: Determining Cause or Drilling Down

The eight tools in this category provide a wide range of methods to get to the root cause or essence of a problem or opportunity:

Ref No.	Tool Description	Snapshot
3	Appreciation	Generating Ideas
4	Ask "Why" Five Times	Simple path to root cause
6	Cause and Effect Diagram	Structured path to root cause
15	Drill Down	Deconstruction to basic elements
17	Force Field Analysis	Understanding driving and restraining forces
19	Hypothesis Testing	Structured path to correct problem statement

21	Ladder of Inference	Understanding team members' beliefs and assumptions
26	Pareto Analysis	Determining key problem to be solved using the 80/20 rule

Need 5: Generic Formats

While the three tools in this grouping could be considered universal, they are often misused or ignored altogether. When applied effectively, however, they provide clarity and simplicity to the analysis and presentation of information:

Ref No.	Tool Description	Snapshot
20	Information Analysis Standards	Checklist for assessing the quality of your reasoning and information
22	Matrix and Grids	Visual structure for comparison and analysis of data
40	Weighted Ranking	Quantitative approach for comparing various options

Need 6: Action Enablers

The five tools in this grouping provide the traction necessary to overcome the inertia of "getting started" and provide the structure to keep things moving in the right direction:

Ref No.	Tool Description	Snapshot
1	Action Planning	Establish a step-by-step road map
9	Debrief	Validating your outcome
16	Facilitation	Help others complete their work and improve the way they work together
31	Problem Solving	Finding root cause
34	Risk Assessment	Protecting your plans

Need 7: Decision Making

The nine tools in this grouping provide a range of methods designed to help you make decisions or to test that a decision was, in fact, a good one:

Ref No.	Tool Description	Snapshot
3	Appreciation	Generating Ideas
4	Ask "Why" Five Times	Simple path to root cause
6	Cause and Effect Diagram	Structured path to root cause
15	Drill Down	Deconstruction to basic elements
17	Force Field Analysis	Understanding driving and restraining forces
19	Hypothesis Testing	Structured path to correct problem statement
21	Ladder of Inference	Understanding team members' beliefs and assumptions
26	Pareto Analysis	Determining key problem to be solved using 80/20 rule
39	Utility Tree/Matrix	Visual display of analysis to identify

Each tool or technique profiled in the following pages is organized alphabetically. Reference information is included with each profile when more detailed information is available from additional source material. Wherever possible, a template, diagram, or example has been taken from the three scenarios in Chapter 6, so that you can see the tool, and how to use it, in an active context.

7.2 The TOP Toolkit

TOP Tool 1: Action Planning (AP)

Purpose:

"Action Enabler" tool, used to establish a step-by-step road map for accomplishing a deliverable or objective.

Summary:

Action planning is the process that guides the day-to-day activities of an organization or project. It is the process of planning what needs to be done, when it needs to be done, by whom it needs to be done, and what resources or inputs are needed to do it. It is the process of operationalizing your objectives.

Most action plans consist of the following elements:

- A statement of what must be achieved.
- A delineation of the steps that have to be followed to reach this objective.
- A clarification of who is responsible for making sure that each step is completed.
- A clarification of the inputs/resources required.

When you go through an action planning process, you should end up with a practical plan that will enable you to resource and carry out the steps needed to achieve your objective.

Steps:

1. Draft the plan—Aimed at getting "first draft" into play by asking the key questions:
    - What are the objectives to be achieved?
    - What action steps are required to meet your objectives?
    - When must each step be completed?
    - Who will be responsible for each step?
2. Anticipate changes—Aimed at applying foresight by asking the key question:
    - What dependency or sequence is likely to change?
3. Revise the plan—Aimed at refining the plan as required by asking the key question:
    - Are logic and flow still intact?

4. Set a baseline for measurement of results—Aimed at establishing the benchmark for measuring progress and quality of the planning, by asking the key question:
    - Which is the dominant driver: time, cost, or scope?

Guidelines/Options:

There are different methods to identifying and recording tasks:

- Identifying tasks can be completed by brainstorming about past experience with your team.
- Tasks can be identified using planning tools and planning tool templates that depict the standard types of activities required. As the project manager, you then customize the standard list for the needs of the specific project.
- Tasks can be summarized in matrix format, Gantt chart format, or in network diagrams.

Enablers:

- TOP Tool 23: Mind Mapping can be used to identify tasks.
- TOP Tool 2: Affinity Analysis can be used to cluster the groups of tasks into logical groupings.
- Project management software, like Microsoft Project, can be used to enhance the activity identification, recording and summarization approaches.

References:

- Horine, Gregory M. *Absolute Beginner's Guide to Project Management Templates*. Indiana: Que, 2005.
- Verzuh, Eric. *The Fast Forward MBA in Project Management*. New Jersey: John Wiley and Sons, 2005.
- Project Management Institute. *A Guide to the Project Management Body of Knowledge*. Project Management Institute, 2004.

Applicable Job Aid, Template, Diagram, or Example:

Template:

A completed example using the following template can be found in Chapter 6—Thinking On Purpose in Action.

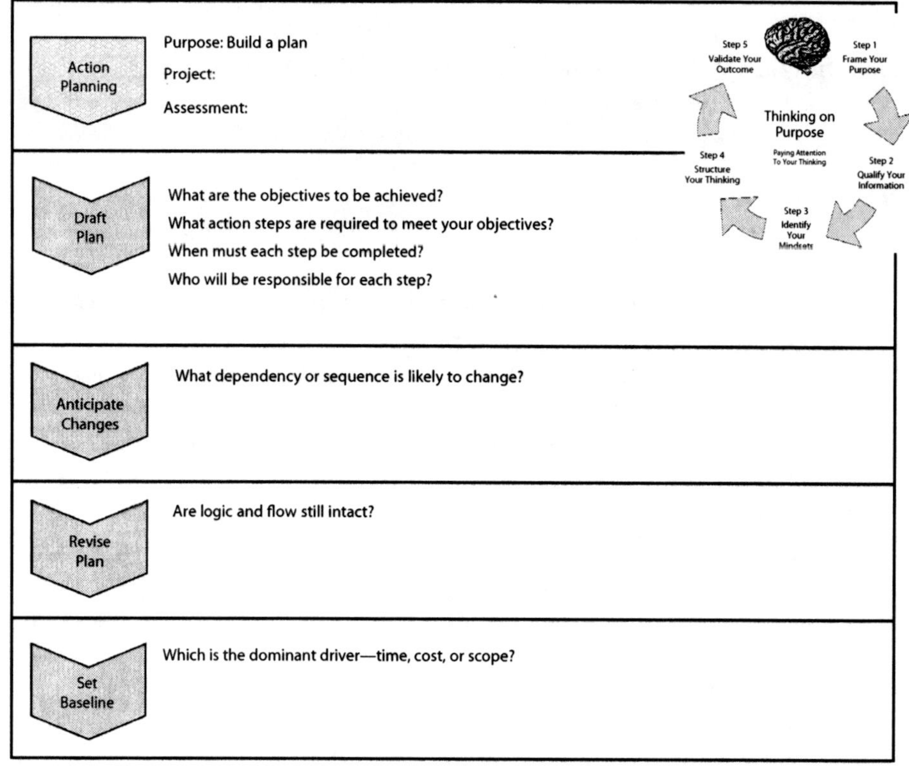
Action Planning
Purpose: Build a plan
Project:
Assessment:
Step 5
Validate Your Outcome
Step 1
Frame Your Purpose
Thinking on Purpose
Paying Attention To Your Thinking
Step 4
Structure Your Thinking
Step 2
Qualify Your Information
Step 3
Identify Your Mindsets
Draft Plan
What are the objectives to be achieved?
What action steps are required to meet your objectives?
When must each step be completed?
Who will be responsible for each step?
Anticipate Changes
What dependency or sequence is likely to change?
Revise Plan
Are logic and flow still intact?
Set Baseline
Which is the dominant driver—time, cost, or scope?

TOP Tool 2: Affinity Analysis

Purpose:

"Establishing Connections" tool to organize several ideas for easier review.

Summary:

Dealing with several ideas can quickly become confusing. An affinity diagram helps you keep track of a large group of ideas.

Steps:

1. Determine what you hope to achieve and what you will do with the answers you get.
2. Use brainstorming to generate your ideas, and put the ideas on cards or sticky notes.
3. Let the group sort the cards or notes one at a time into categories in which the various ideas seem related.
4. Make duplicate cards or notes for ideas that two or more group members place into two or more categories.
5. Talk as a group about the sorting process and its results.
6. Label the categories.
7. Note the category labels and the ideas that come under them.

Guidelines/Options

- Remember your brainstorming rules for step 2.
- The sorting process in step 3 should be silent.
- During sorting, the same item can fall under more than one label or category.
- Divide large groups during the sorting process. Let the first group sort, then the second group. Work together to create a final sorting.
- Use the Decision-Making, Consensus, or Conflict Resolution tools if the group cannot agree on sorting, categories, or labels.

Enablers:

TOP Tool 16: Facilitation

Using sticky notes works well to facilitate clustering.

References

Weaver, Richard G.; Farrell, John D. Managers as Facilitators: *A Practical Guide to Getting Work Done in a Changing Workplace.* San Francisco, CA: Berrett-Koehler Publishers, Inc., 1997.

Applicable Job Aid, Template, Diagram, or Example:

Example:

The affinity process was used by Tom, in *Scenario 3—But Wait, There's More!* as outlined below:

- Tom was apprehensive about getting the team together for a brainstorming session, since it had been difficult to get everyone to agree on the scope and requirements earlier in the project. He felt the best way to get all the issues on the tables was to facilitate an affinity session.
- He gathered all the team members including the Stakeholders into a conference room and provided each of them with yellow sticky notes.
- He asked them to put all the issues and opportunities they could think of on the notes. He suggested that they use phrases and sentences describing the issues.
- After each person had finished recording their issues, he asked them to post the notes randomly on the wall.

Sample of sticky notes

- Increased scope means longer schedule
- More people are needed
- Longer hours
- Committed to another project immediately after this one is complete
- Vacation plans
- Need more money to add functionality
- Need more technical people
- Need people who know about Sox
- Need people who know new technology
- Need more time to add new requirements
- Need to redo requirements
- Need to revisit scope documentation
- This project linked to another project
- Need to reduce hours not increase them

Once the team had put all their ideas on the wall, they all worked as a team to group them. Tom discouraged talking at this point; he knew that the groups would come together very easily.

After they finished grouping the ideas, the team created headings together for each grouping. Typically each heading is three to five words. The results are below:

Extended Timeline

- Increased scope means longer schedule
- Need more time to add new requirements
- Need to redo requirements
- Need to revisit scope documentation

Straining Team Members

- Longer hours
- Need to reduce hours not increase them

Over-budget

- Need more money to add functionality

Cross-impacts on Other Projects

- Committed to another project immediately after this one is complete
- Vacation plans
- This project linked to another project

New Team Members

- More people are needed
- Need more technical people
- Need people who know about Sox
- Need people who know new technology

TOP Tool 3: Appreciation

Purpose:

- "Drill Down" tool for extracting the maximum amount of information from a single fact.

Summary:

- This technique is used by military planners to ensure they know everything possible about the available intelligence and its implications before proceeding.

Steps:

1. Identify the fact for examination.
2. Ask the question "so what?"—i.e. what is the implication of the item being examined?
3. Continue asking the question until you have drawn out all the possible inferences.

Guidelines/Options:

- While it would be possible to reach a conclusion without a formal technique, Appreciation provides a framework to extract information faster and with more reliability.

Enablers:

TOP Tool 16: Facilitation

References

Mind Tools. *Excellent Skills for an Excellent Career*. London, UK: Mind Tools Limited, 2008.

Applicable Job Aid, Template, Diagram, or Example:

Example:

While Appreciation is a technique used by military planners, it does have applications in other disciplines, especially project management.

Example Fact: Our project team is exhausted from many days of long hours.

- So What? The team's ability to handle additional workload is severely compromised.
- So What? Without the ability to respond to the unexpected and identified risks, progress on the project will either slow down significantly or stop with the challenge or realization of a risk.
- So What? Given the risk profile for this project, there is a high probability that we are heading for time or cost implications within the next month that will require Executive Steering Committee approval.
- So What? Either we add resources, or consciously slow things down, or we will be working in an uncontrolled manner with potentially serious HR implications.

TOP Tool 4: Ask "Why" Five Times

Purpose:

"Drill Down" tool for getting to true root cause quickly.

Summary:

This technique is borrowed from Japanese manufacturing management theory. This method is used to help identify the real causes of problems that occur on the manufacturing floor. The goal is not to simply correct the effects of the problem, but to find out the root cause of why the problem is occurring so that you can ensure that it will not happen in the future.

One simple way to do this is called asking "why" five times. The idea is that by the time you have asked "why" the fifth time, you will be at the root cause. It isn't always that simple, but the exercise can be surprisingly insightful in helping you figure out what is really going on, and can help you avoid "quick fix" solutions that are really just Band-Aids that don't resolve anything. It is especially useful for tackling chronic problems that show up over and over again in a system; it is less useful for problems that are unlikely to recur.

Steps:

1. State the problem as known at the present time.
2. Proceed to ask "why" after each answer until root cause is known.

Guidelines/Options:

While five times is not guaranteed, most of the time the fifth round will yield the "nugget."

Enablers:

TOP Tool 16: Facilitation

References

This tool is also considered a Six Sigma tool.

Applicable Job Aid, Template, Diagram, or Example:

Example: Problem Situation:

Your main vendor on your project team is challenging the quality of your acceptance criteria for project documentation. You arrange for a discussion with your vendor offline and proceed with the first why question:

1. Why are you challenging the acceptance criteria?
    - Because the quality is poor.
2. Why is the quality poor?
    - Because they are much too general.
3. Why are they too general?
    - Because they were created by your project team with no consultation with my company.
4. Why was there no consultation with your team (the vendor's team)?
    - Because your development team never provides us any chance to jointly develop things like acceptance criteria.
5. Why doesn't my development team ask for vendor input?
    - Because I have let my personal negative bias toward vendor partnering on creation of acceptance criteria show through. The vendor is right here; our criteria are poor.

TOP Tool 5: Brainstorming

Purpose:

"Expand Possibilities" tool for generating as many ideas as possible.

Summary:

A good brainstorming session produces a long list of ideas. Groups use brainstorming more than any other tool. When a group wants to consider all possibilities, come up with new ideas, and expand beyond current thinking, brainstorming is a good place to start.

Steps:

1. Decide how to use the information—have a purpose for brainstorming.
2. Read the brainstorming guidelines to the group.
3. Give everyone approximately five minutes to silently work alone to generate some ideas.
4. Invite everyone to share his or her ideas and record them exactly as spoken.
5. Stop the session when no one has any more ideas. Be willing to wait through several silent periods so people can think. Do not cut them off too soon.

Guidelines/Options:

- You can record ideas on sticky notes so they can be moved around and grouped together later.
- You may want to use the "nominal group technique" if more vocal team members are dominating the session. In nominal group technique, people take turns sharing their ideas one at a time until all the ideas have been heard.
- When recording ideas on flipcharts, you may want to have two people recording ideas to keep things moving at a fast pace.

Enablers:

Not applicable

References:

Weaver, Richard G.; Farrell, John D. *Managers as Facilitators: A Practical Guide to Getting Work Done in a Changing Workplace.* San Francisco, CA: Berrett-Koehler Publishers, Inc., 1997.

Applicable Job Aid, Template, Diagram, or Example:

Not Applicable

TOP Tool 6: Cause-Effect Diagram (CED)

Purpose:

"Determine Cause/Drill Down" tool for identifying and organizing information about the cause of a problem and possible outcomes.

Summary:

Using a CED helps you discover what's causing your problems and what outcomes you want to achieve. Sometimes it can be hard to pinpoint these causes and their direct effects. This tool makes that process easier.

Steps:

1. Figure out what you hope to achieve and what you will do with the answers you get.
2. Use brainstorming to determine the causes of the effects you are trying to solve
3. Group the results from your brainstorming session by letting everyone have a chance to sort brainstorming results into groups or categories, as they see fit.
4. If more than one person thinks a particular result belongs in more than one category, add it to all relevant categories.
5. Talk as a group about why you sorted the results the way you did.
6. Label each the groupings in a way that makes sense to the group.
7. Keep a record of the results and their labels.
8. Decide which causes to investigate, focusing on the most important issues.

Guidelines/Options:

Create the categories or labels first, then brainstorm under each category.

Restructure an affinity diagram to serve as your cause-effect diagram.

Possible categories:

- Service Industry—4 P's (Policies, Procedures, People, Plant/ Technology)
- Manufacturing Industries—6 M's (Machines, Methods, Materials Measurements, Mother Nature [Environment], Manpower [People])
- Process Steps—Example (Record Change in Change Log, Review Need and Assess Change Impact, Decide on Action, Obtain Financial Authorization, Record in Change Log)

Enablers:

You will be using brainstorming for this tool, so keep in mind the standard rules that apply to that activity.

Suggestions:

- Think globally, act locally—understand the impact of issues beyond your control, but act on those you can control.
- Listen to ideas of participants. Capture their ideas about causes in one or two words.
- Have each person review the CED the next day, or ask each of them to obtain an opinion from one or two other people.
- You have an option to state the desired results instead of a problem. This helps to identify means in place of causes, to achieve the results.

References:

Milosevic, Dragan Z. *Project Management Toolkit*. New Jersey: John Wiley and Sons, 2003.

Kemp, Sid, *Ultimate Guide to Project Management for Small Business.* Madison, WI: Publishing Enterprises, 2005.

Applicable Job Aid, Template, Diagram, or Example:

Example: Scenario 1—Red Light, Green Light

George knew that an effective way to find the root cause of his problems was to do a Cause & Effect diagram, or Ishikawa. By doing so, he quickly realized there were a number of issues that played a role in the timeline slippage. As they went through the various causes, George was completely caught by surprise by the fact that the team could not work on any of the technical deliverables during production, and that this was the biggest reason for the timeline slippage.

The diagram from George's work session is included below:

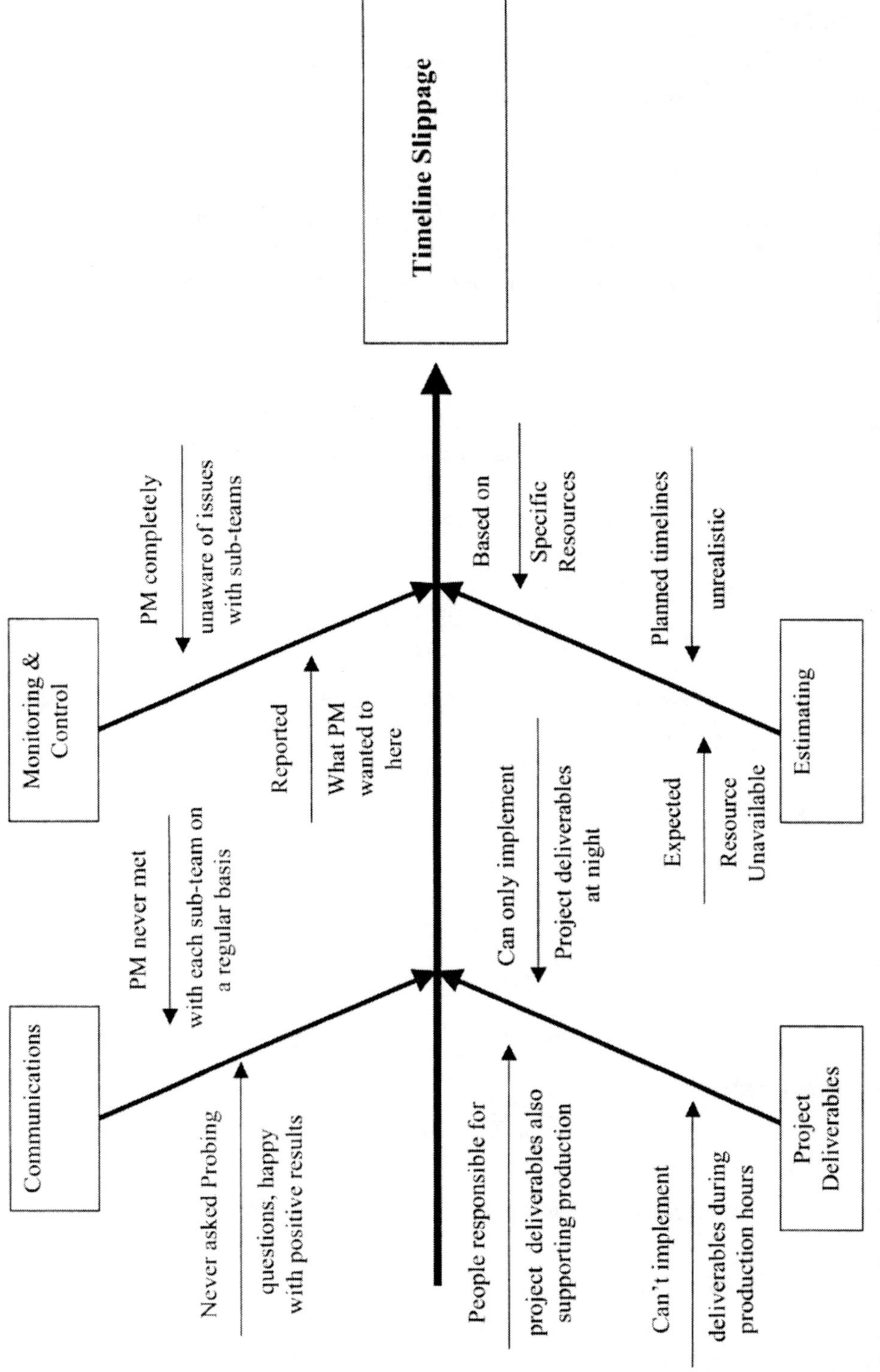

TOP Tool 7: Concept Fan

Purpose:

"Expand Possibilities" tool for finding different approaches to a problem when you have rejected all the obvious solutions.

Summary:

The Concept Fan is a useful technique of widening the search of solutions when you have exhausted all obvious approaches. Its primary result is a clear framework through which you can step back to obtain a different perspective on the problem.

Steps:

1. Write the problem in the middle of a piece of paper.
2. Write possible solutions to this problem on lines radiating from the circle.
3. If no idea works, redefine the problem more broadly. Write the broader definition in the circle to the left of the first one.
4. Draw an arrow from the initial problem definition to the new one to show the linkage between the two problems. Then radiate possible solutions from this broader definition.
5. Keep expanding and redefining the problem until you have a useful solution.

Guidelines/Options:

The idea is to keep stepping back, to provide a broad field of view in which to deal with the problem.

Enablers:

Not Applicable

References

Mind Tools. *Excellent Skills for an Excellent Career*. London: Mind Tools Ltd., 2008.

Applicable Job Aid, Template, Diagram or Example:

Example: Scenario 2—All Together Now

Caroline decided to use a Concept Fan to assist in assessing the situation, and hopefully to look at the issues on the project from a different perspective. As they worked through all the issues, the team quickly came to the conclusion that a lot of the problems could be attributed to the lack of management support for the project. Ultimately, they felt that the project might not even be a strategic fit. The team recommended that project be reviewed at the executive level, and even canceled if deemed not to be a strategic fit.

The diagrams Caroline drew on the whiteboard for the team are outlined below:

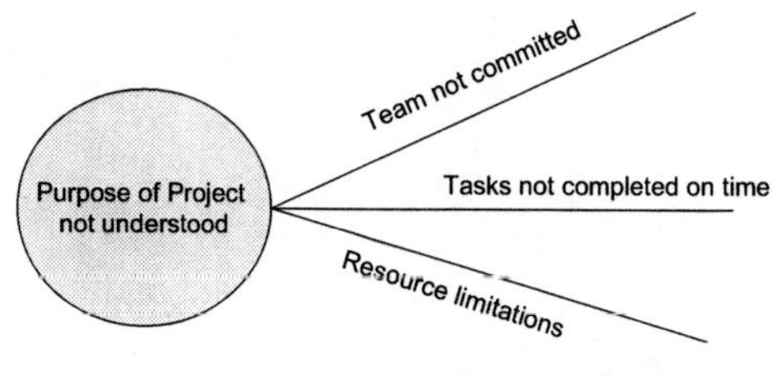

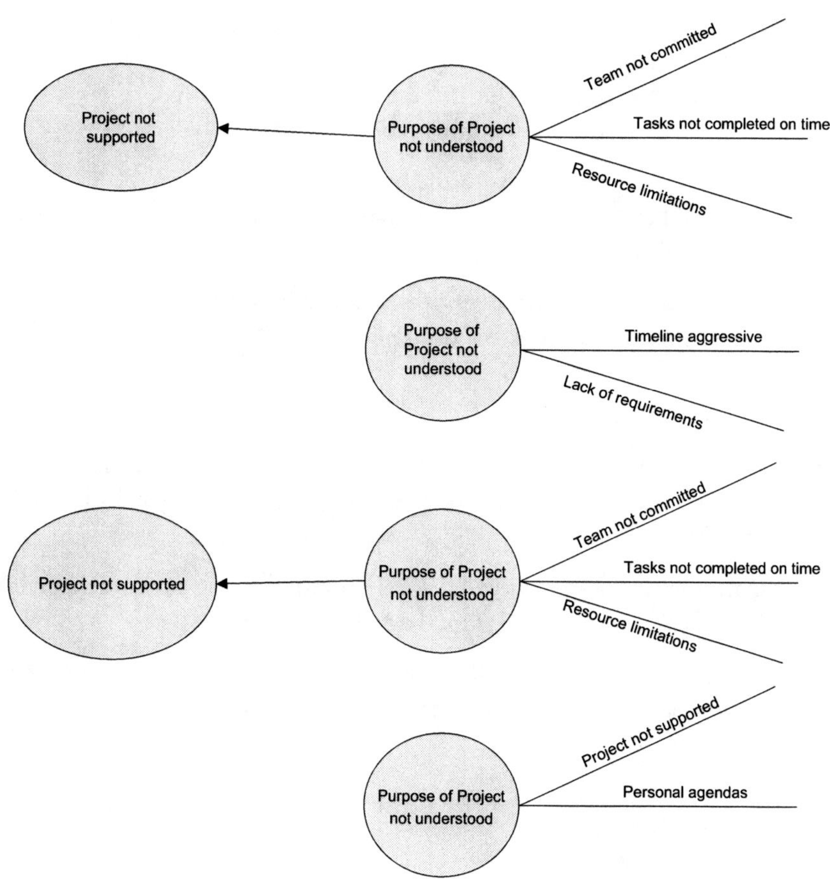

TOP TOOLS

TOP Tool 8: Consensus

Purpose:

"Decision Making" tool to obtain an agreement about a process or decision.

Summary:

When a consensus is reached, all parties agree to commit to and support an action, process, or decision, even if they may not completely agree. This tool is helpful in reaching that consensus within a group.

Steps:

1. Make sure everyone is 100% clear on the subject of the consensus (the action or decision that needs to be taken).
2. Make sure everyone agrees that unanimous commitment is a requirement.
3. Everyone in the group must answer these questions:
   - Is this action something you can agree to?
   - Will you commit to this action within the group?
   - Will you commit to this action away from the group?
4. If anyone answers "no" to the questions above, ask:
   - What needs to happen or change to gain your support for this action?
5. Make sure that everyone agrees that a consensus has been reached and that they are committed to supporting it.

Guidelines/Options

Use this tool only if the consensus of all parties is required. If not, consider a different approach (such as voting). The tool is useful for creating compromise or other related solutions.

Determine how long you will discuss the issue. If you can't reach a consensus by that time, consider a different method of conflict resolution.

Use Vijay K. Verma's Conflict Styles Resolution Grid, outlined in the Template section below, for options depending on the context and situation:

- Competing
- Avoiding
- Accommodating
- Compromising
- Collaborating

Enablers:

TOP Tool 16: Facilitation

References

Weaver, Richard G.; Farrell, John D. *Managers as Facilitators: A Practical Guide to Getting Work Done in a Changing Workplace.* San Francisco, CA: Berrett-Koehler Publishers, Inc., 1997.

Verma, Vijay. *Human Resource Skills for the Project Manager.* Project Management Institute, 1996.

Applicable Job Aid, Template, Diagram or Example:

Example: Scenario 3—But Wait, There's More!

After the team went through the decision-making process, Tom knew it was imperative to have consensus from the group. He needed to know that they were committed to the decision and would support the actions needed to accomplish the action plan. The decision they reached would not be popular with the Stakeholder and possibly not with the senior management, either.

Tom remembered building the scope and requirements at the beginning of the project. It had been very difficult to get everyone to agree on these issues, and he wasn't sure what the outcome of the consensus discussion would be.

When the team came together, Tom established the context by reviewing the decision that they were taking to management. He briefly walked them through the Situational Assessment as well as the Decision Making process. At the end of his overview, he asked if everyone completely understood how they had arrived at the decision, and if they understood the decision itself. Everyone answered in the affirmative on both points.

He then asked if everyone agreed that there needed to be unanimous commitment to the decision. After receiving a positive response from all involved, Tom then directed everyone to three questions written on the white board.

1. Is this action something you can agree to?
2. Will you commit to this action within the group?
3. Will you commit to this action away from the group?
    - Tom was elated to find that everyone quickly agreed on questions 1 and 2. However, he was disappointed to find there was some dissention regarding question 3.
    - After some discussion, it became clear that some of the team members felt that senior management and the sponsor would

pressure them, and that under these circumstances they weren't sure they could commit to the action.

- Although Tom would have liked to have received consensus on the first run, he still needed to find out what it would take to get unanimous support for the decision away from the group. He found himself considering the various styles of Conflict Resolution he might be able to use to achieve consensus (see style matrix below):

Competing, also called Forcing

- Tom had used this in the past, with little success, and he knew that you didn't always get the dedication from the team that you wanted when you used this style.
- There were already enough projects that were done for regulatory reasons, and in which there wasn't room for dissention; this was a Command conflict resolution style.
- This project wasn't like that. Tom needed this team to be ambassadors for their decision and this style wouldn't promote that feeling.

Avoidance

- This wasn't Tom's style at all. He had already taken the time to work through the TOP process, and the last thing he wanted to do was leave everyone hanging.
- Tom couldn't afford to avoid coming to consensus with this team.

Compromise

- Tom knew this style was always attractive, but seldom left anyone completely satisfied.
- Tom felt that compromise was often about giving something up, but after working through the TOP process with the team, he really felt that they could come up with a good solution.

Accommodation, also called Smoothing

- This was another attractive conflict resolution style, because it maintained the relationship going forward. But Tom still felt that through this conflict resolution style, people sometimes gave up to much of their own personal beliefs for the good of the team.

Collaboration, also called Win-Win

- Tom strongly believed that in this situation he needed to take the time to come up with a solution that worked for everyone.
- Tom also realized, as part of the TOP Process, that when people participated in the solution they brought positive energy and good ideas.

After reflection, Tom was confident that using the Collaborative style was going to be a winner.

Conflict Resolution Styles

Concern For Oneself ↑ High	Concern For Others: Low → High	
High	**Compete** • also called forcing • own needs advocated over others • tend to seek control over discussion both in substance and form • relies on aggressive style with low regard for future relationships • tends to result in responses that increase level of threat.	**Collaborate** • Called win-win problem solving • Requires assertive communication and cooperation to achieve a solution better than with side could have achieved alone • Offers chance for consensus, the integration of needs and the potential to exceed the "budget of possibilities" that previously limited our views of the conflict • Brings new time, energy and ideas
(center)	**Compromise** • people gain and give a series of tradeoffs • while satisfactory , generally not satisfying • we remain shaped by our individual perceptions of our needs and don't understand the other position • retain lack of trust • avoid risk taking	
Low	**Avoidance** • common response to negative perception of conflict • feelings get pent up, views go unexpressed and conflict festers until it blows • like a cancer that may have been cured if deal with sooner • because needs and concerns go unexpressed, people often confused and wondering what went wrong	**Accommodate** • also called smoothing • opposite of competing • people in this style yield their needs to those of others trying to be diplomatic • tend to allow the needs of the group to overwhelm their own • preserving the relationship is seen to be most important

TOP Tool 9: Debrief

Purpose:

"Action Enabler" for reviewing a completed action, process or task.

Summary:

Debriefing is a great way to check up on processes and look for ways to improve them. It is also good for acknowledging participation, sharing insights and pinpointing problems areas.

Steps:

1. Ask the following questions:
2. How did you participate and what were your experiences?
3. What worked?
4. What didn't work?
5. What changes would you make or like to see next time?

Guidelines/Options:

- Let everyone involved in the process or task speak. Use debriefing after every major process, task or step.
- Encourage members of the group to take notes before the debriefing and bring them to the meeting.
- Everyone should speak one at a time, and each person should be allowed to speak as often as necessary until all ideas, questions and thoughts have been shared.
- Set a time limit for the debriefing to keep the discussion on track.

Enablers:

Proceduralize and refine the process of debriefing so that it is used when valuable but as efficiently as possible. The debriefing is all about learning and confirming or validating outcomes.

TOP Tool 16: Facilitation

References

Weaver, Richard G.; Farrell, John D. *Managers as Facilitators: A Practical Guide to Getting Work Done in a Changing Workplace*. San Francisco, CA: Berrett-Koehler Publishers, Inc., 1997.

Applicable Job Aid, Template, Diagram, or Example:

Example: Scenario 2—All Together Now

Since Caroline was a seasoned Project Manager, she understood the value of a Post Implementation Review. She always learned so much during the PIR process, and found that she took that learning forward into other projects. She was anxious to talk to the team members who participated in the ***Thinking On Purpose*** Process. She wanted to hold a debrief session as soon as possible, rather than waiting until the end of the project.

When Caroline talked to Brian about this, he was interested but requested a template that he could follow to capture the information. Caroline walked Brian through the steps of ***Thinking On Purpose*** and provided him with templates.

After Brian completed the debriefing session, he met with Caroline to fill her in on the outcome.

Brian told Caroline that the had team agreed to hold a thirty to sixty minute debriefing session, and as a matter of fact had completed the session in forty-five minutes. Everyone had come prepared, and Brian made sure that everyone had an opportunity to provide feedback. Afterward, Brian put together a small report from the debriefing session, below:

***Thinking On Purpose*—Debriefing Session**
Regional Notification Program—Project Team

Attendees:

Bob Keeling, Business Representative
Mel Leung, Facilities Representative
Elaine Lucas, Facilities
Dennis Smith, Technology
Ron Nixon, Technology
Tina Hoffman, Human Resources & Training
Brian Sweet, Project Manager

Things that worked well:

- The ***Thinking On Purpose*** Process helped us come up with good alternatives
- Participating in the Situational Analysis allowed for a better understanding of the problem

- We focused on the issues, not the people
- It was a logical process
- It was easy to follow
- Everyone could participate
- Would follow this process again; it worked!

Things that didn't work well:

- Should have done it sooner
- Should have had a time keeper

What changes would you make or like to see next time?

- Coffee & pastries
- More time for brainstorming
- Next time, invite the sub-teams (they can learn from this process as well)

Brian was happy he did the debriefing; he really liked the TOP Process and it was great to find out the team did as well.

TOP Tool 10: Decision/Event Tree

Purpose:

"Decision Making" tool for illustrating options and alternatives in a situation using a "branching tree" format.

Summary:

A Decision or Event Tree is a way of constructing and identifying alternative scenarios; a flowchart is a type of Decision Tree. To create a Decision Tree, you list all options and connect them with their consequences. You may also include any decisions, factors, or consequences that could alter your options.

Steps:

1. Determine the problem. Let's say, you're trying to determine which software program to buy for tracking clients, and you have three options to choose from.
2. Identify all the major factors. Factors could include price of the software, upgrade fees, platform requirements, ease of use, features, and so on.
3. Determine all the alternatives for each factor. For example, for the factor of price you would list all prices for each of the three programs, including various prices of the same program if it comes in different versions. Then do the same for features, platform requirements, and so on.
4. Create your Decision Tree, laying out all factors and their alternative options by taking all the information you gathered above and put it into an easy-to-analyze Tree.

Guidelines/Options:

You may have other requirements, yes/no decision gates and options to consider (perhaps you can only choose software that comes with multi-user licenses), so you'll have to include these as well.

Principles:

- Two graphical elements—decision points and chance points (after each decision)
- Two data elements—probability and the value of each outcome
- Calculate the expected value for each alternative—probability X equals expected outcome
- Choose option with best expected value

Enablers:

Not applicable

References

Mind Tools. *Excellent Skills for an Excellent Career*.London, UK: Mind Tools Limited 2008.

Applicable Job Aid, Template, Diagram, or Example:

Example: Scenario 1—Red Light, Green Light

George used a Decision Tree structure, below, to explain the alternatives that he and his team considered to his sponsor, and why the team choose "crashing the plan" as the best option.

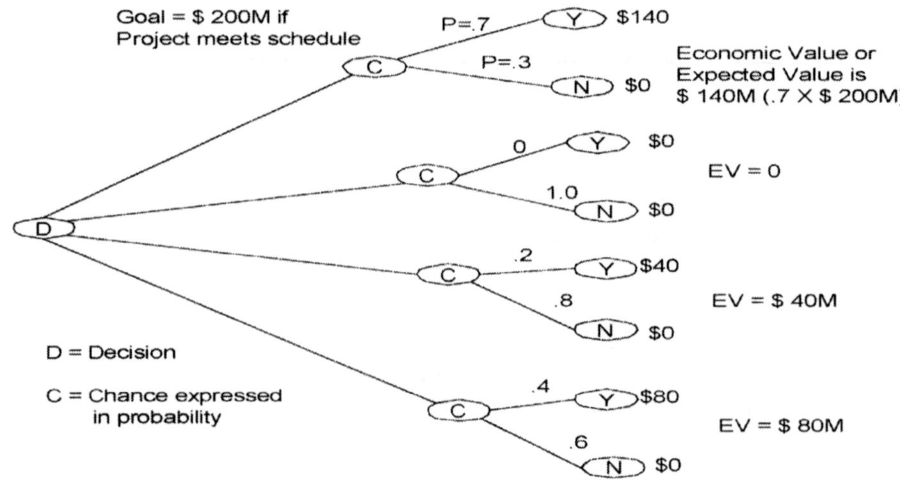

TOP Tool 11: Devil's Advocacy

Purpose:

"Expand Possibilities" tool for challenging the validity or desirability of a particular viewpoint by purposely taking a contrary stance when arguing for or against it.

Summary:

Devil's Advocacy is a valuable process because it helps break participants out of their tendency to focus on the ideas and options they like and not see evidence that could sway the decision. By purposefully taking the contrary stance, you force yourself to step back from defending the solution and instead engage those same tendencies to seek out evidence that negates your viewpoint.

This process also ensures you are far more likely to have a much better understanding of the various arguments for and against all the options. If you are as scrupulous in compiling evidence for one side of the argument as you are for the other, you can be sure that you have a balanced and objective platform for reaching a good decision.

Steps:

Assign an individual or several individuals to argue the opposing view on an issue or decision. This approach can be used for major decisions by using groups of people who are requested to take a Devil's Advocate position that is usually contrary to the conventional wisdom used in making these decisions.

Guidelines/Options:

People often have difficulty arguing against their own position. You may need to be vigilant to ensure that counter-research is thorough, or simply assign the Devil's Advocate position to someone who is neutral about or uninvolved in the process, or who is actively against it.

Enablers:

TOP Tool 16: Facilitation

References:

Not Applicable

Applicable Job Aid, Template, Diagram, or Example:

Example: Scenario 1—Red Light, Green Light

George Green persuaded the senior network representative to take the opposing view in the decision analysis for the plan slippage situation. His Network Leader consciously took the supporting position of outsourcing the solution, which was contrary to his corporate leaning and commitment to his team. The Network Leader's work in arguing this position was instrumental in helping the team cement the "crash the plan" approach as the best option.

TOP Tool 12: Decision Making (DM)

Purpose:

"Decision Making" tool for choosing the best option.

Summary:

There is a difference between making the decision right and making the right decision. Making sure all the possible alternatives are identified will improve the probability of a

good decision, but achieving the desired outcome is by no means guaranteed. On the other hand, simple luck can result in decisions that turn out well even without proper analysis or preparation, because unpredictable factors can also work in your favor. In project management, the key is to make the decision in the right way, and not to rely on hope or luck as the primary strategy.

Once the decision statement has been formalized, proceed with the following steps:

Steps

1. Identify the objectives with key questions:
   - What results do you want, expect or need?
   - What resources can you spend or do you want to conserve?
   - What constraints limit your choices?
2. Generate alternatives with key questions:
   - How have you accomplished these objectives in the past?
   - How could these objectives be accomplished in a new, innovative and creative way?
3. Evaluate alternatives with key questions:
   - Which alternatives pass the Must objectives?
   - Which alternatives pass the Want objective?
   - What are the risks?
4. Choose solution with key questions:
   - Which is the best alternative?
   - Who needs to support, approve, or implement this decision?

Guidelines/Options:

Appropriate objectives can be fleshed out using the 3R approach—Results, Resources, and Restraints (or Limitations):

Results:

- Financial—ROI, cost savings
- Operational—new processes and procedures
- Technological—new technology, new methods, new equipment
- Cultural—new and different norms and ideal behaviors
- Strategic—repositioning the organization: new products and services, new customers, new directions

Resources

- Costs—funds available
- Human Resources—specific skill requirements, especially skills in short supply
- Other Resources—materials, equipment, and facilities

Restraints (or Limitations)

- Physical or technical constraints
- Legal, ethical, or moral considerations
- Organizational values and beliefs, policies, and procedures
- Specific customer and end-user constraints

For decisions requiring more complex analysis of alternatives, Weighed Ranking can be used to more quantitatively assess options. Refer to TOP Tool: 40 for an example using scenario information from this book.

Enablers:

Top Tool 16: Facilitation

Top Tool 27: Plus/Minus/Interesting provides independent validation of the decision.

Top Tool 22: Matrix and Grids provides a format for doing a Weighted Ranking, if required.

Top Tool 40: Weighted Ranking provides a procedure for completing a more quantitative assessment of alternatives, using data from Scenario 2—All Together Now .

References

Harvard Business Review on Decision Making. Boston, MA: Harvard Business School Publishing Corp., 2001.

Hammond, John; Keeney, Ralph; Raiffa, Howard: *Smart Choices—A Practical Guide to Making Better Decisions*. 1999.

Process Design Consultants. *Critical Thinking Participant Workbook*, 1998.

Applicable Job Aid, Template, Diagram, or Example:

Template:

A completed example using the following template can be found in Chapter 6—Thinking On Purpose In action

TOP—DECISION MAKING WORKSHEET

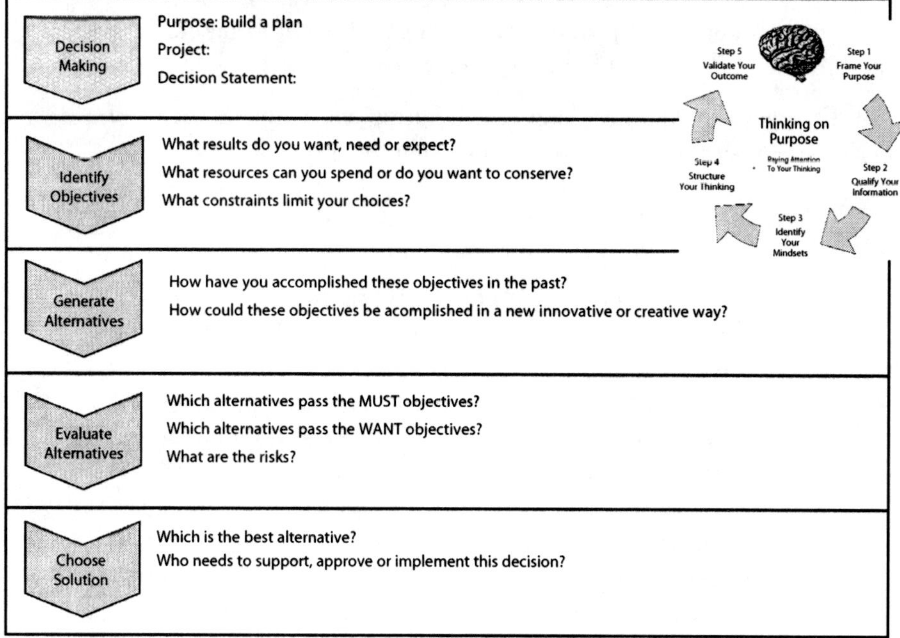

Decision Making
Purpose: Build a plan
Project:
Decision Statement:
Step 5
Validate Your Outcome
Step 1
Frame Your Purpose
Thinking on Purpose
Paying Attention To Your Thinking
Step 4
Structure Your Thinking
Step 2
Qualify Your Information
Step 3
Identify Your Mindsets
Identify Objectives
What results do you want, need or expect?
What resources can you spend or do you want to conserve?
What constraints limit your choices?
Generate Alternatives
How have you accomplished these objectives in the past?
How could these objectives be acomplished in a new innovative or creative way?
Evaluate Alternatives
Which alternatives pass the MUST objectives?
Which alternatives pass the WANT objectives?
What are the risks?
Choose Solution
Which is the best alternative?
Who needs to support, approve or implement this decision?

TOP Tool 13: Divergent/Convergent Thinking

Purpose:

"Expand Possibilities" tool aimed at generating several alternative ideas, options, outcomes, and scenarios.

Summary:

Convergent Thinking is the process of gathering as much information as possible about a situation and using that information to create a solution.

Divergent Thinking is the process of using creativity and brainstorming to spin off as many ideas and concepts about a solution as possible.

Steps:

1. Use Divergent Thinking to brainstorm as many different ideas as possible. *The Thinkers Toolkit* offers the following four commandments for this process:
   - The First Commandment: The more ideas, the better
   - The Second Commandment: Build one idea upon another
   - The Third Commandment: Wacky ideas are okay
   - The Fourth Commandment (Also known as The Golden Rule): Don't evaluate ideas
2. After you have generated several ideas, then it's time to switch to Convergent Thinking. Take all of your ideas and go through them. Organize them into categories. Delete impossible or impractical ideas. Rank or sort the remaining ideas in some way that makes sense for the problem at hand and use the results of this sorting to determine your solution path.

Guidelines/Options:

There are many variations possible with Convergent and Divergent Thinking. One very creative and simple tool is called SCAMPER, which is a checklist of idea-spurring questions that was first suggested by Alex Osborn, a pioneer teacher of creativity. Later,

Bob Eberle arranged it into the mnemonic.
Substitute something
Combine it with something else
Adapt something to it
Modify or **M**agnify it
Put it to some other use

Eliminate something
Reverse or **R**earrange it

To use SCAMPER, isolate the challenge you want to think about and then ask the SCAMPER questions and see what new ideas emerge.

Enablers:

TOP Tool 5: Brainstorming

References

Jones, Morgan D. *The Thinker's Toolkit.* New York: Three Rivers Press, 1998.
Michalko, Michael. *Thinkertoys.* New York: Ten Speed Press, 2006.

Applicable Job Aid, Template, Diagram, or Example:

Diagram: TOP Toolkit, allocated between Divergent and Convergent Thinking

TOP Toolkit Profile	
Divergent Thinking	Convergent Thinking
• Activity Planning	• Affinity Diagram
• Appreciation	• Cause and Effect Diagram
• Ask "Why" Five Times	• Consensus
• Brainstorming	• Debrief
• Concept Fan	• Devil's Advocacy
• Force Field Analysis	• Decision Making
• Decision/Event Tree	• DO IT
• Mind Mapping	• Drill Down
• Pareto Analysis	• Facilitation
• PMI—Plus/Minus/Interesting	• Gap Analysis
• Provocation	• Hypothesis Testing
• Problem Re-Statement	• Information Analysis Standards
• Problem Solving	• Ladder of Inference
• Process Mapping	• Multi-Voting
• Reframing Matrix	• Paired Comparison Analysis
• Situation Assessment	• Probability Tree
• Six Thinking Hats	• Risk Assessment
• SWOT Assessment	• Stakeholder Assessment
	• Utility Tree/Matrix
	• Weighted Ranking

TOP TOOLS

TOP Tool 14: DO IT

Purpose:

"Decision Making" tool that stimulates creative thinking.

Summary:

DO IT bundles a number of techniques together, and introduces formal methods of problem definition and evaluation. DO IT is an acronym for **D**efine the problem, **O**pen mind and apply creative techniques, **I**dentify best solution, and Transform.

Steps:

1. Define the Problem—Concentrate on analyzing the problem to ensure the correct question is being asked.
2. Open Mind—Apply creativity techniques to generate as many answers as possible to the question you are asking. Do not evaluate the answers.
3. Identify Best Solution—Select the best solutions from those identified in Step 2.
4. Transform—Make an action plan for the implementation of the solution and carry it out; without implementation your creativity is sterile.

Guidelines/Options:

DO IT is a structured process for creativity. Using DO IT ensures that you carry out the essential groundwork for getting the most out of the creativity tools.

- When defining the problem, check you are tackling the problem, not the symptom.
- Also make sure to clarify the boundaries of the problem. *Use TOP Tool 30: Problem Restatement.*
- When opening your mind, be mindful of the tendency to create and critique simultaneously.
- This will significantly slow you down. At this stage, your goal is simply to generate as many different ideas as possible using brainstorming. Use *TOP Tool 33: Reframing Matrix.*
- When identifying the best solution, use other tools as appropriate—e.g. *TOP Tool 12: Decision Making.*
- When transforming the idea from concept to reality, make sure your action planning includes the marketing and business side, as well. Use *TOP Tool 1: Action Planning* to lay out the required activities.

Enablers:

TOP Tool 16: Facilitation
TOP Tool 12: Decision Making
TOP Tool 1: Action Planning
TOP Tool 30: Problem Restatement
TOP Tool 33: Reframing Matrix

References

Olsen, Robert W. *The Art of Creative Thinking.*

Applicable Job Aid, Template, Diagram, or Example:

While there is no job aid, template, etc., for this tool, the acronym DO IT is an excellent example of what Topper does on an ongoing basis, i.e. monitor and control Auto Pilot.

Over time, APT will erode your good intentions regarding each aspect of the DO IT philosophy:

- **Definition of the Problem**—Pattern recognition will eventually lead you down the path of, "I have seen this before and therefore I know exactly what the problem is." Step One of TOP, Frame Your Purpose, forces you to "reset" your thinking, or more specifically your state of mind surrounding the problem, so that you are consciously aware of the importance of defining the problem.
- **Open the Mind**—Biases, emotions, and habits close the mind to information that doesn't match your expectations or existing mindset. Topper thinks "reset" while Auto Pilot thinks, "repeat." Go with Topper!
- **Identify Best Solution**—Step Four of TOP, Structure Your Thinking, provides a host of tools and techniques for identifying the best solution. These tools assist you in identifying multiple alternatives, versus considering only one option, which is Auto Pilot's favorite approach.
- **Transform**—OPT helps you identify the activities required to transform ideas into reality. OPT is predicated on foresight and proactivity, versus hindsight and reactivity.

Make DO IT your primary mental model!

TOP Tool 15: Drill Down

Purpose:

"Determine Cause/Drill Down" tool for breaking complex problems into progressively smaller parts.

Summary:

The process for breaking the problem into its component parts is called "drilling down."

Steps:

1. Start by writing the problem down on the left hand side of a sheet of paper.
2. Write down the points that make up the next level of detail on the problem to the right; these may be factors contributing to the problem, information relating to it, or questions raised by it.
3. For each of the points in Step 2 repeat the process and continue drilling down until you fully understand the factors contributing to the problem.
4. If you can't break the issues down using the knowledge you have, then do the necessary research to gather that information

Guidelines/Options:

Drilling into the question deeply increases your understanding. Drill Down also prompts you to link information that might not have been previously associated with the problem. It also shows you exactly where you need further information.

Enablers:

TOP Tool 16: Facilitation

References

Mind Tools. *Excellent Skills for an Excellent Career.* London, UK: Mind Tools, Limited 2008.

Applicable Job Aid, Template, Diagram, or Example:

Example: Scenario 1—Green Light, Red Light

George Green was distressed that his team hadn't disclosed the deterioration of the situation to him until it was too late. Before he approached the team, however, he decided to perform a Drill Down on the problem himself. He followed the drill-down process to the letter and discovered some valuable information and perspectives. George's Drill Down network is recorded below:

Two key revelations came out of this simple but effective exercise:

1. George had never questioned or pushed back on any of the updates that were exclusively verbal in nature.
2. No team member had been required to put his or her status in writing and refer to it in the meeting. Instead, it was a simple conversation.

After this exercise, George changed his mind about pursuing the possibility of negligence or even sabotage. He would start improving the team from the "inside out" by talking about what he was going to do differently going forward at the next team meeting. He would then circle back with each team lead as necessary during their regular one-on-one sessions.

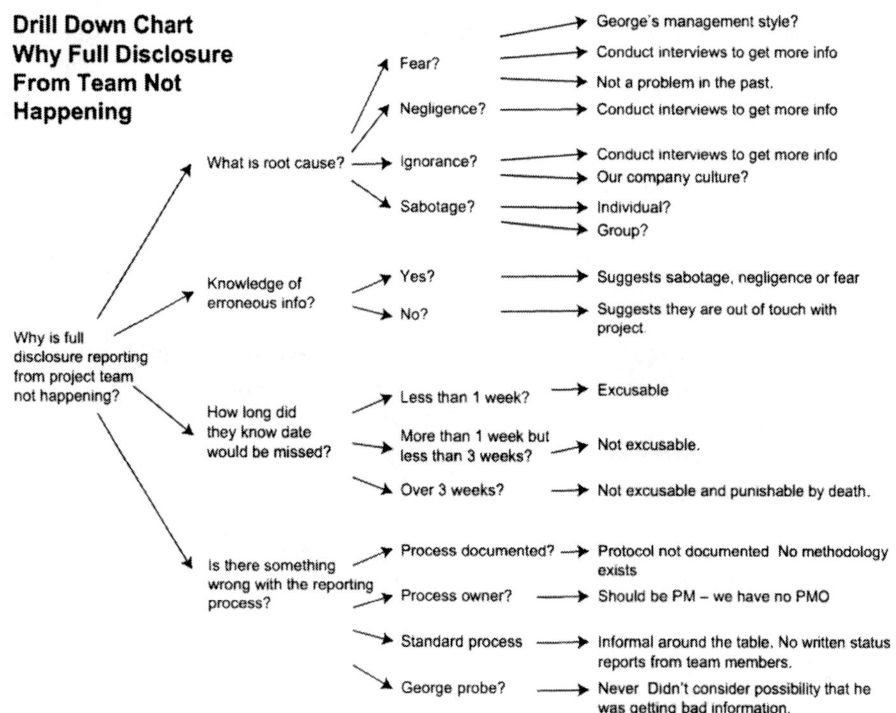

TOP Tool 16: Facilitation

Purpose:

"Action Enabler" tool that helps others complete their work and improve the way they work together.

Summary:

Facilitation needs to be a signature skill for every project or program manager. It takes knowledge, experience and hard work to reach a high level of proficiency in facilitation. Your ability to use TOP is directly linked to your skill as a facilitator. Facilitation is, in turn, linked to how you lead and manage your team. Remember that TOP is a T.E.A.M game: Teach It, Expect It, Anchor It, Model It.

Steps:

While there are no steps per se in the tool summary, there are four elements that underpin being a proficient facilitator:

1. Task—The work the group is trying to get done.
2. Process—Actions and tools that help a group get the work done
3. Group—Understanding group dynamics
4. Self—Use yourself as an instrument

The process in TOP of identifying your mindsets also applies to your team, both as individuals and collectively. (In the collective sense, mindsets are often referred to as "group think.")

Guidelines/Options:

I recommend two excellent books that every project or program manager should own, both physically and intellectually. I recommend you read them in the order given below:

1. *Managers as Facilitators*, by Richard G. Weaver and John D. Farrell, is a solid and practically written primer on what good facilitation looks like.
2. *The Skilled Facilitator*, by Roger Schwarz, builds on the previous book, and takes facilitation to a much deeper level.

I believe you can get by with the only the first book. But to excel in this area, I recommend that you study the second, as well.

Enablers:

Simply put, learn the basics, practice regularly and constantly ask for feedback.

References

Weaver, Richard G.; Farrell, John D. Managers as Facilitators: *A Practical Guide To Getting Work Done in a Changing Workplace.* San Francisco, CA: Berrett-Koehler Publishers, Inc., 1997.

Schwarz, Roger. *The Skilled Facilitator: A Comprehensive Resource for Consultants Facilitators, Managers, Trainers and Coaches.* San Francisco, CA.

Applicable Job Aid, Template, Diagram, or Example:

Job Aid: Summary of Facilitation Skills For Project Managers Engaging Facilitation Skills

These skills invite members to be a part of a group. They encourage a member to feel included and valued within the group context. They help group members reflect on what they already know and prepare them for interactive learning. Engaging skills are used to create curiosity, interest and energy. They encourage the discovery of personal meaning and interpersonal connections.

Demonstrating Leadership—This skill identifies you as the leader and lets group members know that you'll provide guidance, support, and structure for the group. Example: "Hey everybody, I'd like your attention! I'm Jordan and I'm going to be your orientation leader for the next two days."

Creating an Open Environment—There are things you can do as a leader to welcome new members to the group and make them feel included. Example: "I'm really glad that each of you are going to be living on the 9th floor of Aloha Tower this year. I think we're going to have a great time together. I'd like to go around the group and have everyone share one thing they're looking forward to at UH this year."

Encouraging Connections—In order to feel connected to a group, members need to get to know one another and see what they have in common. Example: "I'd like each of the representatives here to introduce themselves and say a few things about the group they represent, and what other groups here they interact with the most."

Building Group Rapport—One of the challenges of group leadership is creating camaraderie and good will within the group. It is important to encourage positive interactions that make members feel good about being part of the group. Example: "Thanks for coming to this time management workshop. Since I'm sure we all procrastinate, I'd like each of us to share one thing that we do to waste time when we're avoiding something more important."

Defining Group Identity—Every group has an identity and an atmosphere. As a leader, you will set the tone for defining what the group is all about and what it will feel like to be a member. Example: "Let me tell you about what the kayak club has been like and what we've done in the past, and then we can talk about whether we want to do the same things this year."

Informing Facilitation Skills

These are used to provide a group with information from outside the group and to help the group learn about itself.

Providing Information—Leadership often involves providing the group with pertinent information that they don't already have. This information might include facts, resources, knowledge, theories, or data. A lecture is one of many ways to provide information. Example: "There are several resources on campus that can help support our group activities. Let me tell you about some of them..."

Soliciting Information—A leader often needs to collect information from the group members. This can be done by asking open-ended questions, surveying ideas, or gathering data. Example: "What kinds of things have you done to effectively manage your stress in the past? Can I have two or three people share what has worked for them?"

Clarifying Ideas or Concepts—This skill involves making sure everyone understands what is being said or agreed upon. One way to clarify is to summarize the concept or idea and see if there are any misunderstandings. Example: "Let me make sure that I am clear on this. We would like to have quiet hours from 6:30 p.m. to 9:30 p.m. and then from 10:00 p.m. to 8:00 a.m. Is that what we're all agreeing on?"

Conceptualizing—Being a leader sometimes involves using new or outside knowledge to help the group better understand itself. Looking at the group using a particular theory, model, or concept is one example of conceptualizing. Example: "In my leadership class, I just learned about three styles of leadership. In our group, I think there is a conflict between those who favor an authoritarian style and those who prefer laissez-faire leadership."

Learning from Within the Group—In addition to providing information from outside the group, you can survey group members or gather information about the group itself. You might also use your observation skills to identify group characteristics, themes, or processes. Example: "In addition to the examples of study skills from the book, I'd like for us to identify our own skills. Let's go around the group and have each person identify one good study habit and one bad study habit they need to change."

Involving Facilitation Skills

These encourage positive interaction and learning between group members. These skills create an opportunity for active experimentation and encourage learning by practice and allow group members to put new knowledge to practical use. Because involvement occurs when group members themselves practice and gain hands-on experience, these facilitation skills require a shift in focus away from the leader and toward the group and the members within the group.

Inviting Participation and Interaction—Leadership often involves prompting group members to take action or to interact with one another. This interaction can occur within the present group or in the future. Example: "Let's break down into small groups so that everyone can share their ideas about how to better promote spiritual growth on campus."

Bouncing Back to the Group—The group's attention may naturally gravitate toward you as the leader. However, it is often helpful for you to deflect this attention and "bounce" the focus or energy back to the group itself to keep interaction and involvement high. Example: "That's a really good question. What have other people's experiences been in this situation?"

Recognizing Commonalities and Promoting Consensus—Promoting involvement often involves helping group members find similarities in ideas, interests, values, and plans. Conflicts often arise when the group focuses on differences rather than common ground. Identifying similarities can be used to support common goals. Example: "It sounds like you have different ideas about how clean you need your room to be but you both agree that you want to work this out and maintain a friendship. After hearing from both of you, let's agree on some minimum standards that would be mutually agreeable."

Supporting Cooperation and Group Cohesion—As the identity of the group continues to form and strengthen, a key leadership skill is to encourage supportive interactions and nurture the ongoing interdependence of the members so that they feel like they can accomplish more as a group than individually. Example: "As we continue to lobby against tuition raises, it is important that we show a united front. We need to make sure that we are supporting each other and communicating the same message. How should we present our collective point of view?"

Experimenting with New Behavior—Group learning often involves encouraging members to try new things. Experimenting can include role plays, work sheets, or other exercises, as well as simply suggesting alternate behaviors for members to try. Example: "Now that we've talked about different ways to meet people on campus, I'd like to do some role plays. Who would like to practice some of these skills?"

TOP TOOLS

Planning Facilitation Skills

These focus on planning for the future and applying learning from the group to other contexts. These skills encourage members to work together to make specific plans to accomplish group or individual goals. Planning skills prepare group members to move from active experimentation within the group to concrete experience beyond the group.

Brainstorming—One of the best ways for a group to start the planning process is by generating lots of ideas in a non-evaluative manner. Brainstorming allows a group to think of a diverse and large number of ideas in a short period of time without rejecting ideas too quickly. Example: "We need to think of some possible fund-raisers for the Spring semester. Let's shout out as many different ideas as possible without criticizing the ideas. We can go back and evaluate how realistic each idea is later."

Generalizing—This skill involves taking a successful behavior from one area and trying it in a new area. Example: "Now that we've all identified strategies that we used to achieve important goals in the past, let's see which of these strategies will help you achieve academic success here at UH."

Strategizing—After analyz Writing—Writing can be used as a way for members to privately organize their thoughts before sharing with the larger group. One way to do this is by handing out index cards and having members record their thoughts. (Supports all four facilitation skills.)

Applying—Once knowledge has been shared in a group, it should be put into action in a way that directly relates to the experience of the group. In this way, group members can take new learning home with them. Example: "Now that we've talked about the importance of verbally communicating about sex in order to prevent negative consequences like STDs and coercion, I'd like each of you to write down some things a student could actually say to a dating partner to bring up these topics...does anyone want to share what they've written?"

Making Specific Plans—Creating an action plan with specific steps, a time-line, and designation of who is going to take the lead on each section is a crucial skill in helping a group realize its goals. Example: "Now that we have passed legislation to spend money on improving library services, what specific steps are we going to take to accomplish this goal? Let's write them on the board and then assign leaders and a time-line."

Leadership Techniques that Support Group Facilitation

Checking-In/Round Robin—To ensure complete participation, it may be helpful to go around the group and have each member take a turn sharing. (Supports all four facilitation skills.)

Writing—Writing can be used as a way for members to privately organize their thoughts before sharing with the larger group. One way to do this is by handing out index cards and having members record their thoughts. (Supports all four facilitation skills.)

Using Humor—To build group rapport, you may want to use some moderate and appropriate humor. Humor should be used to create safety and not alienate or offend people in the group. (Engaging)

Self-Disclosing—At times, it is appropriate to share your own experience as an example or model. Self-disclosure can also be used to build rapport with the group by highlighting your similarity to group members. (Engaging/Informing)

Surveying/Voting—One way to gather information about a group is to survey all the members or to have them vote on a particular issue or idea. (Informing)

Modeling—Demonstrating skills and/or behavior is an active way of providing information to a group that prepares them for practice or other forms of involvement. (Informing / Involving)

Sharing in Pairs/Small Groups—Breaking the group into pairs or small groups allows all members to share their ideas in a less-threatening environment. After sharing in a small group, some members may find it more comfortable to share their ideas with the large group. Common themes can then be identified in an open discussion. (Involving)

Critiquing/Giving Feedback—One way to involve group members is to ask them to give feedback or to critique what you or others have said or done. It is important to encourage the group to start with strengths or positive feedback before suggesting areas for improvement. (Involving)

Role Playing—A great way to encourage new behavior is to ask group members to actually act out what they would do or say in a particular situation. Other group members can play other roles to flesh out the situation. (Involving /Planning)

Strategies for Improving Your Facilitation Skills

Identify Your Own Personality & Learning Style—This is important to know because your leadership style is likely to emphasize your preferences and overlook the needs of other styles.

Consider the Diversity of Learning Styles & Personality Types in Your Group— This will help you adapt various approaches to facilitation that meet diverse learning needs.

Reflect on Your Strengths and Weaknesses—Review the list of twenty facilitation

skills and make note of those that you consider personal strengths and those that need the most improvement.

Target Specific Skills for Practice—Look over the skills you have identified for improvement or addition and decide which skills you should work on first. It is best to target no more than two or three at a time.

Practice Skills in a Safe Environment—Identify a safe place, such as a leadership class, where it is okay to make mistakes and experiment with new techniques. This is the ideal way to start practicing new skills.

Identify Opportunities in Your Group to Improve or Try New Skills—Seek out diverse opportunities to practice facilitation in your group. Volunteer to facilitate a portion of your next meeting or give a presentation. Look for opportunities to practice facilitation skills in informal interactions with group members as well.

Ask Someone to Observe and Give You Feedback—Ask another leader to observe your facilitation skills and give you constructive feedback on what you did well and what you can improve.

Observe Other Leaders—Watch other leaders facilitate a group to discover ways to enhance your own skills. Use the Group Facilitation Skills Checklist to keep track of the skills you observe.

Videotape Yourself and Evaluate Your Skill Usage—Observe yourself on videotape to assess and improve your leadership.

The Nine Ground Rules, below, are excerpted from Roger Schwarz's book, and are a good set of guideposts for facilitating effectively:

1. Test assumptions and inferences
2. Share all relevant information
3. Use specific examples and agree on what important words mean
4. Explain your reasoning and intent
5. Focus on interests not positions
6. Combine advocacy and inquiry
7. Jointly design next steps and ways to test disagreements
8. Discuss undiscussable issues

Use a decision making rule that generates the level of commitment needed.

TOP Tool 17: Force Field Analysis

Purpose:

"Determine Cause/Drill Down" tool for showing which forces are working to stabilize a situation, and which ones are working to change it.

Summary:

Every situation has inherent stability as well as influences that are working to destabilize it. Understanding these are important for determining the forces at work in your situation so that you can plan for them or around them.

Steps:

1. Determine how you will use this information.
2. Outline the current situation.
3. Determine how you want to change the situation, and what your desired outcome looks like.
4. List forces at play that are destabilizing, or trying to create change.
5. List forces at play that are stabilizing, or resistant to change.
6. Create a plan to leverage or increase destabilizing or change-promoting, forces, and limit the effect of stabilizing or change resistant forces.

Guidelines/Options:

- After finishing this analysis, create a plan to incorporate your findings.
- Keep in mind that it's easier to identify destabilizing forces than it is to identify stabilizing ones, and so you may need to use questioning or other prompts to get past this blind spot.
- Brainstorming can help when using this tool, especially during steps 4 and 5.
- Stabilizing forces are difficult to spot, because they are part of the background assumptions of any situation. Use careful questioning and provocative questions to help your team isolate these forces.

Enablers:

TOP Tool 16: Facilitation

References

Jones, Morgan D. *The Thinker's Toolkit.*
New York: Three Rivers Press, 1998

Applicable Job Aid, Template, Diagram, or Example:

Diagram:

Force Field Diagram

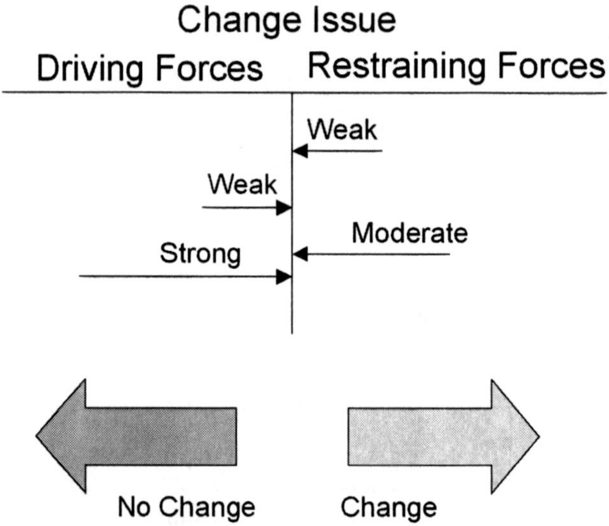

***Example from** Scenario 3—But Wait There's More!*

Tom used the Force Field Analysis technique to analyze the request for electronic signature capabilities from the sponsor, Karen Reid. Tom assembled his team and, after briefing them on the Force Field Analysis tool, facilitated a teamworking session focused on the situation. He used this technique to objectively uncover all the factors as part of his Situational Assessment. Once the list was assembled, he facilitated a second pass on the list to determine strong (S), moderate (M), and weak (W) factors.

Team List of Driving Forces

- Sponsor request itself, as she is a very senior executive (M)
- Sponsor's desire for a leading edge solution (W)
- Sponsors need for elimination of workload for signature verification (S)
- SVP Operation's (Tom's boss) strong desire to repair damage in the relationship with the Sponsor caused by a project disaster last year in the Audit line of the business (S)

Team List of Restraining Forces

- Strain on an already overworked team (S)
- Timeline extension inevitability, which would have a domino effect on other projects that require the same key resources (S)
- Need to take on new resources who have expertise in the new functionally and which is not available in the existing team (M)
- Budget increase inevitability, given resourcing and timeline requirements (W)
- Increased technology risk due to adding an unproven technology solution (M)

Tom used the output of this exercise to complete the TOP Situational Assessment.

TOP TOOLS

TOP Tool 18: Gap Analysis

Objective:

"Getting Started" tool for determining the difference between present state and desired state in an operation or process.

Summary:

Gap Analysis consists of defining the present state, the desired or "target" state and the gap between them. In the later stages of problem solving, the aim is to look at ways to bridge this gap.

Steps:

1. Current state:
   - Where are we now?
   - What are we doing now?
   - How are we doing it now?
2. Future State:
   - Where do we want to be?
   - What do we want to be doing?
   - How do we want to be doing it?
3. Performance Plan—how we intend to get there.

Guidelines/Options:

Gap Analysis alone is not adequate for all problem situations. As goals evolve and emerge during the course of problem solving, "what ought to be" can be a highly variable target. Also, some problems have many alternative solutions, in which case backward-chaining search strategies will have little practical use.

Enablers:

TOP Tool 16: Facilitation

References:

Not applicable.

Applicable Job Aid, Template, Diagram, or Example:

Example: *Gap Analysis from* *Scenario 2—All Together Now*

Caroline realized that the Project Charter was lacking a lot of key information, and she wanted the team to help her build a more comprehensive version. She decided to use a Gap Analysis approach, which allowed everyone to see what information was missing and how additional information would help increase the overall team understanding of the project. Her approach is outlined below, for the Regional Notification Program (RNP) Charter:

Example: Gap Analysis from Scenario 2—All Together Now

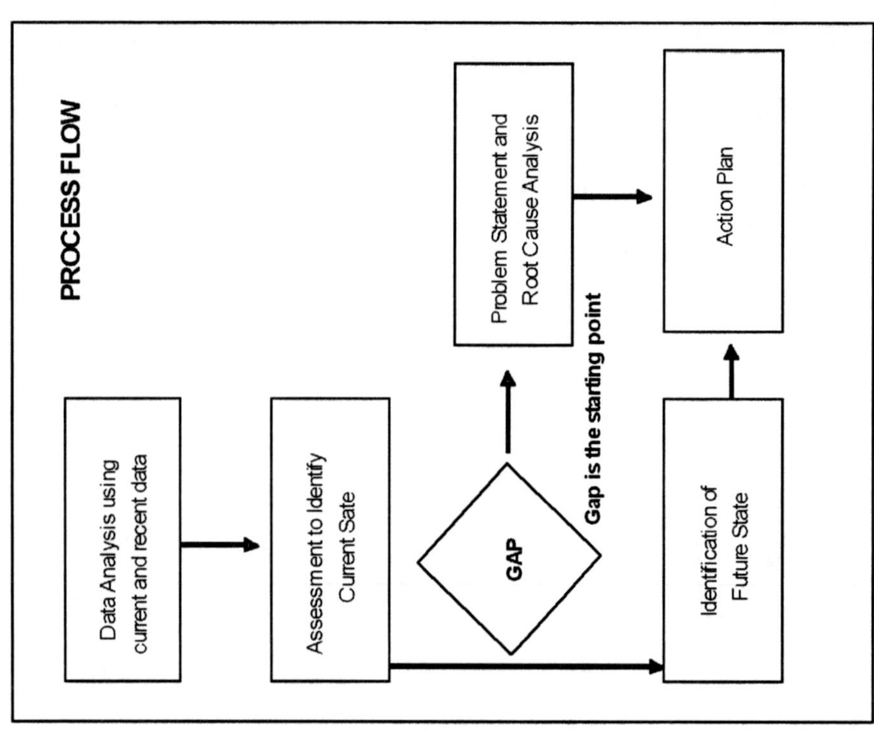

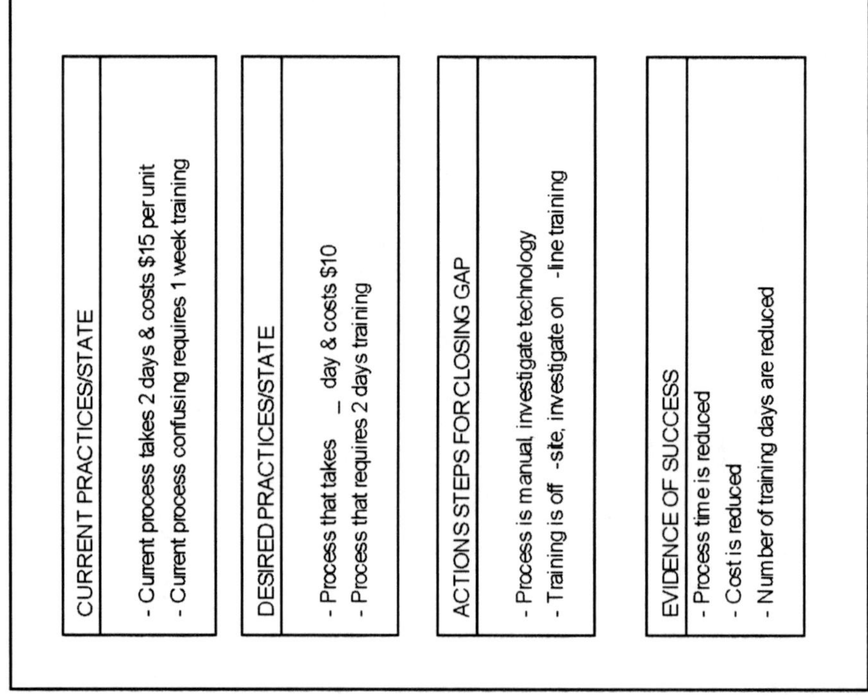

CURRENT PRACTICES/STATE
- Current process takes 2 days & costs $15 per unit
- Current process confusing requires 1 week training
DESIRED PRACTICES/STATE
- Process that takes _ day & costs $10
- Process that requires 2 days training
ACTIONS STEPS FOR CLOSING GAP
- Process is manual, investigate technology
- Training is off -site, investigate on -line training
EVIDENCE OF SUCCESS
- Process time is reduced
- Cost is reduced
- Number of training days are reduced

TOP Tool 19: Hypothesis Testing

Purpose:

"Determine Cause/Drill Down" tool for testing various hypotheses, in order to come to the correct problem statement.

Summary:

A hypothesis is a statement that we may believe to be true, but which has not yet been verified. In order to get to the truth of the matter, we need to move from unproven hypotheses to proven facts. We do this by testing our hypotheses until we discover which ones are true and which ones are not.

Steps:

1. List your hypotheses. For example, let's assume your car won't start. To find out why, you make a list of all the possible reasons: out of gas, bad ignition, bad battery, etc.
2. Build a matrix (see Matrix tool in this chapter). The first column of your matrix should be labeled Evidence. The remaining columns should each contain one hypothesis.
3. Down the left side of your matrix, enter your evidence for each hypothesis, including evidence you don't have. In our example, you would enter things like, "Car tried to turn over when key was turned, but didn't catch," and "I filled up the tank two days ago." Keep going until all of the evidence you currently have is listed.
4. Going across the matrix, determine if the evidence in each row is consistent or inconsistent with each hypothesis. Mark each box with a "C" or an "I" accordingly.
5. Go back and refine your matrix. Maybe a hypothesis needs to be reworded, or a bit of evidence added. Perhaps you've thought of further hypotheses that could be the culprit. Add these to your matrix.
6. Evaluate your work. Go through and eliminate any hypothesis that has little or no consistent evidence. Double-check your evidence and assumptions to make sure you aren't drawing any unwarranted conclusions.
7. Rank your results. The hypothesis with the most consistent evidence and least inconsistent evidence is your most likely answer.
8. Perform a sanity/reality check. Step back and review your conclusions. Do they fit the real world? Are they really possible and likely, or could

they be merely circumstantially supported by existing evidence? If you're convinced your answer is correct, go with it.

Guidelines/Options:

Hypothesis testing can be used as both a diagnostic and a decision making tool (it plays the role of decision maker by eliminating all but one of the hypotheses). Remember the main purpose of this tool is to disprove, not prove, a hypothesis and it is a powerful, versatile tool that can be used to analyze past, present, and future events.

Enablers:

TOP Tool 16: Facilitation
TOP Tool 22: Matrix and Grids

References

Jones, Morgan D. The Thinker's Toolkit. New York: Three Rivers Press, 1998

Applicable Job Aid, Template, Diagram, or Example:

Example: Scenario 1—Red Light, Green Light

George Green used Hypothesis Testing as a way of getting to the bottom of the problem in Red Light, Green Light. While the evidence clearly showed that the cause of the problem was lack of staffing in Network and Development, poor project management fundamentals played a big hand in preventing the exposure of these issues earlier in the project life cycle, when there was more time left in the schedule to fix it.

The matrix used by George as part of his problem solving process is below:

REF	EVIDENCE	HYPOTHESES		
		Poor Project Management (Plan, Monitor, Control)	Poor Reporting by Team Leads	Staffing: Lack of required resources, i.e. Network and Development
1	Project activities are slipping	I	I	C
2	Inaccurate and inconsistent project reporting	C	C	C
3	Junior developer not able to work at same speed as senior	I	I	C
4	Time lines unrealistic given resourcing	C	I	C
5	Over allocated resources	C	I	C
6	Network staff diverted from project deliverables due to support day to day production	I	C	C
7	Late start on project activities due to unexpected training requirements for junior developer	I	I	C
8	PM "full empowerment" management style—minimal follow-up	C	C	I
9	PM did not establish exception reporting criteria	C	C	I
10	Experienced developer not available	I	I	C
11	Change process stopped all project activities being completed during the day	I	I	C
LEGEND C = CONSISTENT, I = INCONSISTENT				

TOP Tool 20: Information Analysis Standards

Purpose:

"Generic Format" tool for assessing the quality of your reasoning.

Summary:

Intellectual standards are concepts and principles by which reasoning should be judged, in order to determine its quality or value.

Steps:

There are nine intellectual standard areas with a set of questions implied for each standard:

- Clarity
  - Could you elaborate?
  - Could you illustrate what you mean?
  - Could you give me an example?
- Relevance
  - How does this relate to the problem?
  - How does that bear on the question?
  - How does that help us with the issue?
- Logic
  - Does all of this make sense together?
  - Does your first paragraph fit with your last?
  - Does what you say follow from the evidence?
- Accuracy
  - How could we check on that?
  - How could we find out if that is true?
  - How could we verify or test that?
- Depth
  - What factors make this a difficult problem?
  - What are some of the complexities of this question?
  - What are some of the difficulties we need to deal with?
- Significance
  - Is this the most important problem to consider?
  - Is this the central idea to focus on?
  - Which of these facts are the most important?
- Precision
  - Could you be more specific?
  - Could you give me more details?
  - Could you be more exact?

- Breadth
    - o Do we need to look at this from another perspective?
    - o Do we need to consider another point of view?
    - o Do we need to look at this in other ways?
- Fairness
    - o Is my thinking justifiable in context?
    - o Are my assumptions supported by evidence?
    - o Is my purpose fair given the situation?
    - o Am I using my concepts in keeping with educated usage or am I distorting them to get what I want?
- Precedence
    - o Has somebody in our organization done this before?
    - o Do we have a framework or template?
    - o Have "lessons learned" been recorded?
    - o Who would be "best in class" at doing this?

Guidelines/Options:

Apply these standards consistently.

Enablers:

TOP Tool 16: Facilitation

References

Paul, Richard W.; Elder, Linda. *Critical Thinking*. Upper Saddle River, NJ: Financial Times Prentice Hall, 2002.

Applicable Job Aid, Template, Diagram, or Example:

Job Aid: See Appendix 8—Information Analysis Standards

TOP TOOLS

TOP Tool 21: Ladder of Inference

Purpose:

"Determine Cause/Drill Down" tool for gaining understanding about beliefs and assumptions in play from either a personal or team perspective.

Summary:

The ladder of inference is a model that describes an individual's mental process while observing situations, drawing conclusions and taking action. When we say, "the fact is …" what we are often saying is, "the fact [as I understand it based upon my data selection process, cultural and personal background, judgments, beliefs, and assumptions] is..."

Steps:

1. **Directly Observable Data**—In conversation we are faced with a lot of directly observable data, including what people are saying as well as their non-verbal behavior. A metaphor for Directly Observable Data would be whatever a camcorder can record.
2. **Observe and Select Data**—Since you can't attend to everything on the first rung of the ladder of inference, you observe and select certain data to pay attention to while ignoring other data. Some of what you choose to pay attention to is selected consciously, but much of it happens outside of your awareness.
3. **Translate and Label Data**—In the second rung, you begin to infer meaning from the data by translating it into your own words and labeling it. Essentially, you say to yourself, "What does it really mean when this person says or does this?"
4. **Evaluate and Explain**—At the third rung, you evaluate and explain what you have translated and labeled at the second rung. Whereas on the second rung, you describe what is occurring, on this rung you judge it and create a causal explanation. You ask yourself, "In what way is this positive or negative?"
5. **Decide How To Respond**—On the fourth and final rung, you decide whether and how to respond.
6. **Our Inferences Become Data**—The ladder of inference is not linear. You turn the inferences that you make into facts that influence what you observe, and this becomes the basis for further inference. This is called a reflexive loop.

Guidelines/Options:

A very powerful application of the ladder of inference is to introduce it at the beginning of a project. When team members commit to individually and collectively examining their beliefs and assumptions and making them explicit, a great deal of time spent arguing and going around in circles can be eliminated.

Enablers:

TOP Tool 16: Facilitation

References:

Adapted from Argyris, 1985, and Action Design, 1997

Applicable Job Aid, Template, Diagram, or Example:

Diagram:

The following concept diagram can be used in any situation to understand the beliefs and assumptions in play during a one-on-one or team discussion:

Ladder of Inference

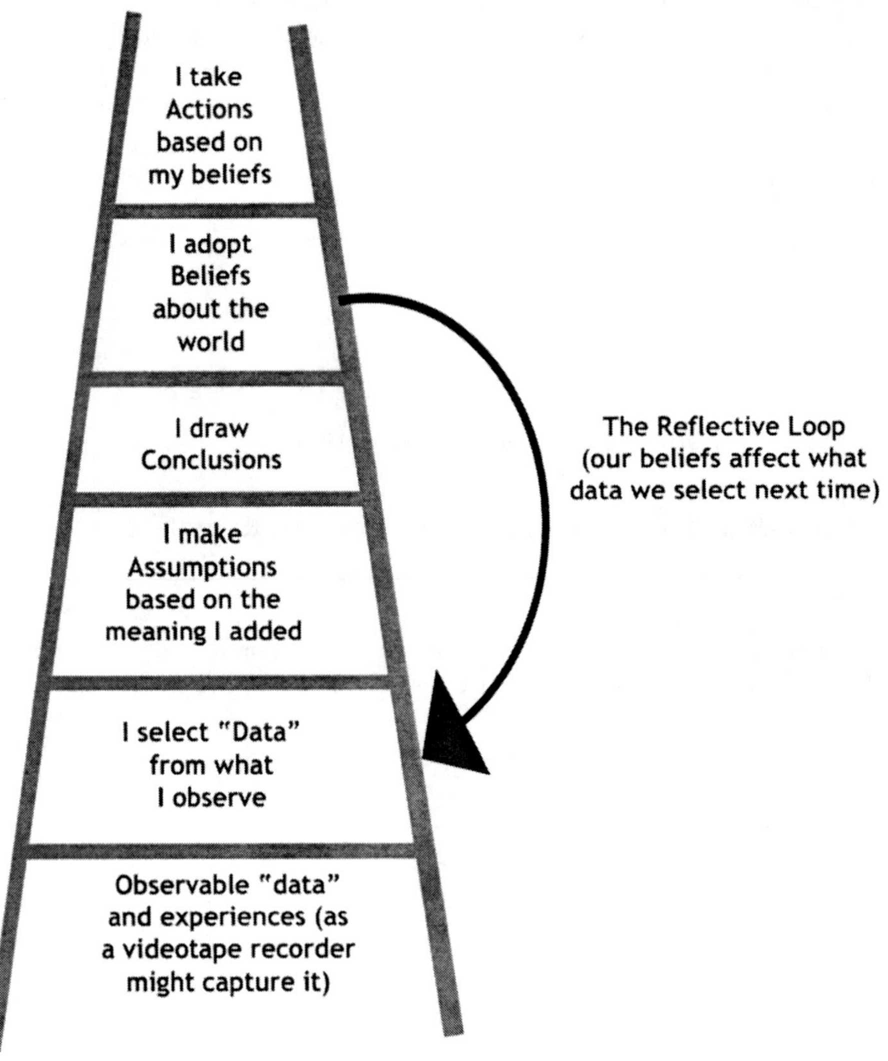
I take
Actions
based on
my beliefs
I adopt
Beliefs
about the
world
I draw
Conclusions
I make
Assumptions
based on the
meaning I added
I select "Data"
from what
I observe
Observable "data"
and experiences (as
a videotape recorder
might capture it)
The Reflective Loop
(our beliefs affect what
data we select next time)

TOP Tool 22: Matrix and Grids

Purpose:

"Generic Formats" tool for creating a visual structure to enable you to examine many different aspects of available information comparatively and quantitatively.

Summary:

A Matrix is just a grid or table. It is a handy format for laying out information that you need to compare or correlate. A spreadsheet is an example of a Matrix, as are tables and comparison charts. You've probably also used Matrices when solving logic puzzles that involve cross-referencing clues (e.g. Jane has red hair. The girl with blonde hair does not have a car. Bob rides a bike.).

To create a Matrix, you simply draw a table that contains as many rows and columns as you require and arrange the information within the table so that it makes sense and allows you to compare the data effectively. It is a quick and easy way to get a feel for a lot of complex and interwoven information at one time.

Steps:

Not Applicable

Guidelines/Options:

Enablers:

Microsoft Office Suite—Power Point, Excel, Word etc

References

Jones, Morgan D. The Thinker's Toolkit. New York: Three Rivers Press, 1998

Applicable Job Aid, Template, Diagram, or Example:

Example:

Where Matrices Are Applied in TOP Toolkit

TOP Tool 19: Hypothesis Testing
TOP Tool 25: Paired Comparison Analysis
TOP Tool 33: Reframing Matrix
TOP Tool 37 Stakeholder Assessment
TOP Tool 39: Utility Matrix

TOP Tool 40: Weighted Ranking

TOP TOOLS

Where Grids Are Applied in TOP Toolkit

TOP Tool 17 Force Field Analysis
TOP Tool 38: SWOT Analysis

TOP Tool 23: Mind Mapping

Purpose:

"Establishing Connections" tool for helping project managers order and structure their thinking by mapping words and concepts.

Summary:

Mind Mapping is a technique for recording and displaying information that is radically different from the more traditional, linear methods. It allows for information to be associated in a visual, free-form manner. It provides a much more flexible approach to showing connections between pieces of information and events. Mind Mapping is different from concept mapping, in that a mind map has only one main concept while a concept map may have several. Mind Mapping can be applied in strategizing, planning, requirements analysis and execution activities within a project.

Steps:

1. Define your purpose for taking notes.
    - Bloom of ideas
    - Flow of ideas
2. Where your brain goes, you will follow.
    - Bloom plus flow of ideas
3. Two individuals' mind maps on an identical topic will look different.
4. Just capture ideas. Order comes later.
5. Starting position—follow the laws for now.
6. Use key words, identify main branches versus sub branches, and learn to draw simple icons.
7. Single key word generates more thoughts than a phrase.
8. Get ideas for idea-mapping applications by seeing others' examples.
9. Try using mind-mapping software for different mind mapping options.
10. Be patient with yourself. You're learning a new skill.
11. Clearly identify a single, simple, and specific topic for the Team Mapping Method.
12. Always start the team mapping process by asking each participant to create an individual map around the defined topic.

Guidelines/Options:

Possible Mind Mapping applications:

- To do list
- Decision making

- Keeping a journal
- Personal planning
- Vision or Mission
- Goals
- Client
- Project Plan
- Problem solving
- Book
- Preparing and delivering a presentation
- Article
- Phone calls
- Job or process description
- Writing a document
- Status meeting
- Study notes
- Team Mind Map
- Study Notes
- Capturing notes during a team meeting

Additional Options:

- Use single words or simple phrases for information
- Print words
- Use color to separate different ideas
- Use symbols and images
- Use shapes, circles, and boundaries to connect information
- Use arrows to show cause and effect

Enablers:

Software tools are available to enhance the creation, maintenance and display of mind maps.

References

Buzan, Tony. *The Ultimate Book of Mind Mapping.* London, Harper Thorsons, 2006.

Nast, Jamie. *Idea Mapping – How to Access Your Hidden Brain Power.* Hoboken, New Jersey: John Wiley and Sons, 2006.

Applicable Job Aid, Template, Diagram, or Example:

Example #1:

The following is an example of a mind map for De Bono's Six Thinking hats which is also TOP Tool #36.

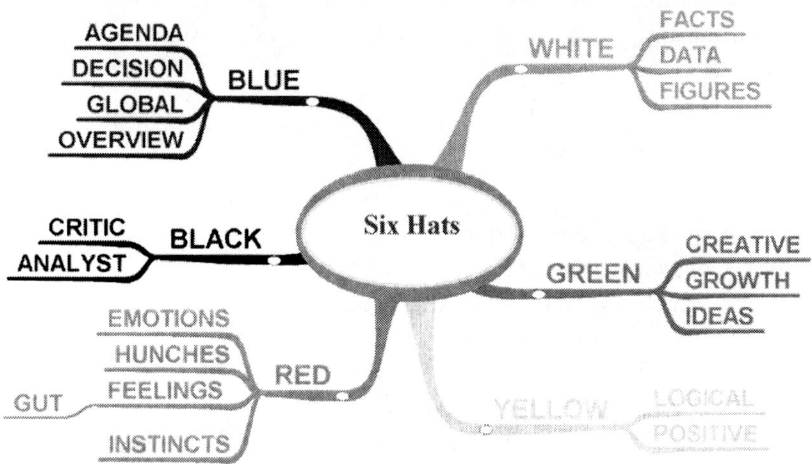

Example #2:

Using Mind Mapping to Plan a Business Trip

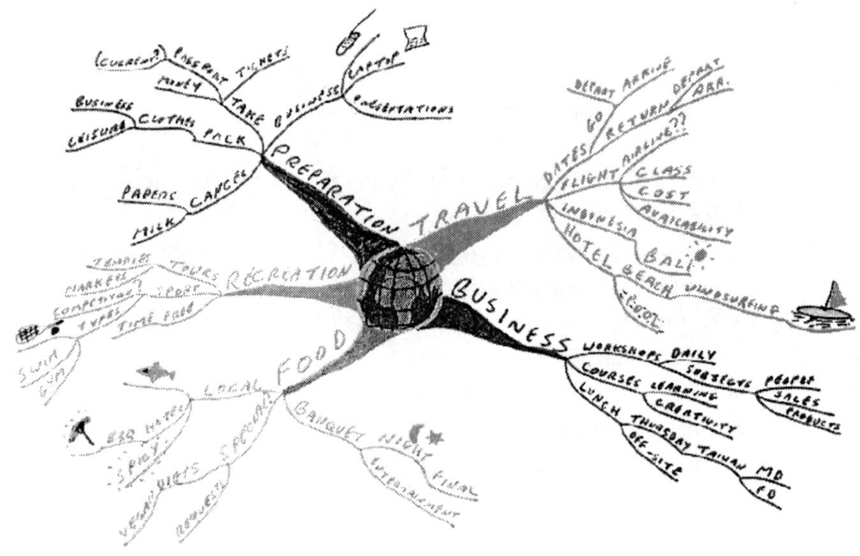

TOP Tool 24: Multi-Voting

Purpose:

"Decision Making" tool for organizing, sorting, prioritizing and consolidating a list.

Summary:

Multi-Voting is a "rough and ready" tool for taking a large list of items, for example from a brainstorming session, and using ranking/consolidation techniques to reduce and organize those items.

Steps:

1. Determine the purpose for the exercise (i.e. sorting, consolidating, reducing, a combination, etc.)
2. Consolidate like items.
3. Decide on voting criteria (i.e. vote for ideas with the greatest perceived value, or lowest cost)
4. Decide how many votes there will be, how many votes can be cast for an item and who will be voting.
5. Let everyone know how many votes they will be casting (remember, everyone gets the same number of votes).
6. Take a few moments to let everyone decide how he or she will vote.
7. Vote.
8. Examine the results and sort or reduce the items according to those results.
9. Repeat as necessary.

Guidelines/Options:

- Everyone gets the same number of votes.
- The number of votes per person = 1/2 to 1/3 the total list.
- Number or otherwise identify the items before voting to avoid confusion.
- If necessary, hold the voting in secret. Otherwise, a show of hands or other public voting is fine.
- Make sure there is agreement on how many votes can be cast per item, or if there will be a specific vote distribution (i.e. three votes for first choice, two for second and one for third). Also determine if voters can cast all their votes for a single option, or if they must be spread out.

Enablers:

TOP Tool 16: Facilitation

References

Weaver, Richard G.; Farrell, John D. *Managers as Facilitators: A Practical Guide To Getting Work Done in a Changing Workplace.* San Francisco, CA: Berrett-Koehler Publishers, Inc., 1997.

Applicable Job Aid, Template, Diagram, or Example:

Not Applicable

TOP Tool 25: Paired Comparison Analysis (PCA)

Purpose:

"Decision Making" tool for working out the importance of a number of options relative to each other, especially when the data available is generally subjective.

Summary:

PCA helps assists in the selection of the most important problem to solve or selecting the best solution.

Steps:

1. List the options you need to compare and letter each option.
2. Mark the options as row and column headings on the worksheet.
3. Block out cells in the matrix where a option is being compared to itself.
4. For applicable cells, compare the option in the row with the option in the column. For each cell comparison, decide which of the two options is the most important.
5. Record the option that is more important in the cell and decide the degree of difference between the two options using a scale of 0 to 3. (0 means no difference, 3 means significant difference.
6. Consolidate the results by adding up the total of all values for each of the options.

Guidelines/Options:

Matrix cells containing options that are compared to themelves or for a second time can be darkened for clarity.

To enhance contrast, you can convert the values to a percentage of the total score. Can be used in a team environment, either as a collective whole or individually, to facilitate comparison.

Enablers:

TOP Tool 16: Facilitation
TOP Tool 22: Matrix and Grids

References

Mind Tools. Excellent Skills for an Excellent Career. London, Mind Tools Limited 2008

Applicable Job Aid, Template, Diagram, or Example:

Example: Scenario 2—All Together Now

Caroline used the Paired Comparison Analysis tool to determine the ranking of the four "want" criteria in her decision analysis. She recorded the four criteria down the left hand side and along the top of a plain matrix. She then compared the options against each other to determine a suggested ranking in her decision approach when using the Weighted Ranking option, as illustrated in TOP Tool 40: Weighted Ranking

DECISION CRITERIA

	Available Budget For Contractor (A)	Benefits Clearly Understood (B)	Unanimous Agreement (C)	Available Budget for Outsourcing (D)
Available Budget For Contractor (A)		A1	C3	0
Benefits Clearly Understood (B)			C2 B3	
Unanimous Agreement (C)				C1
Available Budget for Outsourcing (D)				

A = 1—rank 3rd

B = 3—rank 2nd

C = 6—rank 1st

D = 0—rank 4th

TOP Tool 26: Pareto Analysis

Purpose:

"Determine Cause/Drill Down" tool for identifying the most important problem to solve

Summary:

This tool uses the *Pareto Principle*, which says that by doing 20% of the work, you can generate 80% of the value. Essentially, this is a technique for finding the changes or impacts that will give the biggest benefits. It is useful in situation where there are many possible courses of action or possibilities.

Steps:

1. List the problems you face or the options you have available.
2. Group options where they are facets of the same larger problem.
3. Apply the appropriate score to each group.
4. Work on the group with the highest score.

Guidelines/Options:

The scoring mechanism mentioned in Step #3 above depends on the kind of problem you are trying to solve. For example, if you were trying to improve wait times for your customers, you would score options on the basis of time waited. If you were trying to improve turnaround on change records, you would score options on the basis of time taken to fix the problem.

Enablers:

Application of the Matrix Tool to summarize and analyze data

References:

Koch, Richard. *The 80/20 Principle—The Secret to Success by Achieving More With Less.* New York, NY: Doubleday, 1998.

Applicable Job Aid, Template, Diagram, or Example:

Example: Scenario 1—Red Light Green Light

After George Green, the project manager, had completed the Situational Assessment for the project, it was clear to him that the quality of the time estimates from Network and Development were a problem. Fortunately, the Development resources (five developers) had been asked to document their estimates and rationale for this project as part of a new estimating improvement initiative. Their estimates had been summarized, by job code and by individual, into a centralized database for the purposes of the estimating pilot.

With a quick phone call, George was able to obtain a matrix showing the components worked on by each development team member, along with the costs and schedule information to date. George received the following report showing baseline estimates and up-to-date information by developer for their respective components of the build.

Element	Development Team					
	Dean Jones	Harley Richards	Bill Jamieson	Peter Simpson	Gerrard Wiemer	Total
Baseline Effort Estimate	10 Days	14 Days	9 Days	8 Days	12 Days	53 Days
Current Effort Estimate	11 Days	15 Days	24 Days	9 Days	11 Days	70 Days
Variance	+1 Day	+1 Day	+15 Days	+1 Day	-1 Day	-17 Days

Clearly, George had lucked out by finding the estimating pilot, since its information reports allowed him to discover that Bill Jamieson's component was a big contributor to the problem. This quick analysis is a good example of the 80/20 rule: Over 80% of the delays in the project came from 20% of team members. Interestingly, subsequent analysis revealed that the information reports were being produced regularly, but were not being communicated to George. Had they been so communicated, these reports would have triggered an investigation several weeks earlier and potentially prevented this problem from showing up so abruptly.

TOP TOOLS

TOP Tool 27: PMI—Plus/Minus/Interesting

Purpose:

"Decision Making" tool for confirming viability of decision before moving to action

Summary:

This technique is a refinement on the centuries old pros and cons approach. After a decision analysis has been completed with a course of action selected, Plus/Minus/ Interesting provides a "smell test" that the recommended decision is the correct one. It is always better to confirm that taking the action you are planning is better than a "do nothing" option.

Steps:

1. Draw a table with three columns headed Plus, Minus and Interesting.
2. Under the appropriate heading, write down the positive, the negative and all other interesting implications and possible outcomes.

Guidelines/Options:

If the decision is still not obvious or clear, you can score (numerically plus or minus) the table to show the importance of individual items. The total score should provide a perspective on whether the decision should be implemented or not.

Enablers:

TOP Tool 16: Facilitation

References

De Bono, Eward. *Serious Creativity: Using The Power of Lateral Thinking To Create New Ideas.* London: Penquin 1993

Applicable Job Aid, Template, Diagram, or Example:

Example: Scenario 3—But Wait, There's More!

Decision: **Complete the first project. Start up a new project to deliver the new functionality.**		
Plus	**Minus**	**Interesting**
All objectives are met for the first project. +5	New functionality that would help the sponsor is not being implemented in the first project. -3	The second project could leverage the technology and learnings from the first project and may come in under budget and in a reduced timeframe. +3
Project Manager and stakeholders transfer knowledge to the second project. +3	Subject matter experts (SMEs) could be moved to other initiatives and may not be available for the second project. -3	Availability of SMEs outside of the organization means less cost that doing it "in house." +2
Stakeholder forced to address SPOK. +2	SPOK (Single Point of Knowledge) unavailable. -4	Alternative technology provides solutions that are off the shelf and which don't rely on SPOK. +2
Budget met for the first project. +5	Costs more to initiate a second project than to add to the first. -2	Project Manager could spend more time controlling expenditures. +2
TOTAL = +15	TOTAL = -12	TOTAL = +9

TOP Tool 28: Provocation

Purpose:

"Expand Possibilities" tool for moving your thinking outside of the established patterns you use to solve problems.

Summary:

As explained in Chapter 3, we think by recognizing patterns and reacting to them. Our reactions are heavily influenced by our biases, which come from our past experiences and our logical extensions of those experiences. Often we do not think outside these patterns

and while we may know the answer as part of another problem, the structure of our brain does not make the connection. Provocation is a tool we can use to link these patterns by using a ridiculous statement or provocation to shock our brain out of its patterned thinking.

Once a provocative statement is made, we suspend judgment and use the statement to generate ideas. Edward De Bono developed this concept, and included it his book Serious Creativity as a means of developing more creative solutions to problems.

Steps:

1. Make a ridiculous statement or provocation in which something about the situation we take for granted is not true.
2. Examine the statement from a number of perspectives:
   - The consequences of the statement
   - What the benefits would be
   - What special circumstances would make it a sensible solution
   - The principles needed to support it and make it work
   - How it would work moment to moment
   - What would happen if a sequence of events was changed

Guidelines/Options:

While Provocation does not always produce good or relevant ideas, it often does.

Enablers:

Application does rely on all members of your team understanding how this technique works.

TOP Tool 16: Facilitation

References

De Bono, Edward. *Serious Creativity: Using The Power of Lateral Thinking to Create New Ideas*. London, UK: Penguin 1993.

Applicable Job Aid, Template, Diagram, or Example:

Not applicable

TOP Tool 29: Probability Tree

Purpose:

"Decision Making" tool for determining the probability that various individual scenarios will occur.

Summary:

A Probability Tree is simply a Decision Tree that is designed to illustrate the probability of something happening. You can use it to help you predict things like who will win an election.

Steps:

1. Identify the problem you are trying to solve.
2. Identify the events and factors you need to evaluate.
3. Build a Decision Tree portraying all reasonable alternatives, making sure that events or alternatives at each new branch are both mutually exclusive and collectively exhaustive.
4. Give each event or decision a probability, totaling 100%.
5. Determine the conditional probability of each situation.
6. Calculate the probability of each event or decision.

Guidelines/Options

- There are two types of probability events: mutually exclusive events, in which one result or the other must occur (either a match lights, or it doesn't), and conditionally dependent events, in which one event must happen in order for the next event to happen (the key must be inserted into the lock and turned, which lifts the tumblers and unlocks the door).

- It is useful to remember that in order to calculate mutually exclusive probabilities, you break down the total probability (100%) based on the number of options and their percentage of probability. (If you have four events that are equally possible, then each has a 25% chance of happening, since 100% divided by 4 is 25%.) In order to calculate the probability of conditionally dependent events, you multiply the probability of each event. (If you have two events which are each 50% likely to occur, the probability of both occurring is 25%, since .5 x .5 = .25.) Also, if you have no information as to the likelihood of events, for these purposes, you should assign them all equal probability.

- A Probability Tree, in addition to the attributes of a Decision Tree, enables analysis of the entire Tree and any of its elements from the perspective of probability. In addition, it enables you to estimate which scenarios are most and least likely.

Enablers:

TOP Tool 16: Facilitation

References

Jones, Morgan D. The Thinker's Toolkit. New York: Three Rivers Press, 1998.

Applicable Job Aid, Template, Diagram, or Example:

Example: Scenario 3—But Wait, There's More!

Tom's boss, Dave Moody, asked Tom for his assessment of the likely outcome of the proposed presentation to the Steering Committee. Tom used the Probability Tree to develop a quick assessment for his boss.

Tom drew the diagram below on Dave's office white board, and then talked through how the Probability Tree demonstrated his projection that the probability of their recommendation being accepted was 50/50. Tom also explained that if the recommendation was rejected there was a very good chance (80 %) that further discussion would be possible.

His final projections were:

- Accepted outcome: 50 %
- Reject by further discussion: 40 %
- Reject and mandatory implementation of the additional functionality: 10 %

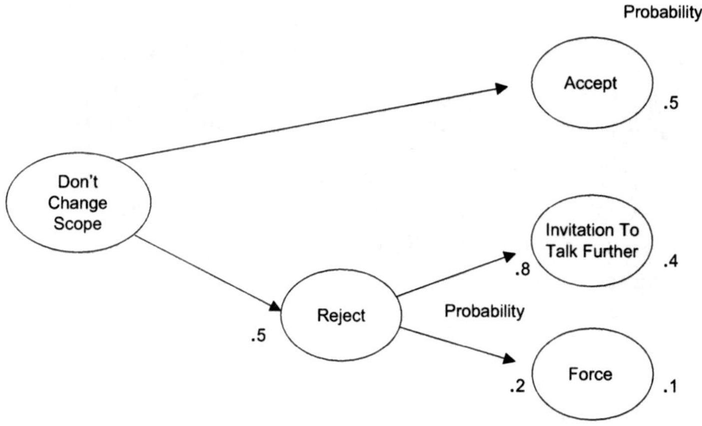

TOP TOOLS

TOP Tool 30: Problem Restatement

Purpose:

"Expand Possibilities" tool that helps determine the actual root cause of a problem.

Summary:

One of the biggest reasons that solutions fail is because they solve the wrong problems. For example, if you were hired by a client who has problems with a slow assembly line, you might start out by trying to solve the problem of how to speed the line up. But if the root cause of the slowdown is shoddy parts that don't fit well, simply moving things faster won't help.

By restating a problem, you can make sure you're solving the true root cause and not just the symptoms.

Steps:

1. Paraphrase: Restate the problem in your own words. Try to find several different ways to say the same thing.
2. 180 Degrees: State the reverse of the current problem. For example, in our current scenario, you might ask, "How can we slow the line down?" By answering that question, you can develop a better insight as to what the root cause might be, and you may turn up problems no one was aware of.
3. Broaden Your Focus: Think about your problems in a bigger picture. For example, instead of asking, "Should I take this client?" you might restate the question as, "What direction do I want my business to take, and what sort of clients best support that vision?"
4. Redirect Your Focus: Completely change the problem. Instead of asking, "How can we make the assembly line go faster?" you might ask, "How can we improve employee job satisfaction?" This option can open your eyes to other methods of solving the problem.
5. Ask Why: Sometimes, acting like a five-year-old can be useful. For each problem statement, ask "Why?" Use the answer to that question to restate the problem. Repeat. This helps you identify root causes and alternate solution paths.

"How can we speed up the line?"

"Why?"

"We are losing customers to late shipments."

"How can we avoid losing customers?"

"Why?"

"The cost of losing customers and finding new ones is wiping out our profit margin."

"How can we prevent losing customers from impacting the bottom line?" ...and so on.

In this example, the real problem is money lost to dissatisfied customers, and you may find that it's simply easier and cheaper to reset customer expectations of delivery time, or increase customer service elsewhere to make up for slower assembly times. Or not. But either way, you have new avenues to explore.

Guidelines/Options:

- Reframing a problem in a number of different ways before selecting a problem statement helps you make sure that you've best captured the essence of the problem. Be sure to reframe as many times as necessary until you feel positive you have reached the true root cause.
- Repeating this process several times during the problem-solving process is also helpful, since there are various stages of a problem-solving process where root causes or motivator might be obscured by assumption or other MindFields.

Enablers:

TOP Tool 18: Gap Analysis

References

Jones, Morgan D. *The Thinker's Toolkit.* New York: Three Rivers Press, 1998

Applicable Job Aid, Template, Diagram, or Example:

Example: Scenario 3—But Wait, There's More!

Tom knew that one of the ways to get to the root cause of a problem was a simple process called Problem Restatement. He liked the tool because you could do it by yourself or with a group. In this case, he decided to do a Problem Restatement with the project team.

He began the process by stating the problem in his own words: *The project sponsor wants to add new functionality to the project, which is well underway.*

- **Paraphrase—Create alternative ways to describe the problem**
  - Scope creep
  - Project sponsor wants more deliverables
  - Project sponsor wants to add more features after the scope has already been established
  - Project being impacted by scope creep
- **180 Degrees—State the reverse of the problem**
  - Be happy the sponsor has requested new functionality after the scope has already been established.
- **Broaden Your Focus—Think of the problem in a bigger picture**
  - What value will the new functionality bring to our company?
  - How could the changes to the project affect other projects?
- **Redirect Your Focus—Change the problem**
  - How can we improve the current deliverables?
  - How can we use the project team more efficiently?
  - Are there any other projects doing something similar?

Ask Why

"The Project Sponsor wants to add new functionality to the project, which is well underway."

"Why?"

"To add an electronic signature and additional audits."

"Why?

"To save hours chasing down signatures and establish one repository that would be the book of record."

Result: How can we reduce approval time without adding technology immediately?

Result: Where can we store additional audits until the system is set up to add capacity?

Tom was amazed how simply restating the problem and asking questions could bring so much information forward. This was definitely a process he would use again.

TOP Tool 31: Problem Solving (PA)

Purpose:

"Action Enabler" tool that facilitates identifying root cause of a problem.

Summary:

Problem Solving is a structured process designed to neutralize the effects of APT by using a four-step process along with probing questions:

Steps:

1. **Describe the problem**—Aimed at obtaining clarity about what is the problem through questions like 1) What is and what is not happening, 2) Where is it and where is it not happening, and 3) When is it and is it not happening?
2. **Generate possible causes**—Aimed at using brainstorming techniques to identify all the possible causes of symptoms of the problem.
3. **Test possible causes**—Aimed at systematically testing each possible cause to either identify it for further analysis or rule it out completely.
4. **Confirm root cause**—Aimed at definitively stating the root cause of the problem and where necessary, if not confirmed, degree of probability. The idea is to be sure that corrective action being taken is solving the root cause.

Guidelines/Options:

Where possible, problem solving should be a team game.

Enablers:

TOP Tool 5: Brainstrorming

TOP Tool 16: Facilitation

TOP Tool 20: Information Analysis Standards

References

Not Applicable

TOP TOOLS

Applicable Job Aid, Template, Diagram, or Example:

Template: A completed example using the following template can be found in Chapter 6—Thinking On Purpose in Action

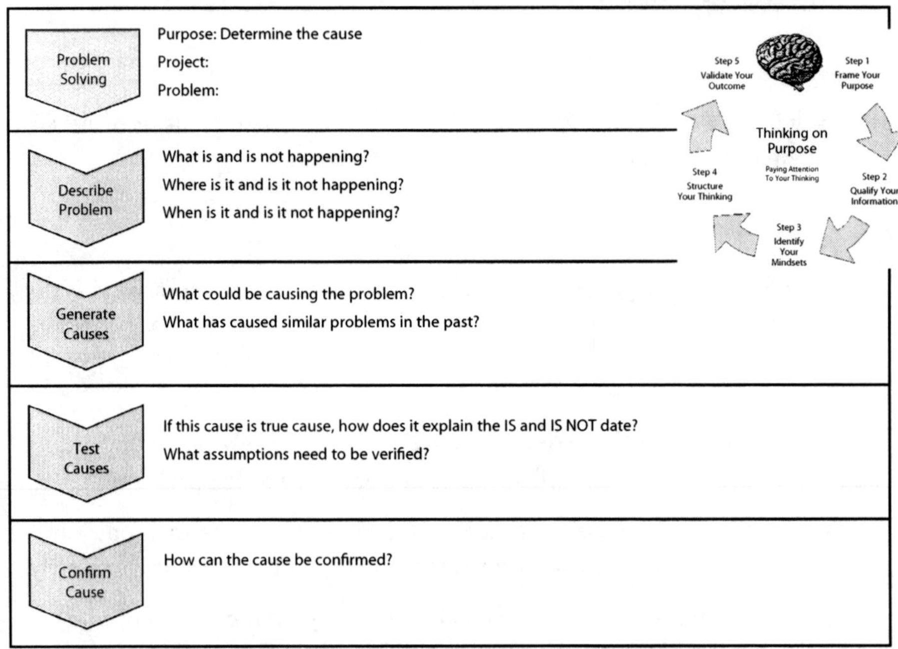

Problem Solving
Purpose: Determine the cause
Project:
Problem:
Describe Problem
What is and is not happening?
Where is it and is it not happening?
When is it and is it not happening?
Generate Causes
What could be causing the problem?
What has caused similar problems in the past?
Test Causes
If this cause is true cause, how does it explain the IS and IS NOT date?
What assumptions need to be verified?
Confirm Cause
How can the cause be confirmed?
Thinking on Purpose
Paying Attention To Your Thinking
Step 1 Frame Your Purpose
Step 2 Qualify Your Information
Step 3 Identify Your Mindsets
Step 4 Structure Your Thinking
Step 5 Validate Your Outcome

TOP Tool 32: Process Mapping

Purpose:

"Establishing Connections" tool that creates a step-by-step map of a process.

Summary:

Before beginning any project, it is often valuable to map out the processes involved in that project before work begins. This ensures that all steps are accounted for and are completed in order, that the best process is determined, that any redundant or unnecessary steps are eliminated, and that problems areas are identified and steps taken to mitigate them.

Steps:

1. Identify the reasons for creating the map.
2. Summarize the process to be mapped in a few sentences.
3. Decide how detailed you want to get, but be flexible. You may need to go into further detail in some areas, while others can be dealt with at a higher level.
4. Set down the start and finish points of the process.
5. Let each person responsible for specific tasks outline their own areas of responsibility in front of the rest of the participants. This way, everybody understands what is involved in these tasks and how they will be done.
6. Use the Consensus tool to make sure that the process map is complete and accurate.
7. Answer these questions based on the map to make sure everyone understands their responsibilities and next steps:
   - Does every task or job have someone responsible for completing it?
   - Are there any gaps, overlaps, or other discrepancies?
   - Are the biggest problem areas identified?
   - Are all steps necessary and unique, or can we drop some?

Guideline/Options

- Disagreements about the process being mapped often highlight problem areas. Pay special attention to these issues to ensure everyone is on the same page when the work begins.
- Make sure that those responsible for completing different jobs or processes are identified.
- List each step individually on a sticky note or card, so it can be moved around during the discussion process

- Set out metrics or other ways of measuring the process to make sure it is proceeding according to plan.
- Consider creating an "ideal process" map after you complete the actual process map. The differences may provide food for thought.

Enablers:

- Mind Mapping techniques can be used to identify tasks.
- Affinity analysis can be used to cluster the groups of tasks into logical groupings.
- Project management software, like Microsoft Project, can be used to enhance the activity identification, recording and summarization approaches.
- Flow Charting Symbols.

A flowchart is a pictorial identification of the steps or tasks in a process using boxes or other symbols to represent steps.

While symbols vary, the following are common:

⬬ An ellipse may be used to identify inputs (tasks, information, etc.) necessary to start the process.

■ A step or task, or activity in the process can be shown with a box or triangle.

◆ A diamond designates a point where a decision has to be made.

● A circle with a letter, number, or both shows a continuation point that will have a corresponding point somewhere else on the diagram.

→ An arrow defines the direction or flow of the process.

Information on additional flow-charting symbols can be obtained at: http://www.nos.org/htm/basic2.htm

References

Jones, Morgan D. *The Thinker's Toolkit.* New York: Three Rivers Press, 1998.

Applicable Job Aid, Template, Diagram, or Example:

Example: Scenario 1—Red Light, Green Light

George knew that some people were very visually oriented, so he decided to put together a simple flow chart to depict what activities needed to take place in order to implement the technical activities.

He showed the team this first page to see if a flow chart would help them with their planning. They all agreed that the chart would help them complete the process.

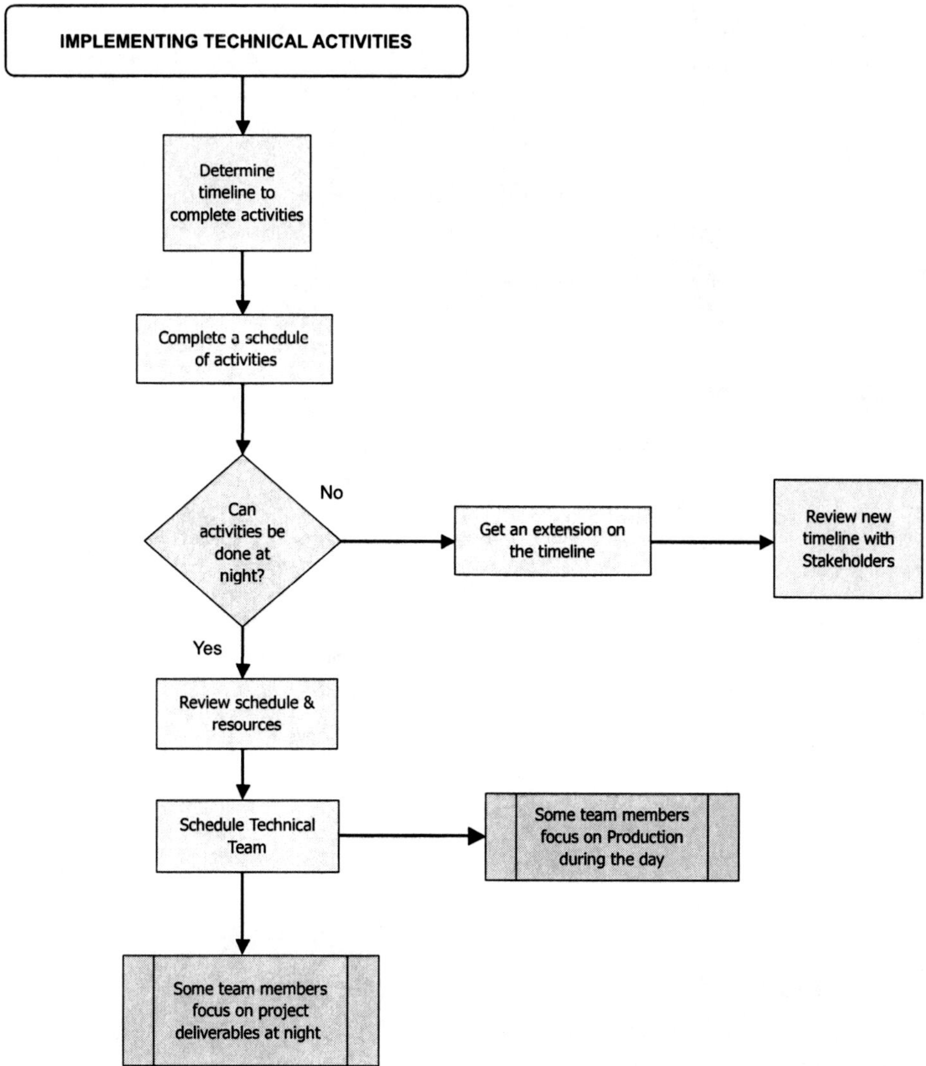

TOP Tool 33: Reframing Matrix

Purpose:

"Expand Possibilities" tool that looks at business problems from a number of different perspectives.

Summary:

This approach relies on the fact that different people with different experiences will probably approach similar problems in different ways. This technique helps you put yourself into the minds of different people and imagine the solutions they would come up with.

Steps:

1. Put the problem or question to be asked in the middle of a grid.
2. Use boxes around the grid for the different perspectives.
3. Four Ps Approach:
    - Product Perspective: Is there something wrong with the product.
    - Planning Perspective: Are our business plans or marketing plans at fault?
    - Potential Perspective: If we were to seriously increase our targets, how would we achieve these increases?
    - People Perspective: Why do people choose one product over another?
4. Professions Approach:
    - Look at the situation from the viewpoint of different professions.
    - For example, a doctor would have a different perspective than a civil engineer than a sales person.

Guidelines/Options:

In project management, the professions approach could be replaced by Stakeholders or other functional groups—e.g. marketing, sales, IT, finance.

Enablers:

TOP Tool 16: Facilitation

References

Morgan, Michael. *Creating Workforce Innovation: Turning Individual Innovation into Organizational Innovation.* 1983.

Applicable Job Aid, Template, Diagram, or Example:

Job Aid:

In this hypothetical project, the project is now forecast to go over budget.

The grid opposite provides a framework for looking at the potential problem from multiple perspectives—Product, Planning, Potential, and People. For example, in this situation it might be that the root cause of the problem is the wrong vendor being chosen, which could very well be outside the accountability of the project manager.

Product Perspective :	**Planning Perspective:**
Are the requirements correct? Is the right technology being used? Was the right vendor selected?	Is the Project Plan optimized? Are the deliverables being tracked? Is the scope being maintained?
Potential Perspective:	**People Perspective:**
Can the Project Plan be crashed? Are there more resources available? Can the timeline be extended?	Are the right people in the right roles? Are the stakeholders engaged? Is Senior Management supportive?

Problem:
Project is forecasting to be over budget

TOP Tool 34: Risk Assessment

Purpose:

"Action Enabler" tool that provides a rudimentary framework for assessing the level of risk in either a decision-making or action-planning situation.

Summary:

While assessing risk is good practice in every situation, scale is the variable factor. The degree of intensity to be applied in a risk assessment for a major IT project would be greater than for a ten-activity work plan to move furniture in the office. The same mechanics are applied to both but in different degrees. The real purpose of assessing risk is to answer these questions in advance: "What could go wrong?" "What could we do to prevent it?" and "If it did go wrong, what would we do about it?" Risk assessment is a dynamic process that should have energy throughout the life cycle of the initiative or project.

Steps:

1. Identify the risks by asking the question—What could go wrong?
2. Qualify or prioritize the risk by asking the questions—What is the probability and what is the impact?
3. Plan the response by asking the questions—What can be done to reduce the probability and what can be done to reduce the impact?
4. Monitor and control the risk by asking the question—Who is monitoring the risk?

Guidelines/Options:

The key is making Risk Assessment an ongoing activity that is focused on preventing problems or negative situations. Risk Assessment is simply foresight being applied situationally. For complex project situations there will be a need to apply a more detailed and rigorous Risk Assessment. Don't forget about the opportunities perspective on risk analysis.

Enablers:

A "risk register" is used in both manual and computer applications for identifying and managing risk. Essentially, the risk register provides a common tool for both identification and communication of risks. The magic of the risk register is that as risks are identified, the form provides a trigger or template for recording the results of the following steps in the process. This upfront part is often referred to as risk planning.

A risk register usually records the output of the following:

- Identify the risks
- Qualify the risks (What are the most important risks to consider?)
- Quantify the risks (How much money is at stake and how much needs to be put away in a contingency plan?)
- Response Strategy (How will the risks be responded to if they did happen?)
- Monitoring and Control (Who and when?)

An example risk register from *Scenario 2—All Together Now* is included after the template below.

References:

Project Management Institute. *Project and Program Risk Management—A Guide to Managing Project Risks and Opportunities* Project Management Institute, 1992.

Project Management Institute. *A Guide to the Project Management Body of Knowledge*. Project Management Institute, 2004.

Kenrick, Tom. Identifying and Managing Project Risk. New York: AMACOM, 2003.

Applicable Job Aid, Template, Diagram, or Example:

Template: A completed example using the following template can be found in Chapter 6—Thinking On Purpose in Action.

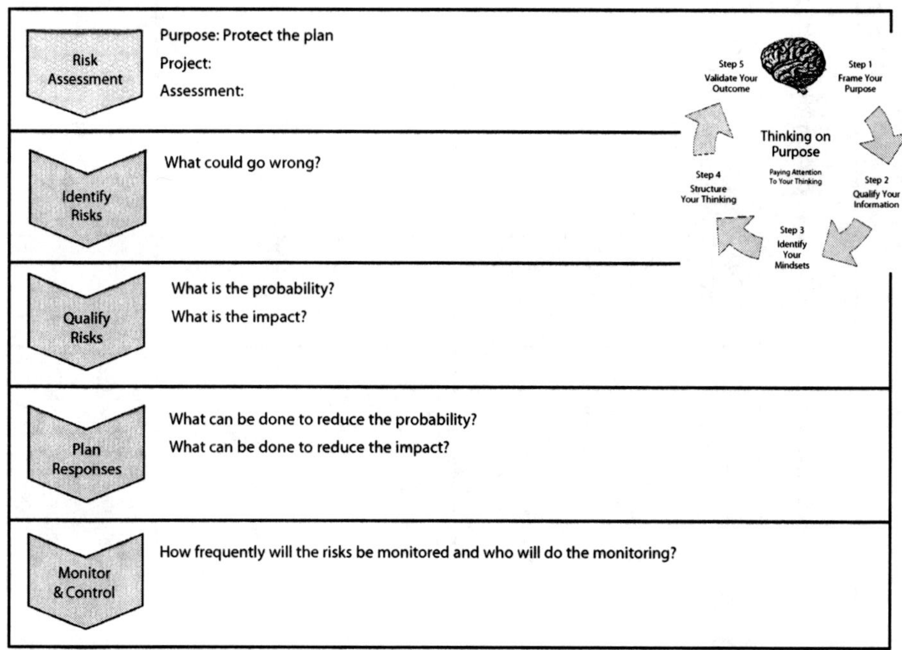
Risk Assessment
Purpose: Protect the plan
Project:
Assessment:
Step 5
Validate Your Outcome
Step 1
Frame Your Purpose
Thinking on Purpose
Paying Attention To Your Thinking
Step 4
Structure Your Thinking
Step 2
Qualify Your Information
Step 3
Identify Your Mindsets
Identify Risks
What could go wrong?
Qualify Risks
What is the probability?
What is the impact?
Plan Responses
What can be done to reduce the probability?
What can be done to reduce the impact?
Monitor & Control
How frequently will the risks be monitored and who will do the monitoring?

Risk Register

Example: from All Together Now—Scenario #2

Risk Management Template — Risk Register All Together Now — Scenario #2								
Decision: **A major project review at the executive level weighing this project against all other projects in the organization with the option of cancellation if not a strategic fit.**								
Ref #	**Risk Event & Description**	**Prob. (HML)**	**Impact (HML)**	**Overall (HML)**	**If Risk Occurs, Action Required by:**	**If Risk Occurs, Escalate to:**	**Risk Response (Avoid, Accept, Mitigate, Transfer)**	**Risk Reponse Description**
1	Loss of team members to other projects while executive project review is being completed.	H	H	H	Brian (Project Manager)	Caroline (Program Manager)	Transfer	Start negotiations with contractors/ outsourcer to replace project team members if necessary. Possibly outsource development and hire contractors to replace Project Manager.
2	Loss of funding to other initiatives.	M	H	H	Caroline (Program Manager)	Mike Kelly (Project Sponsor)	Accept	Depending on the outcome of the executive review, the project could be cancelled. It makes sense to release the funds for other projects and resubmit funding proposals if necessary.
3	Strong negative executive reaction.	M	M	M	Caroline (Program Manager)	Mike Kelly (Project Sponsor)	Mitigate	Prepare a briefing for the executive team prior to the "official" project review, providing context and clarifying issues.
4	Lack of stakeholder support in the preparation of the executive discussion package	L	H	M	Brian (Project Manager)	Caroline (Program Manager)	Avoid	Collaborate with the stakeholders on the building of the discussion paper, thereby allowing their point of view to be heard in order to do the "right thing" for the company.

TOP Tool 35: Situational Assessment (SA)

Purpose: "Getting Started" tool for gathering information and determining if root cause of a problem is known.

Summary:

Situational Assessment provides a structured approach to getting all the facts on the table and beginning the process of prioritizing and identifying where further information is required or additional questions need to be asked.

Steps:

SA is also one of the five possible "frames" in the Frame Your Purpose step of ***Thinking On Purpose***. The template below helps to structure your thinking to help mitigate the effects of autopilot thinking—e.g. jumping to cause or solution without getting the facts.

1. Identify issues with key questions.
    - What is happening?
    - What could happen in the future?
    - What is deviating from plan or expectations?
2. Clarify issues with key questions.
    - What evidence do we have?
3. Prioritize the issues with key questions.
    - How important is the issue?
    - How urgent is the issue?
4. Assess root cause with key question.
    - Is root cause known?
    - If it is not, then the next logical "purpose" will be problem solving. If root cause is known, the next logical "purpose" will be decision making, i.e. what is the best way to fix the identified cause?

Guidelines/Options:

SA is most often executed in a team environment using brainstorming or nomimal brainstorming techniques.

A prerequisite to performing a SA effectively is knowing that the right people are in the room to participate in the process and, of course, to identify issues. *TOP Tool 37: Stakeholder Assessment* is an important companion tool to SA as a means of making sure the right people are in the room or being consulted.

The third support element to completing an effective Situational Assessment is making sure that that you have the facts straight. *TOP Tool #20: Information Analysis Standards* provides an excellent set of probing questions to help make sure both your reasoning is sound and your facts have been qualified.

When all else fails, start with the "5 Ws and How" approach

Who?	
What?	
When?	
Where?	
Why?	
How?	

Enablers:

TOP Tool 16: Facilitation Skills

References

Process Design Consultants. *Critical Thinking—Certificate in Continuing Studies in Strategic Leadership*, 1998.

Applicable Job Aid, Template, Diagram, or Example:

Template: A completed example using the following template can be found in Chapter 6—Thinking On Purpose in Action.

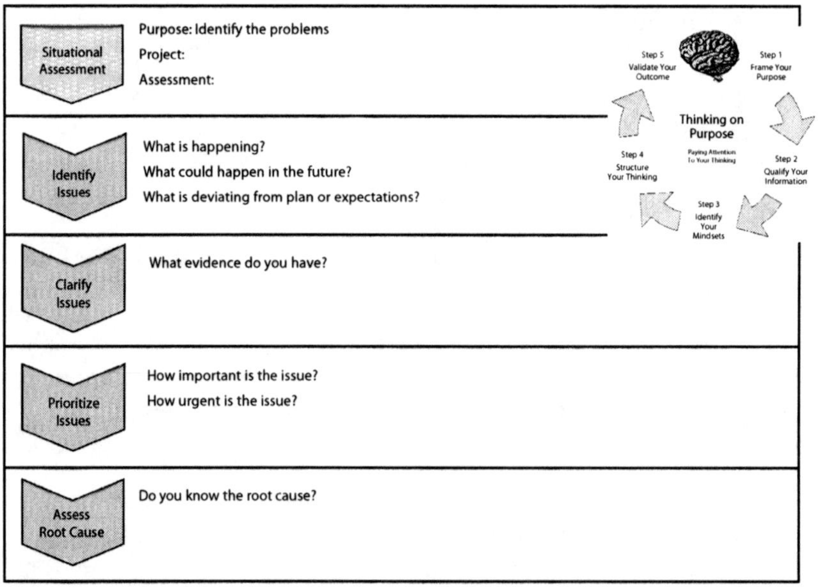

Situational Assessment	Purpose: Identify the problems Project: Assessment:
Identify Issues	What is happening? What could happen in the future? What is deviating from plan or expectations?
Clarify Issues	What evidence do you have?
Prioritize Issues	How important is the issue? How urgent is the issue?
Assess Root Cause	Do you know the root cause?

Thinking on Purpose
Paying Attention To Your Thinking
Step 1 Frame Your Purpose
Step 2 Qualify Your Information
Step 3 Identify Your Mindsets
Step 4 Structure Your Thinking
Step 5 Validate Your Outcome

TOP Tool 36: Six Thinking Hats

Purpose:

"Expand Possibilities" tool to help you make better decisions by forcing you to move outside your habitual ways of thinking.

Summary:

Created by Edward De Bono is his book, Six Thinking Hats, this tool helps you understand the full complexity of the decision and spot issues and opportunities to which you might otherwise be blind. While many successful people think from a rational, positive viewpoint, they may, due to biases and habit, fail to look at the problem from an emotional, intuitive, or creative point of view.

Using the Six Thinking Hats technique, you can use multiple approaches so that your decisions will mix ambition, skill in execution, sensitivity, creativity and good contingency planning.

Steps:

Each "Thinking Hat" has a different thinking style:

1. **White Hat** is neutral and objective. The white hat is concerned with objective facts and figures.
2. **Red Hat** suggests anger (seeing red), rage and emotions. The red hat gives the emotional view.
3. **Black Hat** is gloomy and negative. The black hat covers the negative aspects—why it can't be done.
4. **Yellow Hat** is sunny and positive. The yellow hat is optimistic and covers hope and positive thinking.
5. **Green Hat** is grass, vegetation, and abundant, fertile growth. The green hat indicates creativity and new ideas.
6. **Blue Hat** is cool and is also the color of the sky, which is above every thing else. The blue hat is concerned with control and the organization of the thinking process, as well as the use of other hats.

Guidelines/Options:

In meetings, this tool can have the benefit of blocking confrontations that happen when people use different thinking styles while looking at the same problem.

A variant of the application of this technique is to look at problems from the perspective of different professions (i.e. something other than project management). Application of the Six Thinking Hats is a proactive rather than a reactive process.

The key point is that a hat is a direction to think, rather than a label for thinking. The key theoretical reasons to use the Six Thinking Hats are to:

- Encourage parallel thinking
- Encourage full-spectrum thinking
- Separate ego from performance

Enablers:

All team members should be briefed on the concept and application of this technique before it is used in a practical situation.

TOP Tool 16: Facilitation Skills

References:

De Bono, Edward. Six Thinking Hats. Toronto, Canada: Key Porter Books Limited 1985.

Applicable Job Aid, Template, Diagram, or Example:

Example: Scenario 2—All Together Now

Once Caroline, the project manager in this scenario, was satisfied that her team had nailed down the cause of the problems, i.e. no one really understood the reason for the project etc., she used De Bono's Six Thinking Hats to help her team think in different directions.

First, she gave her team a primer in De Bono's concepts before the decision-making discussions. Interestingly enough, it was the White Hat thinking (let's drop the arguments and proposals and look at the data or facts) that let the team to realize that a complete executive review of the project was a viable option, within the set of decision alternatives.

(The White Hat should always be in play in any decision to help ensure that data and facts are being interpreted appropriately, i.e. not emotionally.)

TOP Tool 37: Stakeholder Assessment

Purpose:

"Getting Started" tool for identifying and assessing the importance of key people, groups of people, or institutions that may significantly influence the success of your activity or project. You can use this technique alone or with your team members.

Summary:

Stakeholder Assessment is used to: 1) identify people, groups, and institutions that will influence your initiative (either positively or negatively), 2) anticipate the kind of influence, positive or negative, that these groups will have on your initiative, and 3) develop strategies to get the most effective support possible for your initiative and reduce any obstacles to successful implementation of your program.

Steps:

1. Identify Stakeholders, people, groups, and institutions that will affect or be affected by the situation and list them in the column under "Stakeholder" in a matrix chart. (example given below)
2. Review the list and identify the specific interests these Stakeholders have in your initiative. Consider issues like: the project's benefit(s) to the Stakeholder; the changes that the project might require the Stakeholder to make; and the project activities that might cause damage or conflict for the Stakeholder. Record these under the column "Stakeholder Interest(s) in the Project."
3. Review each Stakeholder listed in column one. Ask the question: How important are this Stakeholder's interests to the resolution of the current situation?

   Consider:

   - The role the key Stakeholder must play for the project to be successful, and the likelihood that the Stakeholder will play this role.
   - The likelihood and impact of a Stakeholder's negative responses to the situation.

Assign the label A for Advocate, S for Supporter, N for Neutral, C for Critic, and B for Blocker. Record these letters in the column entitled "Assessment of Impact."

4. Identify the methods or strategies that you could use to increase Stakeholder support and reduce opposition. Consider how you might approach each of the Stakeholders. What kind of information will they need? How important is it to involve the Stakeholder in the planning

process? Are there other groups or individuals that might influence the Stakeholder to support your initiative? Record your strategies for obtaining support or reducing obstacles to your project in the last column in the matrix.

Stakeholder Analysis Matrix

Stakeholder	Stakeholder Interest(s) in the project	Assessment of Impact (Advocate, Supporter, Neutral, Critic, Blocker)	Potential Strategies for Obtaining Support or Reducing Obstacles

Guidelines/Options: The Power of the Right Question

You need to know more about your key Stakeholders: You need to know how they are likely to feel about and react to your project. You also need to know how best to engage them in your project and how best to communicate with them.

Key questions that can help you understand your Stakeholders are:

- What financial or emotional interest do they have in the outcome of your work? Is it positive or negative?
- What motivates them most of all?
- What information do they want from you?
- How do they want to receive information from you? What is the best way of communicating your message to them?
- What is their current opinion of your work? Is it based on good information?
- Who influences their opinions generally, and who influences their opinion of you? Do some of these influencers therefore become important Stakeholders in their own right?
- If they are not likely to be positive, what will win them around to support your project?
- If you don't think you will be able to win them around, how will you manage their opposition?
- Who else might be influenced by their opinions? Do these people become Stakeholders in their own right?

A good way of answering these questions is to talk to your Stakeholders directly— people are often quite open about their views, and asking people's opinions is often the first step to building a successful relationship with them.

Where appropriate for the situation, it can also be helpful to calibrate power and interest for each Stakeholder using a four-box grid, or Stakeholder Map, as follows:

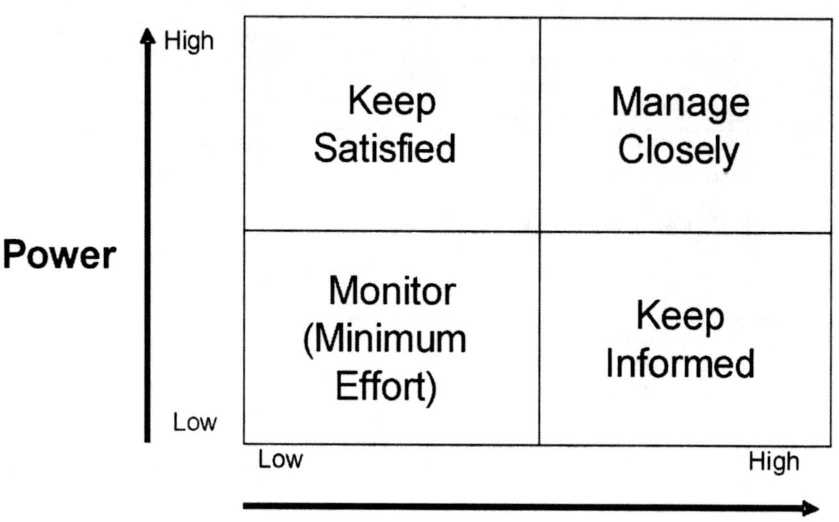

Enablers:

TOP Tool 16: Facilitation

References

Mind Tools. *Excellent Skills for an Excellent Career.* London, UK: Mind Tools Limited 2008.

Applicable Job Aid, Template, Diagram, or Example:

Example: Scenario 2—All Together Now

When Caroline joined the Regional Notification Program, she decided that one of her first steps should be to do a Stakeholder Assessment. She needed to understand what each Stakeholder's role was and better understand who would influence the team in a positive or negative way.

Stakeholder	Stakeholder Interests in the Project	Impact Assessment	Potential Strategies for Obtaining Support or Reducing Obstacles
Bob Keeling	• Little interest • Project unnecessary • Project was adding risk • Didn't have time to devote to the project • Bigger priorities than the project	B	• Needs to understand how the project fits into the organizational strategy • Needs to be involved in planning, especially around the timeline and risk assessment
Mel Leung	• Not fully engaged • Couldn't commit his time due to shortage of staff • Didn't feel respected by the team • Wasn't really paying attention to any of the details of the projects	C	• Needs to understand the purpose of the project • Needs to be involved in the planning, especially roles and responsibilities, and timelines
Elaine Lucas	• Very engaged • Loves projects with "cool" technology • Completely understands what has to be done • Her chance to shine in the organization	A	• Ambassador for the project • Will assist in dealing with technical team members • Strong relationship with vendor • Looking for opportunities to stretch her skills • Will be helpful in presentations
Dennis Smith	• Not engaged at all • Doesn't believe in the project • Not a team player • Too busy	B	• Needs to understand how the project fits into the organizational strategy • Needs to understand the purpose of the project • Needs to be involved in the planning, especially in the requirements, scope and timeline
Ron Nixon	• Technical SME • Delivers tasks in a linear fashion • Doesn't work with ambiguity • Conflict with another project	S	• Needs to understand the purpose of the project • Knowledge and possible advocate • Always needs to know reasons for decisions • Needs to be involved in the planning, especially in the requirements, scope and timeline
Yvonne Brown	• Somewhat engaged • Skeptical of project's need • Concerned about additional workload • Concerned about impact to the budget	N	• Needs to understand how the project fits into the organizational strategy • Needs to understand the business case for the project • Needs to be updated on financials frequently
Brian Sweet	• Fully engaged • Good chance to showcase his talent • Solution to problems is to work harder • Prefers one-on-ones to team meetings • Works best in isolation • People skills need improvement	S	• Isn't using all his PM tools • Needs to work throug the *Thinking on Purpose* processes • Needs some "quick wins" to give him some confidence • Needs to lead more rather than trying to do everything himself
Impact Assessment Legend A = Advocate S = Supporter N = Neutral C = Critic B = Blocker			

After she did the Stakeholder Assessment, Caroline realized that she needed something to help keep all the good information she had collected at the front of her mind.

She completed the Stakeholder Map below and she kept it close for all project meetings. It proved to be an excellent reminder of what the Stakeholders required and why.

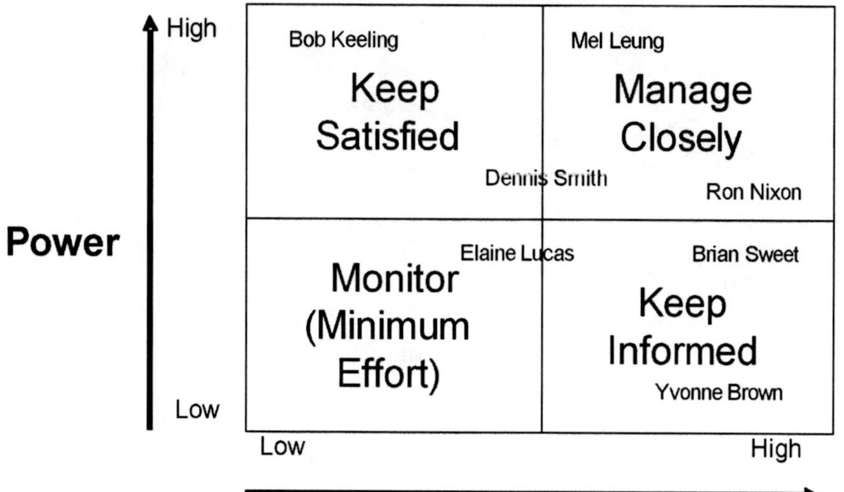

TOP Tool 38: SWOT Analysis

Purpose:

"Getting Started" tool for understanding your **S**trengths and **W**eaknesses and for looking at **O**pportunities and **T**hreats.

Summary:

SWOT Analysis can help uncover opportunities that you are well positioned to take advantage of and potentially eliminate threats that might catch you off guard. SWOT can also serve to assist in establishing a strategy that can help you distinguish yourself from your competitors.

Steps:

Using probing questions:

1. Examine Strengths. Consider this from an internal and external perspective:
   - What advantages does your company have?
   - What do you do better than anyone else?
   - What unique or lowest-cost resources do you have access to?
   - What do people in your market see as your strengths?
2. Examine Weaknesses:
   - What could you improve?
   - What should you avoid?
   - What are people in the market place likely to see as weaknesses?
   - Do other people seem to perceive weaknesses that you do not perceive?
   - Are your competitors doing any better than you?
3. Examine Opportunities:
   - Where are the good opportunities facing you?
   - What are the interesting trends you are aware of?
   - Do my strengths open up any opportunities?
   - If I could eliminate my weaknesses, what opportunities would I open up?
4. Examine Threats:
   - What obstacles do you face?
   - What is your competition doing?
   - Are the required specifications for your job, products, or services changing?
   - Is changing technology threatening your position?
   - Do you have bad debt or cash-flow problems?
   - Could any of your weaknesses seriously threaten your business?

Guidelines/Options:

Strengths and weaknesses typically orient to the internal aspects of your company. Opportunities and threats orient to external factors.

Apply SWOT to a company, a project/program, or for an individual career.

Enablers:

TOP Tool 16: Facilitation

References

Mind Tools. *Excellent Skills for an Excellent Career.* London: Mind Tools Ltd. 2008.

Applicable Job Aid, Template, Diagram, or Example:

In the *Red Light, Green Light scenario*, George found out his project was going to miss key dates. He might even miss his implementation window, making it impossible to deliver the project on time. George was caught off guard and he needed to act quickly. A SWOT Analysis was a quick way to find opportunities that he might otherwise miss, so George gathered the team together to work through the analysis, asking probing questions to draw out the relevant information.

The result, outlined below, gave George the confidence to pursue opportunities to "crash the plan" that he would not have considered without this structured approach. (For example, this process showing him clearly that the level of experience and expertise of his team would provide the means to crash the plan quickly and effectively.)

Strengths • What do you do well? • What unique resources can you draw on? • What do others see as your strengths?	**Weaknesses** • What could you improve? • Where do you have fewer resources than others? • What are others likely to see as weaknesses?
• Strong project management skills • Experienced subject matter experts (SMEs) • Open to new ideas • Strong management support • Team is motivated to find a solution	• Weak monitoring and control • Poor communication because the PM didn't spend enough time with the team • Team told the PM what they thought he wanted to hear rather than the truth • Team members didn't always take accountability for their deliverables
Opportunities • What good opportunities are open to you? • What trends could you take advantage of? • How can you turn your strengths into opportunities?	**Threats** • What trends could harm you? • What is your competition doing? • What threats do your weaknesses expose you to?
• Strong PM has had experience with crashing the plan • SMEs have a good network who can assist • Management may provide more resources/budget • Team wants to succeed and will do what it takes to remedy the situation	• Estimating has to be realistic • Plan needs to be monitored closely • Reduced quality • Cost overruns • Burnout

TOP Tool 39: Utility Tree/Matrix

Purpose:

"Decision Making" tool for evaluating alternatives in order to pinpoint the option with the most utility or benefits.

Summary:

A Utility Tree/Matrix allows you to choose from among alternative options or alternative courses of action by separately evaluating their respective benefits (their utilities) and the probability of achieving those benefits. The option with the most utility, or favorable options, is the best choice.

Steps:

1. List the options and outcomes to be considered. Let's say you are planning a vacation. Your options list might include all the potential destinations, while the outcomes might include travel modes, financial considerations, and possible activities (playing tennis or golf, for example).

2. Determine whose perspective you're analyzing for. Is this vacation to please you, a surprise for your spouse, or a group trip for a club you belong to? Each of these perspectives would provide different weights to different outcomes and options.

3. Build a Utility Tree/Matrix for each option. For each destination, for example, you would create a Tree or Matrix that would allow you to compare financial considerations, activities, and travel modes for each destination.

4. Determine a utility value for each option-outcome pair—each cell of the Matrix or each branch of the Tree—based on its value to the perspective you are analyzing from. If you are planning this trip as a surprise for your spouse, then outcomes that include many of his or her interests (say, playing tennis and paying less than $300 per day) would score higher than those that suited your own (playing golf and paying between $400 and $600 per day).

5. Determine the probability of each outcome. The probabilities of the various outcomes depend on the options—if you choose a winery tour and the hotel package doesn't include a tennis court, then the outcome of "playing tennis" is 0%. On the other hand, if it is near a golf course, but the golf course is only open for two of the four days of the tour, then the outcome of "playing golf" would be 50%. The total of all outcomes combined must equal 100%.

6. Determine the "expected values" of outcomes. Expected values are the utility multiplied by the probability—you only get value out of an outcome if it is both of interest (high utility) *and* available (high probability). Total up all of the expected values for each option.
7. Rank the options by score.
8. Do a sanity/reality check to make sure that your numbers haven't led you to choose an option that isn't actually the best (for example, choosing a trip that is already sold out).

Guidelines/Options:

The three basic elements of utility analysis are options, outcomes, and perspectives.

- Options are the choices you are faced with.
- Outcomes are the results of choosing those options.
- Perspectives are viewpoints that you or others have about those outcomes.

Enablers:

TOP Tool 22: Matrix and Grids

References

Jones, Morgan D. *The Thinker's Toolkit.* New York: Three Rivers Press, 1998.

Applicable Job Aid, Template, Diagram or Example:

Template: Scenario 1—Red Light, Green Light

While George Green and his team reached the conclusion to "crash the plan," using the high-level TOP decision template they could have applied a Utility Tree/Matrix analysis, as outlined below, to explain the economic impacts of the decision.

UTILITY MATRIX ANALYSIS—RED LIGHT, GREEN LIGHT

Perspective: Project Benefits	Outcome	Make the Schedule	Total EV	Rank
	Yes (Ms)	No (Ms)		
Crash the Plan	U $200 P .7 EV $140	0 .3 0	$140	1
Extend Timeline	U $200 P .0 EV $0	0 1.0 0	$ 0	4
New Project Manager	U $200 P .2 EV $40	0 .8 0	$ 40	3
Outsource Development	U $200 P .4 EV $100	0 .6 0	$ 80	2

The creation of the matrix using the eight steps above is outlined below:

- The Perpective in the top left hand corner represents the benefit to the project of meeting the schedule. In this case, $200,000.
- The Outcome (meet the schedule) means that whatever option is chosen, the deadline will either be met, or not met.
- The Total EV means economic value of the alternative.
- The four options in this scenario have been recorded down the left-hand side of the matrix.
- For each option, the U (utility or benefit) is multiplied by the probability of success, which is a subjective calculation by the PM and/or his team. For option one, the U is $200,000 and the probability is rated at .7 or 70 %. The multiplication of U x P is $140,000. The relatively high probability is based on the high level of motivation in the team to accomplish this task. This is referred to as the EV or economic value. In this option, the probability of not meeting the schedule is .3 or 30% and because not reaching the schedule will not deliver the benefit, the product of U x P is $0.
- Each of the other three options is examined in a similar way also calculating the relative EV.The team felt that, given their experience

with outsourcing and the tight lead-time, outsourcing was a low probability option. The team also rationalized the "change the PM" option as being even more problematic and therefore scored it appropriately.

- Using the EV as the indicator, option one is the best option.
- The Utility Tree/Matrix can be used as a focused and concise communication tool with senior management to explain a decision on alternatives.

TOP Tool 40: Weighted Ranking

Purpose:

"Generic Format" to for ranking various options to determine relative merit and utility.

Summary:

Weighted Ranking is the process of evaluating competing options using the same criteria. Humans naturally rank options every day. You may decide to pick a bagel instead of a doughnut to go with your morning coffee, or choose a particular album from your musical library to listen to while you work out. Weighted Ranking structures this natural process for maximum effectiveness.

Steps:

1. List all the reasons for choosing one option over another. For example, in *Scenario 2—All Together Now*, Caroline is deciding on the best course of action for her company. She identified Must and Want criteria that would apply to any alternative.
2. Use "pair-ranking" to determine the priority of your criteria. Pair-ranking is simply comparing each criteria against another one at a time, until you can list them in order of importance. The key is that you must rank each item against every other item in turn (item 1 vs. item 2, item 1 vs. item 3, item 2 vs. item 3, etc). See *TOP Tool 25: Paired Comparison Analysis*.
3. Assign each criterion a value of 1-10, based on your perceived value. For example, "unanimous agreement on the project" was considered the most important in *Scenario 2—All Together Now* and was assigned a 10. The remaining criteria were assessed a value less than 10, depending on relative importance.
4. Draw up a matrix and enter your options along the top and your criteria down the left side, along with their weightings.
5. Multiply the percentage weighting of the criteria (agreement worth 10) times the degree that each particular option satisfies those criteria (also ranked 1-10; a good fit might get a 9 or 10 while a bad fit could get a 2 or 3). Repeat for each criteria and option.
6. Total the values for each option. Enter the total score into the appropriate area.
7. Use these totals to determine a final, Weighted Ranking of each option.

8. Do a sanity/reality check. Make sure that the raw numbers don't throw up an undesirable option (a company with a great location, for example, but with a salary that won't let you live there comfortably). Sometimes a Weighted Ranking will create a result that is counter to your intuitive preferences, as well. Exploring why this is so may provide some insight into your own mindsets and other mental processes that may surprise you. Or it may simply be a trick of the numbers. That's why you have to check your results against reality to see if they make sense before acting on them. Refer to *TOP Tool 27: PMI* to do a sanity check on the decision.

Guidelines/Options:

This tool is often used in conjunction with decision making to facilitate evaluating different options in a decision making situation. Refer to TOP Tool 10: Decision Making.

Enablers:

TOP Tool 22: Matrix and Grids

References

Jones, Morgan D. *The Thinker's Toolkit.* New York: Three Rivers Press, 1998

Applicable Job Aid, Template, Diagram, or Example:

Example: Scenario 2—All Together Now

Although Caroline was able to work through to a good decision using the TOP Decision Making template, a Weighted Ranking analysis for the same decision is outlined below to illustrate how a Weighted Ranking can be used in more complex situations.

Caroline used Weighted Ranking as a means to decide in which order to interview each of the team members on the Regional Notification Program (RNP) project. The steps she took are outlined below:

Step 1

She listed all major criteria for ranking—organizational level, depth of knowledge about the project, influence level, likely availability, etc.

Step 2

She pair ranked the criteria:

A—Organization Level - √ √
B—Knowledge Depth - √
C—Influence Level √√√
D—Availability

Which is more relevant:

A or B—A—she put a check mark beside A
A or C—C
A or D—A
B or C—C
B or D—B
C or D—C

Criteria ranking
Influence Level
Organization Level
Knowledge Depth
Availability

Step 3

She established weightings out of 100:
Influence—40
Organizational—30
Knowledge—20
Availability—10

Step 4

She established a Weighted Ranking Matrix and pair-ranked the potential interviewees for each criteria and calculated the scores (see pages 266 & 267)

Step 5

She did a "smell test" to make sure this sequence made sense.

Items To Be Ranked	Criteria				Votes	Final Seq.
	Influence .4	Org .3	Knowl .2	Avail .1		
Bob K	7 x .4= 2.8	7 x .3= 2.1	5 x .2= 1.0	1 = .1	6.0	1
Mel L	4 x .4= 1.6	4 x .3= 1.2	1 x .2= .2	4 = .4	3.2	4
Elaine L	2 x .4= .8	3 x .3= .9	3 x .2= .6	2 = .2	2.5	6
Dennis S	3 x .4= 1.2	2 x .3= .6	4 x .2= .8	3 = .3	2.9	5
Ron N	1 x .4= .4	1 x .3= .3	2 x .2= .4	6 = .6	1.5	7
Yvonne B	6 x .4= 2.4	5 x .3= 1.5	6 x .2= 1.2	5 = .5	5.6	3

Weighted Ranking Matrix

Weighted Ranking Decision Tree													
Decision Matrix													
Scenario #2 – All Together Now													
Decision Statement:													
What is the best course of action for the Regional Notification Project (RNP)													
Set Objectives		Generate and Evaluate Alternatives											
		A: Redo Initial Steps			B: Major Project Review			C: New Project Manager			D: Postpone Project		
	Musts	Information	Y	N	Information	Y	N	Information	Y	N	Information	Y	N
	Respect the business cycle		X			X				X		X	
	Clear articulation of purpose and strategic fit of project		X			X				X			X
	Team involvement in requirement process		X			X				X			X
	Senior Management Support		X			X				X			X
WT	Wants	Information	S	WS	Information	S	WS	Information	S	WS	Information	S	WS
10	Unanimous agreement to project	Mandated review	6	60	Fully supported review	9	90						
7	Benefits clearly understood	Only high level review (if at all)	8	56	Detailed review of project benefits	10	70						
6	Available budget for contractor	Only current available budget assigned	3	18	Will have appropriate budget assigned	8	48						
4	Available budget for outsourcing	Only current available budget assigned	3	18	Will have appropriate budget assigned	8	48						
	Total Score			152			256						
Decision		Go with the major project review at the executive level weighing this project against all other projects in the organization with the option of cancellation if not a strategic fit.											
S = Score (Satisfaction)		WS = Weighted Score (Satisfaction X Desirability)											

Bibliography

Amen, Daniel G., MD. *Making a Good Brain Great: The Amen Clinic Program for Achieving and Sustaining Optimal Mental Performance.* New York: Harmony Books, 2005.

Bradberry, Travis and Greaves, Jean. *The Emotional Intelligence Quick Book.* New York: Fireside, 2003.

Brown, M. Neil and Keeley, Stuart M. *Asking the Right Questions: A Guide to Critical Thinking.* New Jersey: Pearson/Prentice Hall, 2004.

Brue, Greg. *Six Sigma for Managers.* Madison, WI: CWL Publishing Enterprises, Inc., 2002.

Butler, Gillian, PhD. and Hope, Tony, MD. *Managing Your Mind: The Mental Fitness Guide.* New York: Oxford University Press, 2007.

Conlan, Roberta. *States of Mind: New Discoveries about How Our Brains Make Us Who We Are.* New York: John Wiley & Sons Inc., 1999.

De Bono, Edward. *Six Thinking Hats.* Toronto, Ontario: Key Porter Books Limited, 1985.

De Bono, Edward. *Serious Creativity.* Toronto, Ontario: Key Porter Books Limited, 1985.

Dixit, Avinash K. and Nalebuff, Barry J. *Thinking Strategically: The Competitive Edge in Business, Politics, and Everyday Life.* New York: W. W. Norton & Company, 1991.

Dweck, Carol S., PhD. *Mindset: The New Psychology of Success.* New York: Ballantine Books, 2008.

Fine, Cordelia. *A Mind of Its Own: How Your Brain Distorts and Deceives.* New York: W.W. Norton & Company Inc., 2006.

Ford, Debbie. *The Right Questions: Ten Essential Questions to Guide you to an Extraordinary Life*. New York: HarperCollins Publishers Inc., 2003.

Gardner, Howard. *Changing Minds: The Art and Science of Changing Our Own and Other People's Minds*. Boston, MA: Harvard Business School Press, 2006.

Gilovich, Thomas. *How We Know What Isn't So: The Fallibility of Human Reason in Everyday Life*. New York: The Free Press, 1991.

Gladwell, Malcolm. *Blink: The Power of Thinking Without Thinking*. New York: Little, Brown and Company, 2005.

Goleman, Daniel. *Emotional Intelligence*. New York: Bantam Books, 1995.

Goleman, Daniel. *Working with Emotional Intelligence*. New York: Bantam Books, 1998.

Gregory, Richard L. *The Oxford Companion to the Mind*. New York: Oxford University Press, 1998.

Hammond, John S. Keeney, Ralph L. and Raiffa, Howard. *Smart Choices: A Practical Guide to Making Better Decisions*. 1999.

Drucker, Peter F.; Hammond, John; Keeny, Ralph; Raiffa, Howard. *Harvard Business Review on Decision Making*. Boston, MA: Harvard Business School Publishing Corp., 2001.

Horine, Gregory M. *Absolute Beginner's Guide to Project Management*. Indianapolis, IN: Que Publishing, 2005.

Hurson, Tim. *Think Better: An Innovator's Guide to Productive Thinking*. New York: The McGraw- Hill Companies, 2008.

Ingram, Jay. *Theatre of the Mind: Raising the Curtain on Consciousness*. Toronto, Ontario: HarperCollins Publishers Ltd., 2005.

Jones, Morgan D. *The Thinker's Toolkit: 14 Powerful Techniques for Problem Solving*. New York: Three Rivers Press, 1998.

Katzenbach, Jon R. and Smith, Douglas K. *The Wisdom of Teams: Creating the High-Performance Organization*. New York: HarperCollins Publishers, Inc., 1993.

Kayser, Thomas A. *Mining Group Gold: How to Cash in on the Collaborative Brain Power of a Group*. El Segundo, CA: Serif Publishing, 1990.

Kendrick, Tom. *Identifying and Managing Project Risk: Essential Tools for Failure-Proofing Your Project*. New York: AMACOM, a division of American Management Association, 2003.

Kepner, Charles H. and Tregoe, Benjamin B. *The New Rational Manager*. Princeton, NJ: Princeton Research Press, 1981.

Kliem, Ralph L. and Ludin, Irwin S. *Tools and Tips for Today's Project Manager.* Newtown Square, PA: The Project Management Institute, 1999.

Koch, Richard. *The 80/20 Principle: The Secret of Achieving More with Less.* New York: Doubleday, 1998.

Longman, Andrew and Mullins, Jim. *The Rational Project Manager: A Thinking Team's Guide to Getting Work Done.* Hoboken, NJ: John Wiley & Sons, Inc., 2005.

Marcum, Dave; Smith, Steve; Khalsa, Mahan. *BusinessThink: Rules for Getting It Right—Now, and No Matter What*! New York: John Wiley & Sons, Inc., 2002.

Margolis, Howard. *Patterns, Thinking, and Cognition: A Theory of Judgment.* Chicago, IL: The University of Chicago Press, 1987.

Maxwell, John C. *Thinking for a Change: 11 Ways Highly Successful People Approach Life and Work.* USA: Warner Books, 2003.

Middleton, John. *Upgrade Your Brain: Boost Your Memory, Think More Clearly, and Discovert Your Inner Einstein.* New York: The Penguin Group, 2006.

Milosevic, Dragan Z. *Project Management ToolBox: Tools and Techniques for the Practicing Project Manager.* Hoboken, NJ: John Wiley & Sons, Inc., 2003.

Naisbitt, John. *Mind Set! Reset Your Thinking and See the Future.* New York: HarperCollins Publishers, 2006.

Nast, Jamie. *Idea Mapping: How to Access Your Hidden Brain Power, Learn Faster, Remember More, and Achieve Success in Business.* Hoboken, NJ: John Wiley & Sons, Inc., 2006.

Nutt, Paul C. *Why Decisions Fail.* San Francisco, CA: Berrett-Koehler Publishers, Inc., 2002.

Paul, Richard W. and Elder, Linda. *Critical Thinking: Tools for Taking Charge of Your Professional and Personal Life.* Upper Saddle River, NJ: Financial Times Prentice Hall, 2002.

Project Management Institute. *A Guide to the Project Management Body of Knowledge.* Newtown Square, PA: The Project Management Institute, 2004.

Project Management Institute. *Projects & Program Risk Management: A Guide to Managing Project Risks & Opportunities.* Newtown Square, PA: The Project Management Institute, 1992.

Restak, Richard MD. *The Naked Brain: How the Emerging Neurosociety is Changing How We Live, Work, and Love.* New York: Three Rivers Press, 2006.

Robbins, Stephen P. *Decide & Conquer: Make Winning Decisions and Take Control of Your Life*. Upper Saddle River, NJ: Financial Times Prentice Hall, 2004.

Rosinski, Philippe. *Coaching Across Cultures: New Tools for Leveraging National, Corporate, and Professional Differences*. Boston, MA: Nicholas Brealey Publishing, 2004.

Rouse, William B. *Don't Jump to Solutions: Thirteen Delusions That Undermine Strategic Thinking*. San Francisco, CA: Jossey-Bass Inc., 1998.

Schwarz, Roger. *The Skilled Facilitator: A Comprehensive Resource for Consultants, Facilitators, Managers, Trainers and Coaches*. San Francisco, CA: Jossey-Bass, 2002.

Stein, Steven J., PhD. and Book, Howard E., MD. *The EQ Edge: Emotional Intelligence and Your Success*. Mississauga, Ontario: John Wiley & Sons Canada, Ltd., 2006.

Thomas, David C. and Inkson, Kerr. *Cultural Intelligence: People Skills for Global Business*. San Francisco, CA: Berrett-Koehler Publishers, Inc., 2004.

Van Hecke, Madeleine L., PhD. *Blind Spots: Why Smart People Do Dumb Things*. Amherst, NY: Prometheus Books, 2007.

Verma, Vijay K. *Human Resource Skills For the Project Manager*. Newtown Square, PA: The Project Management Institute, 1996.

Verzuh, Eric. *The Fast Forward MBA in Project Management: Second Edition*. Hoboken, NJ: John Wiley & Sons, Inc., 2005.

Wansink, Brian PhD. *Mindless Eating: Why We Eat More Than We Think*. New York: Bantam Dell, 2006.

Weaver, Richard G. and Farrell, John D. *Managers as Facilitators: A Practical Guide to Getting Work Done in a Changing Workplace*. San Francisco, CA: Berrett-Koehler Publishers, Inc., 1997.

APPENDIX ONE

Common Biases

Actor-observer bias: The tendency to blame the actions of others on their personalities, rather than their situations, while at the same time blaming our own actions on our situations rather than our personality.

Ambiguity effect: The tendency to avoid making a decision if missing information makes the probability difficult to determine.

Anchoring: The tendency to rely on one piece of data or one trait when making a decision. For example, a person may refuse to buy any versions or years of a particular brand of vehicle because they have heard of a problematic issue with one model from one year.

Attentional bias: The tendency to ignore or neglect important or relevant data when it is associated with less relevant data that we perceive as threatening or more interesting. For example, in one study participants were presented with words printed in various colors, and were told to name the color of each word. Those participants with spider phobias had more trouble naming the color of words that related to spiders than they did words that were of little interest. Attentional bias is also the reason you suddenly see, for example, a particular make or model of car everywhere when you yourself are driving one or are considering purchasing one, when previously you didn't notice them.

Availability heuristic: The tendency to believe that something is more likely as it is more clearly remembered. This bias tends to make us feel that uncommon, but remarkable and vividly remembered, events are more likely to recur than more common, but less memorable ones.

Availability cascade: The tendency for something to become more credible or plausible the more it is repeated, with no regard to its actual merit.

Bandwagon effect: This is groupthink. It involves believing or preferring ideas because others around you do. The more people who believe in or espouse an idea, the harder it is to be "the odd man out."

Base rate fallacy: The tendency to put greater weight to evidence of minor or no validity for the purposes of creating a probability judgment, while ignoring stronger evidence. For example, most parents have a stronger belief in "stranger danger" when it comes to crimes against their children, even though statistically almost all of these crimes are committed by friends and family members.

Beneffectance: The tendency to believe yourself responsible for positive events, but not for negative ones. Related to self-serving bias.

Blind spot: The tendency to miss important information due to existing biases and beliefs. A person who believes they are a great manager may miss indications that their subordinates are unhappy until serious problems arise. Even then, the manager may not be able to see how their actions precipitated the issues even when presented with direct evidence, simply because their biases will prompt them to interpret that evidence based on their beliefs about their own skills.

Choice-supportive bias: The tendency to perceive your decisions and choices as being better or based on better evidence than they actually were. For example, if you hire based on a set of criteria, you will remember past hires as passing more of those criteria than they did. Since you chose to hire them, your bias encourages you to believe that your choices were the best you could make.

Clustering illusion: Seeing patterns or groupings that aren't really there.

Confirmation bias: The tendency to accept information or evidence that supports your preconceived beliefs, while ignoring evidence to the contrary. If you believe a particular political candidate is the best, you will seek out and give greater weight to information praising them, and ignore or dismiss information that highlights their shortfalls.

Congruence bias: The tendency to confirm beliefs or hypotheses through direct testing, while ignoring indirect testing. For example, if we are presented with two levers and told to find the one that will provide a reward, we will make a guess about which one is the correct lever (say, lever A) and then pull lever A (a direct test) rather than pulling lever B, which we believe to be a dummy (an indirect test). If we then state that Lever A is the reward lever and are told we are wrong, we either become confused or assume the person is lying rather than pulling Lever B (an indirect test of Lever A), only to discover that they both provide a reward.

Consistency bias: The tendency to remember your past actions as being more similar to your current ones than they really were.

Contrast effect: The enhancement or lessening of our perception of value for one object in contrast to another of greater or lesser value. For example, a supermodel will be perceived as more attractive when contrasted with a regular person than on her own. Likewise, an inexpensive suit appears shabbier when contrasted against a more expensive suit than it would by itself.

Cryptomnesia: Mistaking memory for imagination. You might cope with a bad memory by "remembering" it being a fictional story or make-believe event.

Distinction bias: The tendency to perceive two alternatives as having greater disparity when considered together than when considered separately. For example, two high-end computers will appear to be distinctly different when displayed together, whereas if displayed separately, we would perceive their differences as minimal.

Dunning-Kruger effect: The tendency of incompetent people to be unable to grasp the level of their own incompetence, as well as being incapable of recognizing superior competence in others. This is the "you don't know what you don't know" bias.

Egocentric bias: The tendency to believe that we have more impact on or responsibility for a group effort than an indifferent observer would assign to us.

Endowment effect: The tendency to place greater value on something you possess than you would place on it if someone else possessed it. People often price their houses far higher, for example, than they would be willing to pay for the same property if they were buying.

Extremes aversion: The tendency to prefer the middle ground or choice rather than either extreme.

False consensus effect: The tendency to believe that others agree with us more than they do.

Focusing effect: The tendency to place too much weight on one single aspect of an event or prediction, resulting in incorrect predictions and assumptions. People tend to assume that owning a luxury car will make them happier than owning a nice but mid-range car, but forget that such aspects as higher taxes, insurance, and repair bills will probably cancel out the glamour of the flashier version. They also forget that people tend to have a baseline of happiness to which they will return after any swing in any direction. So even if the car makes them happier to begin with, they will very shortly return to their baseline happiness.

Forer or Barnum Effect: The tendency to rate descriptions supposedly tailored to our personalities as highly accurate, when in fact they are general and can apply to anyone. Horoscopes are a good example of this.

Framing bias or effect: The tendency to come to conclusions based on how the data is delivered. For example, saying that a surgery has a 10% failure rate is the same as saying it has a 90% success rate. But the latter statement seems far more favorable than the former.

Fundamental attribution error: The tendency to believe that others are acting based on personal motivations, rather than situational ones, regardless of their true motive. For example, you might believe someone who cuts you off in traffic does it because he's an irresponsible jerk, when in fact he simply may not have seen you, or miss-guessed your distance.

Halo effect: The tendency to allow our perception of someone's personal traits in one area (physically attractiveness, for example) to color our viewpoint of their traits in other areas (personality or competence).

Hawthorne effect: The tendency of people to change their behavior, usually for the better, when they are observed or think they are observed.

Herd instinct: The urge to follow the crowd and do as others do.

Hindsight bias: The tendency to believe that past events were more predictable than they actually were.

Hyperbolic discounting: Giving lesser weight to events or consequences in the far future than to those in the immediate future. When asked if they would prefer to receive $100 now or $200 next week, most people will take the $100. Likewise, when faced with a minor embarrassment now or the potential for a major disaster later, many people will act to avoid the immediate discomfort and prefer to risk the larger consequences later.

Illusion of asymmetric insight: The tendency to think you know more about your peers than they know about you.

Illusion of control: The belief that we can exert some measure of control over situations or events we clearly do not. For example, the belief that wearing "lucky" clothes while we watch our favorite sports will influence the outcome of the games.

Illusion of transparency: The illusion that everybody knows more about everybody else than they do.

Illusory correlation: Believing two events to be related when they are not. Pavlov's dogs believe that the ringing of a bell is directly related to the appearance of food, when this is actually not the case.

Impact bias: The tendency to believe that your emotional response to future events will take longer to resolve or experience than it actually does. A bride will believe that her wedding will make her happy for a very long time, when in fact, the joy of the event will wear off as quickly as her enjoyment of any recent happy day.

Information bias: The belief that more information is better, even when that information can have no bearing on the results or answers.

Ingroup bias: The tendency to prefer and behave preferentially to others of your own group over outsiders.

Irrational escalation: The tendency to take irrational action based on rational prior actions, or to justify prior actions. Bidding wars are an example of irrational escalation. Just-world phenomenon: The tendency for people to believe that people get what they deserve.

Loss aversion: The tendency to feel more pain about losing something than you gain pleasure from keeping. For example, someone may not care one way or another about a jacket, until someone tries to steal it. At that point, the pain of losing the object far outweighs the prior benefits of having it.

Mere exposure effect: The tendency for people to prefer something simply because it's familiar. This is the bias behind "name recognition" advertising. The more often you hear of something, the more favorable your impression of it.

Moral credential effect: People who have a history of non-prejudicial behavior are more willing to express prejudicial views at a later time. For example, in one study people who were given an opportunity to view and reject a blatantly sexist statement prior to testing were more inclined to select a Caucasian male for a job opening later.

Need for closure: The drive to have an answer or explanation for an event or happening.

Neglect of probability: The tendency to ignore probability when making a decision. For instance, if a person has heard of a rare case where wearing a seatbelt caused injury rather than preventing it, they might decide not to wear their seatbelt, even though seatbelts prevent injury in almost all accidents.

Notational bias: The tendency of notation, or how something is written down or encoded, to affect how things are recorded using that notation. For example, Western musical notation does not adequately represent the notes and tonal variations of Eastern music, and so music written in Western notation tends to sound more recognizably Western.

Observer-expectancy/subject-expectancy effect: The tendency of an expected result to alter behavior to produce that result. Often seen in scientific experiments. When a researcher believes a certain hypothesis to be true, they will often alter the experiment to make it true (even without realizing it). This is also the phenomenon behind Clever Hans the Counting Horse. Hans was not actually counting, but reacting to subconscious signals from his handlers to stop pawing the ground when he got to the right answer.

Omission bias: The belief that a harmful action is morally worse than an equally harmful inaction. For instance, that shooting someone is morally worse than not preventing someone from being shot.

Optimism bias: The tendency to believe that a plan of action will go as intended.

Outcome bias: The tendency to give more weight to the outcome of an event than the decision-making that went into it. So even if you made the best decision you could given the information you had, a negative outcome will be seen as the result of a poor decision rather than the result of, say, insufficient information or chance.

Outgroup homogeneity bias: The tendency of people in your own ethnic or cultural group to appear more individuated than those of other groups. This is the "All (ethnic group) people look alike to me" bias.

Overconfidence effect: The tendency to overestimate your own skill or ability.

Planning fallacy: The tendency to assume that an activity will take less time than it does.

Positive outcome bias: Wishful thinking. The tendency to predict positive outcomes of events, regardless of evidence or experience to the contrary.

Primacy effect: The tendency to give more weight to the first instance of something than to subsequent instances.

Projection bias: The belief that others share your personal views or feelings.

Pseudo-certainty effect: The tendency to avoid risk to gain a positive outcome, but to accept risk to avoid a negative outcome. People are unwilling to bet when the odds of winning are low (avoiding risk) if they have nothing to lose (positive outcome), but likely to bet heavily (accepting risk) to avoid losing everything (negative outcome), even if the odds of winning remain the same.

Reactance: The desire to rebel against a request or instruction solely to maintain the appearance of control over your actions, or avoid the appearance of giving up control over your actions. Teenage rebellion at its best. Also, the force behind the effectiveness of what is commonly referred to as "reverse psychology."

Recency or peak-end effect: The tendency to give more weight to recent events than to earlier ones. We believe something that happened yesterday to be more likely than something that happened last year.

Rosy retrospection: The tendency to view the past as better than it really was. Also known as "the good old days."

Neglect of regression toward the mean: Believing that extreme behavior or results will continue, despite contrary probabilities.

Selection bias: The distortion of data based on the manner in which the data was collected. If you use a net to sample fish in a lake, then the size of the mesh in the net could skew your data if it let certain fish escape.

Selective perception: The tendency for you to see what you expect to see.

Self-fulfilling prophecy: The tendency to act (consciously or not) in ways that will confirm our predictions or beliefs.

Self-serving bias: The tendency to assign successes to your own actions and failures to outside influences or the actions of others.

Status quo bias: Aversion to change, the preference for things to remain as they are.

Stereotyping: The tendency to make predictions about an individual's behavior or characterisitics without having specific information about that individual.

Subadditivity effect: Predicting the probability of the whole to be less than the probability of its parts. Event A might be predicted to be 55% likely to happen and event B to be 75% likely to happen, even if the probability of both happening are 100%.

Subjective validation: The tendency to believe something is true because our personal belief system demands it to be true. For example, someone who believes that white males are superior at sports will believe that teams featuring white males will be more likely to win, regardless of the teams' actual rankings or statistical merits.

Suggestibility: The tendency to remember suggestions from others as originating in your own mind.

System justification: The tendency to prefer the status quo and dismiss or disparage alternatives even at the expense of personal—or the group's—self-interest.

Telescoping effect: The tendency to believe that recent events happened further back in time than they did, and remote events to be more recent than they are. It is why something that happened last year can seem like it happened yesterday, while something that happened last week may feel like it happened ages ago.

Trait ascription bias: The tendency to perceive yourself as being more flexible and open, while viewing others as set in their ways.

Unit bias: The tendency to believe that a single unit of something, say food or drink, is the proper amount to eat or drink. We will eat the same number of servings, and feel equally full or hungry, even as the serving sizes get bigger and smaller.

Von Restorff effect: An item that stands out in contrast to those around it will be more likely to be remembered. This is why we underline or use bold in text.

Zero-risk bias: The tendency to prefer reducing a small risk to zero rather than reducing a large risk by a percentage, even when that percentage of a larger risk is greater than the total of the smaller risk. We would rather see a 10% chance that we will receive a shock reduced to zero than reduce a 100% chance of a shock to 50%.

APPENDIX TWO

Common Fallacies

Ad hominem: Attacking your opponent, rather than his argument or evidence. This is often used by people to draw attention away from their own insufficient evidence or faulty arguments. The intent is to discredit an argument by discrediting the person arguing, even though the two are not directly correlated (an unpleasant person may have a perfectly valid argument).

Appeal to ignorance: Drawing a conclusion from a lack of evidence, or using a lack of evidence to support a claim. For example, there is no evidence one way or the other about the existence of God. But both sides of the issue use this lack of evidence to support their claims for and against the existence of God.

Appeal to popularity (Ad populum): Trying to validate or justify a claim or argument by appealing to popular opinion; believing that something must be true because it is widely believed to be true. However, popular belief does not a fact make. People have accepted as common wisdom any number of complete fallacies, such as the flat earth or the idea that traveling at speeds of over fifteen miles per hour would be fatal.

Appeal to questionable authority: Resting the validity of an argument on the opinion of someone who does not have the skill, training, education, or expertise required to give a valid opinion in that area. For example, relying on a non-electrician to validate the quality of electrical work.

Begging the question: A fallacy in which the underlying evidence for the reasoning is assumed within the reasoning. For example, "Stealing is wrong, therefore taking extra sugar from the diner is wrong." In this argument, the premise—that taking extra sugar from the diner is stealing—is assumed, but never addressed. Since the premise has not been established as fact, the argument based on it is null and void. This can be a very difficult fallacy to understand and to spot in action. It is very easy to simply accept the underlying assumptions as fact.

Conjunction fallacy: The belief that specific conditions are more probable than general ones. Often used in advertising, since a specific claim (four out of five doctors prefer) is more believable than a general one (doctors agree).

Either/Or (false dilemma or false dichotomy): Giving or assuming only two options when in reality many options may be available.

Equivocation: Using a word that has more than one meaning in an argument. When an alternate meaning is put into play, the argument no longer makes any sense. For example: all men are created equal; women are not men; therefore, women are unequal. In this sense, the word "men" was originally used to infer "mankind," but in the second instance the meaning is changed to mean male humans. In this way, it is easy to twist the meaning of a word to derail or falsely win an argument.

Explaining by naming: The fallacy that because you have labeled something, you have explained it.

Gambler's fallacy: The belief that unique random events or results are caused by or affected by prior unique random events. For example, the belief that a "lucky run of the dice" will positively or negatively influence later rolls, when in fact each roll is individually random and in no way affected by other rolls, or that because a specific string of numbers won in one lottery, it is more likely to win again, when in fact each winning series of lottery numbers is uniquely random and not influenced by any other series.

Glittering generality: Using vague, positive descriptions or emotional appeals to entice someone to approve of something they might disapprove of upon closer, rational examination. "No one will get hurt…it'll be fun!"

Hasty generalization: Assuming something to be true for all members of a group because it is true for some of them. "That manager is great to work with. All the managers at that firm must be great to work with."

Ludic fallacy: The tendency to apply the simpler probabilities of games or models to infinitely more complicated real-world situations; mistaking the model for the system. For example, assuming that because you often win at Monopoly, you should be able to get rich in the real estate market. Also, assuming that something has a far simpler probability structure than it does by ignoring real-world complexities.

Red herring: Introducing an unrelated argument in such a way that it appears related in order to change the subject to one more easily winnable or move the discussion to one more favorable for yourself.

Post hoc: Falsely associating two unrelated events as cause and effect. A new law passed making it illegal to beg on the street. Crime went up. Therefore, outlawing beggars increases crime.

Slippery slope: The belief that one action will set off a cascade of further actions (usually, but not necessarily, negative), when in fact there are safeguards or systems in place to prevent this cascade.

Searching for perfect solutions: The belief that a solution should not be adopted because it does not solve every aspect of a problem. Often used by antagonists as a pseudo-legitimate way to scuttle perfectly good solutions they don't like. In reality, a good solution covers most of the bases, and the remaining issues can then be dealt with one at a time, as needed.

Straw person: Distorting or misrepresenting an opponent's position to make it easier to attack. By doing so, you wind up attacking a position that was never proffered. For example, if someone says that in times of famine, food rationing makes sense, to distort that argument you claim that your opponent supports starving children in order to feed the rich (which no sane person would support) is to use a straw man argument.

Texas sharpshooter: Stating or altering your hypothesis after you've collected the data. For example, changing or taking a political stance after viewing poll results.

Weak analogy: Drawing upon a poor analogy to support a claim. For example, saying that because we have hungry people in North America, we shouldn't send aid to a famine-stricken foreign country. In reality, the analogy is weak because even the poorest people in North America usually have access to at least some food (through food pantries, government programs, soup kitchens, etc.) when there may be little to no food at all in the other country.

Wishful thinking: Assuming something to be true because you want it to be true. When wishful thinking forms the basis of an argument, the entire argument becomes invalid.

APPENDIX THREE

TOP Self-Assessment

Instructions: Rate your current frequency of application for each TOP step in your day to day PM activities. Use the form on the reverse side of this page.

TOP STEP	NEVER			MOST OF THE TIME	ALWAYS
Do you set aside specific time to ensure that you are answering the right question or	1	2	3	4	5
Do you currently spend time assessing and qualifying each piece of information that goes into solving the	1	2	3	4	5
Are you aware of all of the biases, habits and emotions that are in play at anytime during your problem-solving	1	2	3	4	5
Do you use a specific process or approach to ensure that your problem solving, decision-making, and action planning is done in	1	2	3	4	5
Do you use a specific process or approach to review your thinking to verify that you did come to the best conclusion and that your solutions are actually	1	2	3	4	5
TOTAL SCORE:					
Meaning?	You are not TOP and therefore un-protected from	You are inconsistently TOP and at times are unprotected	You are TOP most of the time but APT	You are consistently TOP and are fully aware of APT and
Key Question?	Where do you begin?	When do you need to TOP?	When are you not to TOP?	How are you sharing this with others?
Now What?	Use TOP as "workbook" to develop OPT skills	Use TOP as "guidebook" to successfully develop	Use TOP as "cookbook" to insure OPT in play all the time	Use TOP as "textbook" to support selling and teaching
Vulnerabilities?	Going too deep initially and becoming overwhelmed	Moving too fast and over reliance on process	Settling for "adequate" over "optimum" and over reliance	Over confidence & not sharing or coaching when appropriate for

APPENDIX FOUR

TOP Ten Nuggets

Nugget 1: The 30/60/10 Rule

Planning makes foresight as clear as hindsight. Successful project management is 30 percent insight, 60 percent foresight, and 10 percent hindsight.

Nugget 2: Auto Pilot and Topper

Auto Pilot represents automatic thinking processes hardwired into our brains by evolution. Topper represents mindfulness and critical thinking. Topper and Auto Pilot are interdependent on one another.

Nugget 3: Follow-through and Follow-up (F&F)

Following through and following up are vital aspects of project and general management, as well as a basic life skill. APT encourages complacency and neglect of these actions, while OPT counteracts that tendency.

Nugget 4: Mindsets

Mindsets are an accumulation of biases that have been formed over time as a result of environments and experiences. These mindsets often dictate how we see and act within the world around us. Key concept: If you don't choose your mindset, it will be chosen for you.

Nugget 5: Emotions and Thoughts Are Connected

Emotions can take over the rational parts of your brain during stressful situations. Only conscious attention and control of your emotions allows critical thinking rather than animal reaction to dictate your actions.

Nugget 6: Thinking On Purpose is a T.E.A.M Game

You have an obligation to teach your team TOP and model it yourself. Otherwise, the TOP process starts and stops with you, limiting your ability to succeed.

Nugget 7: Tools and Templates Do Not Replace Thinking

Tools provide a structure to help you reach the best possible conclusion or direction. However, you must provide the brainpower to process that data within the framework effectively.

Nugget 8: "Naming" is First Step in Mitigating the Impact of Biases and Emotions

Becoming aware of and recognizing biases helps you escape the cycle of repeated mistakes, problems, and poor reactions.

Nugget 9: Make Asking the Right Question a Signature Skill

The first step in making "asking the right question" a signature skill is learning the distinction between *having the right answers and answering the right questions.* A companion technique to asking the right questions is *reframing.*

Nugget 10: Get the OPTICS Right

OPTICS is an acronym that stands for Opportunity, Problem, Team, Influence, Change, and Stress. These six elements and the way they play out in action depends on whether you are using APT or OPT.

APPENDIX FIVE

TOP Road Map

See the revse side of this page for the completed TOP Road Map chart.

Purpose / Thinking Step	The Thinking on Purpose Roadmap: Frame Your Purpose	Qualify Your Information	Identify Your Mindsets	Structure Your Thinking	Validate Your Outcome
Situational Assessment	Identify the Problem	• Identify your POV • Confirm fact or fallacy • Confirm needed information is available	• Expand your POV • Sweep for MindFields • Reframe your thinking • Choose your mindset	• Identify the issues • Clarify the issues • Prioritize the issues • Establish if cause is known	• Problem identified?
Problem Solving	Determine the Cause	• Identify your POV • Confirm fact or fallacy • Confirm needed information is available	• Expand your POV • Sweep for MindFields • Reframe your thinking • Choose your mindset	• Describe the problem • List possible causes • Test possible causes • Confirm root cause	• True cause determined?
Decision Making	Choose a Solution	• Identify your POV • Confirm fact or fallacy • Confirm needed information is available • Test information	• Expand your POV • Sweep for MindFields • Reframe your thinking • Choose your mindset	• Identify objectives • Generate alternatives • Evaluate alternatives • Choose solution	• Best solution chosen?
Action Planning	Build a Plan	• Identify your POV • Confirm fact or fallacy • Confirm needed information is available • Test information	• Expand your POV • Sweep for MindFields • Reframe your thinking • Choose your mindset	• Draft a plan • Anticipate changes • Revise the plan • Set a baseline	• Most realistic plan built?
Risk Assessment	Protect the Plan	• Identify your POV • Confirm fact or fallacy • Confirm needed information is available • Test information	• Expand your POV • Sweep for MindFields • Reframe your thinking • Choose your mindset	• Identify the risks • Qualify the risks • Plan responses • Monitor and control	• Plan well protected?

APPENDIX SIX

TOP Toolkit—by Need

40 TOP TOOLS

NEED 1: GETTING STARTED

35 - Situational Assessment
37 - Stakeholder Assessment
18 - Gap Analysis
38 - SWOT Analysis

NEED 2: ESTABLISHING CONNECTIONS

2 - Affinity Diagram
23 - Mind Mapping
33 - Process Mapping

NEED 3: EXPAND POSSIBILITIES

5 - Brainstorming
7 - Concept Fan
11 - Devil's Advocacy
13 - Divergent/Convergent Thinking
28 - Provocation
30 - Problem Re-Statement
33 - Reframing Matrix
36 - Six Thinking Habits

NEED 4: DETERMINE CAUSE / DRILL DOWN

3 - Appreciation
4 - Ask "Why" Five Times
6 - Cause and Effect Diagram
15 - Drill Down
17 - Force Field Analysis
19 - Hypothesis Testing
21 - Ladder of Inference
26 - Pareto Analysis

NEED 5: GENERIC FORMATS

20 - Information Analysis Standards
22 - Matrix and Grids
40 - Weighted Ranking

NEED 6: ACTION ENABLERS

1 - Action Planning
9 - Debrief
16 - Facilitation
31 - Problem Solving
34 - Risk Assessment

NEED 7: DECISION MAKING

8 - Consensus
10 - Decision / Event Tree
12 - Decision Making
14 - DO IT
24 - Multi-Voting
25 - Paired Comparison Analysis
27 - PMI (Plus/Minus/Interesting)
29 - Probability Tree
39 - Utility Tree / Matrix

TOP Toolkit—by Number

Ref	Tool or Technique	Page	Need
1	Action Planning	175	Action Enablers
2	Affinity Diagram	179	Establishing Connections
3	Appreciation	181	Determining Cause/Drill Down
4	Ask Why Five Times	183	Determining Cause/Drill Down
5	Brainstorming	185	Expanding Possibilities
6	Cause and Effect Diagram	187	Determining Cause/Drill Down
7	Concept Fan	190	Expanding Possibilities
8	Consensus	192	Decision Making
9	Debrief	196	Action Enablers
10	Decision/Event Tree	199	Decision Making
11	Devil's Advocacy	201	Expanding Possibilities
12	Decision Making	203	Decision Making
13	Divergent/Convergent Thinking	206	Expanding Possibilities
14	DO IT	208	Decision Making
15	Drill Down	210	Determining Cause/Drill Down
16	Facilitation	212	Action Enablers
17	Force Field Analysis	219	Determining Cause/Drill Down
18	Gap Analysis	222	Getting Started
19	Hypothesis Testing	225	Determining Cause/Drill Down
20	Information Analysis Standards	228	Generic Formats
21	Ladder of Inference	230	Determining Cause/Drill Down
22	Matrix and Grids	233	Generic Formats
23	Mind Mapping	235	Establishing Connections
24	Multi-Voting	238	Decision Making
25	Paired Comparison Analysis	240	Decision Making
26	Pareto Analysis	242	Determining Cause/Drill Down
27	PMI – Plus/Minus/Interesting	244	Decision Making

APPENDIX EIGHT

TOP Information Analaysis Standards

Ref	Standard	Key Questions	Comments
1	Clarity	• Could you elaborate? • Could you illustrate what you mean? • Could you give me an example?	
2	Relevance	• How does this relate to the problem? • How does that bear on the question? • How does that help us with the issue?	
3	Logic	• Does of this make sense together? • Does your first paragraph fit with your last? • Does what you say follow from the evidence?	
4	Accuracy	• How could we check on that? • How could we find out if that is true? • How could we verify or test that?	
5	Depth	• What factors make this a difficult problem? • What are some of the complexities of this question? • What are some of the difficulties we need to deal with?	
6	Significance	• Is this the most important problem to consider • Is this the central idea to focus on? • Which of these facts are the most important?	
7	Precision	• Could you be more specific? • Could you give me more details? • Could you be more exact?	
8	Breadth	• Do we need to look at this from another perspective? • Do we need to consider another point of view? • Do we need to look at this in other ways?	
9	Fairness	• Is my thinking justifiable in this context? • Are my assumptions supported by evidence? • Is my purpose fair given the situation? • Am I using my concepts in keeping with educated usage or am I distorting them to get what I want?	
10	Precedence	• Has somebody in our organization done this before? • Do we have a framework or template? • Have "lessons learned" been recorded? • Who would be the "best in class" at doing this?	

Index

A

B

C

D

E

G

H

J

K

L

M

N

O

P

Q

R

S

T

U

V

W

Y

Z

About the Author

Bill Richardson is an internationally recognized consultant, trainer, speaker and corporate coach who focuses on helping people get better results by doing ordinary things extraordinarily well. One of the ordinary things he focuses on with his clients is thinking effectiveness and how it reverberates through all aspects of personal and professional life. Project managers are a key focus for Bill, and his clientele includes individuals and teams from various size companies from around the world. He has over thirty-five years of experience in Project Management, training and coaching, and is Project Management Professional (PMP) certified.

Bill lives in Port Perry, Ontario, Canada with his wife and family.

Did you like this book?

If you enjoyed this book, you will find more interesting books at

www.MMPubs.com

Please take the time to let us know how you liked this book. Even short reviews of 2-3 sentences can be helpful and may be used in our marketing materials. If you take the time to post a review for this book on Amazon.com, let us know when the review is posted and you will receive a free audiobook or ebook from our catalog. Simply email the link to the review once it is live on Amazon.com, with your name, and your mailing address—send the email to orders@mmpubs.com with the subject line "Book Review Posted on Amazon."

If you have questions about this book, our customer loyalty program, or our review rewards program, please contact us at info@mmpubs.com.

Oshawa, Ontario, Canada

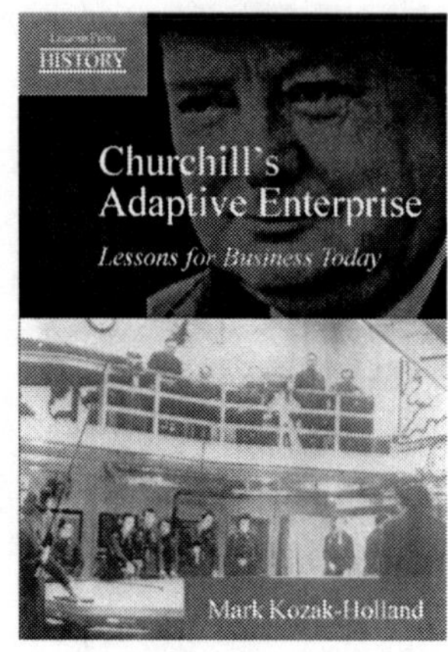

Churchill's Adaptive Enterprise: Lessons for Business Today

This book analyzes a period of time from World War II when Winston Churchill, one of history's most famous leaders, faced near defeat for the British in the face of sustained German attacks. The book describes the strategies he used to overcome incredible odds and turn the tide on the impending invasion. The historical analysis is done through a modern business and information technology lens, describing Churchill's actions and strategy using modern business tools and techniques. Aimed at business executives, IT managers, and project managers, the book extracts learnings from Churchill's experiences that can be applied to business problems today. Particular themes in the book are knowledge management, information portals, adaptive enterprises, and organizational agility.

Eric Hoffer Book Award (2007) Winner

ISBN: 1-895186-19-6 (paperback)
ISBN: 1-895186-20-X (PDF ebook)
http://www.mmpubs.com/churchill

The Elusive Lean Enterprise: Why Companies Struggle to Get the Full Benefits from Lean

In today's fast-paced and volatile business environment, customers are demanding increased flexibility and lower cost, and companies must operate in a waste-free environment to maintain a competitive edge and grow margins. Lean Enterprise is the process that companies are adopting to provide superior customer service and improve bottom line performance.

Are you contemplating Lean Enterprise for your manufacturing or office facility? Are you already implementing Lean, but dissatisfied with the speed of change? Do your employees think that Lean is just the new flavor of the month? Are you being forced to go Lean by your customers? This book is designed to help guide you through the Lean transformation and avoid the pitfalls. Find out why many companies are failing to live up to the promise of Lean, and why there may be alternatives to outsourcing or going offshore.

ISBN: 1-897326-64-5 (paperback)
ISBN: 1-897326-65-3 (hardcover)
ISBN: 1-897326-66-1 (Adobe PDF ebook)

Order from your local bookseller, Amazon.com, or directly from the publisher at **http://www.mmpubs.com**

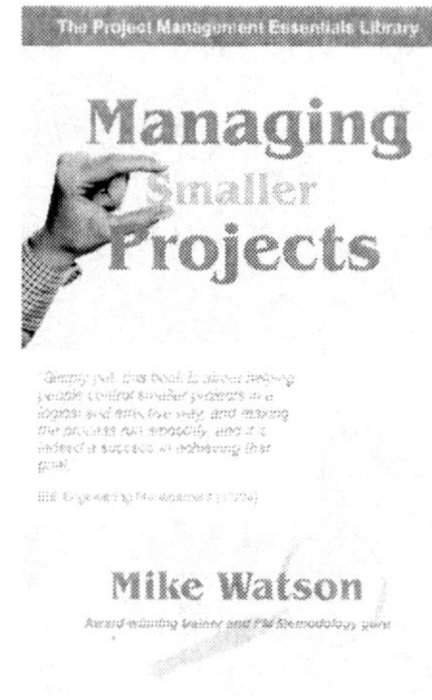
The Project Management Essentials Library
Managing
Smaller
Projects
Mike Watson

Managing Smaller Projects: A Practical Approach

So called "small projects" can have potentially alarming consequences if they go wrong, but their control is often left to chance. The solution is to adapt tried and tested project management techniques.

This book provides a low overhead, highly practical way of looking after small projects. It covers all the essential skills: from project start-up, to managing risk, quality and change, through to controlling the project with a simple control system. It cuts through the jargon of project management and provides a framework that is as useful to those lacking formal training, as it is to those who are skilled project managers and want to control smaller projects without the burden of bureaucracy.

Read this best-selling book from the U.K., now making its North American debut. *IEE Engineering Management* praises the book, noting that "Simply put, this book is about helping people control smaller projects in a logical and effective way, and making the process run smoothly, and is indeed a success in achieving that goal."

Available in print format. Order from your local bookseller, Amazon.com, or directly from the publisher at **www.mmpubs.com/msp**

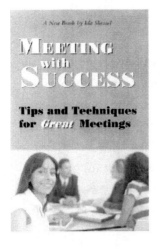

Your wallet is empty? And you still need to boost your team's performance?

Building team morale is difficult in these tough economic times. Author Kevin Aguanno helps you solve the team morale problem with ideas for team rewards that won't break the bank.

Learn over 100 ways you can reward your project team and individual team members for just a few dollars. Full of innovative (and cheap!) ideas. Even with the best reward ideas, rewards can fall flat if they are not suitable to the person, the organization, the situation, or the magnitude of the accomplishment. Learn the four key factors that will *maximize* the impact of your rewards, and *guarantee* delighted recipients.

101 Ways to Reward Team Members for $20 (or Less!) teaches you how to improve employee morale, improve employee motivation, improve departmental and cross-organizational teaming, maximize the benefits of your rewards and recognition programme, and avoid the common mistakes.

ISBN: 1-895186-04-8 (paperback)

Also available in ebook formats. Order from your local bookseller, Amazon.com, or directly from the publisher at **http://www.mmpubs.com/**

Your wallet is empty? And you still need to boost your team's performance?

Building team morale is difficult in these tough economic times. Author Kevin Aguanno helps you solve the team morale problem with ideas for team rewards that won't break the bank.

Learn over 100 ways you can reward your project team and individual team members for just a few dollars. Full of innovative (and cheap!) ideas. Even with the best reward ideas, rewards can fall flat if they are not suitable to the person, the organization, the situation, or the magnitude of the accomplishment. Learn the four key factors that will *maximize* the impact of your rewards, and *guarantee* delighted recipients.

101 Ways to Reward Team Members for $20 (or Less!) teaches you how to improve employee morale, improve employee motivation, improve departmental and cross-organizational teaming, maximize the benefits of your rewards and recognition programme, and avoid the common mistakes.

ISBN: 1-895186-04-8 (paperback)

Also available in ebook formats. Order from your local bookseller, Amazon.com, or directly from the publisher at **http://www.mmpubs.com/**

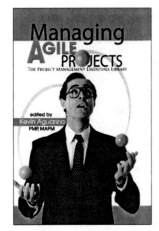

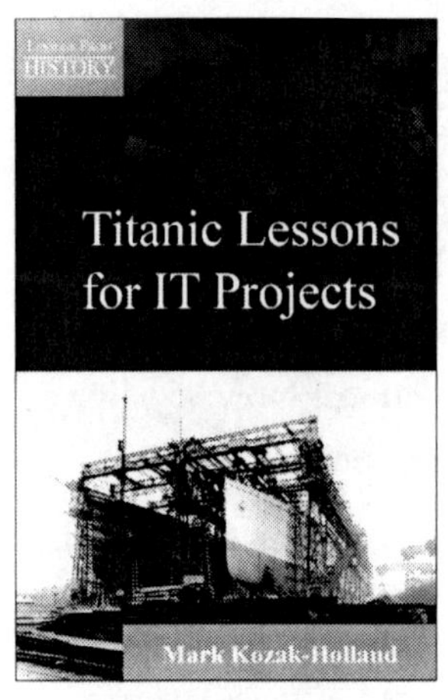

Titanic Lessons for IT Projects

Titanic Lessons for IT Projects analyzes the project that designed, built, and launched the ship, showing how compromises made during early project stages led to serious flaws in this supposedly "perfect ship." In addition, the book explains how major mistakes during the early days of the ship's operations led to the disaster. All of these disasterous compromises and mistakes were fully avoidable.

Entertaining and full of intriguing historical details, this companion book to Avoiding Project Disaster: Titanic Lessons for IT Executives helps project managers and IT executives see the impact of decisions similar to the ones that they make every day. An easy read full of illustrations and photos to help explain the story and to help drive home some simple lessons.

ISBN: 1-895186-26-9 (paperback)

Also available in ebook formats. Order from your local bookseller, Amazon.com, or directly from the publisher at **http://www.mmpubs.com/titanic**

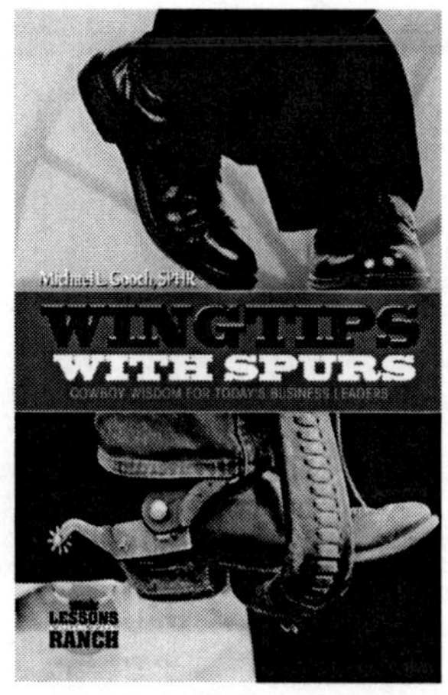

Lessons from the Ranch for Today's Business Manager

The lure of the open plain, boots, chaps and cowboy hats makes us think of a different and better way of life. The cowboy code of honor is an image that is alive and well in our hearts and minds, and its wisdom is timeless.

Using ranch based stories, author Michael Gooch, a ranch owner, tells us how to apply cowboy wisdom to our everyday management challenges. Serving up straight forward, practical advice, the book deals with issues of dealing with conflict, strategic thinking, ethics, having fun at work, hiring and firing, building strong teams, and knowing when to run from trouble.

A unique (and fun!) approach to management training, Wingtips with Spurs is a must read whether you are new to management or a grizzled veteran.

ISBN: 1-897326-88-2 (paperback)

Also available in ebook formats. Order from your local bookseller, Amazon.com, or directly from the publisher at **http://www.mmpubs.com**

CPSIA information can be obtained at www.ICGtesting.com
Printed in the USA
LVOW05s0118230813

349025LV00002B/4/P